Toward Nationalizing Regimes

CENTRAL EURASIA IN CONTEXT SERIES

—

DOUGLAS NORTHROP, EDITOR

TOWARD NATIONALIZING REGIMES

CONCEPTUALIZING POWER AND IDENTITY IN THE POST-SOVIET REALM

DIANA T. KUDAIBERGENOVA

UNIVERSITY OF PITTSBURGH PRESS

Published by the University of Pittsburgh Press, Pittsburgh, Pa., 15260

Copyright © 2020, University of Pittsburgh Press

Manufactured in the United States of America

Printed on acid-free paper

10 9 8 7 6 5 4 3 2 1

Cataloging-in-Publication data is available from the Library of Congress

ISBN 13: 978-0-8229-4617-5
ISBN 10: 0-8229-4617-3

Cover art: Askhat Akhmedyarov, *If the Pain Could Be Burnt Away*

Cover design: Alex Wolfe

To my parents,

Dr. Turarbek Kudaibergenov
&
Raushan Ibragimova-Kudaibergenova

CONTENTS

Figure 1. Map of Eurasia, Latvia, and Kazakhstan, and the former Soviet Union countries. *Sources*: United Nations Statistics Division, CIA World Factbook; Alyson Hurt/NPR.

PREFACE

Nationalism remains one of the most popular forms of political ideologies worldwide, but it is also the source of constant divisions, inequalities, and power struggles. Inspired by new venues in the study of nationalism, this book discusses the paradoxical fluidity and controlled nature of nation-building processes as well as elitist power struggles to define what the nation is. Often during my interviews aimed at defining nation-building discourses and programs, the first question that politicians and policymakers in power directed at me was "What nation do you want to talk about?" although we were discussing the same country, its territory, and its sovereignty. How many nations are there in one state? How and where does one start imagining the limits and boundaries of one nation as it overlaps with *nationality* (also known in some cases as ethnicity), citizenship, communal belonging, and transnational identifications of constant migration flows? The concept and definition of the ever-present "nation" becomes a complex matter that continues influencing the ways power relations are governed from within the power field of each country and its elites. The book also reflects on who decides which national discourse wins and becomes the dominant discourse guiding politics and social relations in the state.

In essence, this book is about these processes of power relations. It is an attempt to explain how power works through the control of "nation" and nation-building as a discourse—in fact, the most powerful discourse guiding elite competition from within and outside the power field.

My study takes the new states and nations of Eurasia that emerged in 1991 as examples to study nationalizing regimes, although this framework is expandable to other cases and contexts (see fig. 1). The collapse of the Soviet Union famously opened new venues for theories of nationalism and the study of processes and actors involved in these new nation-building processes. To date significant discussions have emerged on the matter of Soviet nationalities policy, the codification of ethnicity and citizenship, and the conceptualization of nationalist discourses and the ways these came about during and after the Soviet Union. And plenty of space and demand remain for conceptualizations of key elements such as "state," "elites," "ethnicity," and "nation-building" as a contested and in-flux process that directly influences the rights and freedoms of citizens, and democratization processes on the political and social levels. This is the conceptual and empirical gap I address in this study from a variety of different stances—from the position of the power elites themselves, from the dissection of the hegemonic nationalist discourse and counterdiscourses that surround it, from the voices of the minorities caught between these power struggles, as well as from anxieties associated with regime change.

The selection of Kazakhs and Latvians as case studies was very important for illustrating examples in which the Russian-speaking minority almost outnumbered indigenous "titular ethnic groups" of Kazakhs and Latvians before and after independence in 1991. In more electorally democratic Latvia, where the consolidation of pro-Latvian elites had pursued and developed very exclusivist citizenship and nation-building policies, the regime failed to comply with the demands of its Russian-speaking minority even on matters of minority education and state language provisions. In less democratic Kazakhstan the Russian minority was treated differently. Since the declaration of independence in 1991, universal citizenship, the duality of state (Kazakh) and official (Russian) languages, and minority language schools in which Russophone education dominated were promoted and became the fundamental elements of the multicultural policy of President Nursultan Nazarbayev's regime.

What explains this difference in approaches to nation-building after the collapse of the Soviet Union? What can a study of two very different trajectories of development tell us about the nature of power, state, and nationalizing regimes of the "new" states of Eurasia? I use the concept of "nationalizing regime" to study these processes of elitist nation-building projects, intra-elite competitions, and legitimacy building for ideological regimes (Latvia) or personalized regimes (Kazakhstan). I believe that the study of power mechanisms through an understanding of political decision making at the highest level can tell us more about what governs these very different processes of nation-building, where specific elitist interests lie, and how these processes affect society, polity, and democracy.

Chapter 2, "The Archaeology of Nationalizing Regimes: Narratives, Elites, and Minorities," is a slightly revised version of an article previously published in *Problems of Post-Communism* 64, no. 6: 342–55. I want to thank the editorial board of *Problems of Post-Communism*, Taylor and Francis, and the editor, Dmitry Gorenburg for allowing its reproduction here.

ACKNOWLEDGMENTS

Writing this book was a long journey with unexpected turns and pleasant surprises, all done in the company of great people and mentors to whom I am indebted. I want to thank David Lane, my supervisor in the Department of Sociology at the University of Cambridge for his careful guidance and encouragement throughout my MPhil and doctoral years in the department. The days on deadlines that I spent in different Latvian libraries and spaces writing up chapters to send him still bring back good memories of tireless fieldwork days. His supervision taught me to be meticulous, focused, and always interested in finding new horizons. My sociology faculty adviser Jeffrey Thomas Miley helped me greatly during our methodological and conceptual discussions on nationalism. I thank him for pointing out so many political sociology texts along with the discussions that followed and firsthand experiences. My committee members, Sally N. Cummings and Hazem Kandil offered significant help, advice, and inspiration throughout this period. They were always attentive regarding the development of my work and I am deeply grateful to them for the support and guidance they gave me at every step of my professional development.

Prajakti Kalra and Siddharth Saxena, the heart of the Cambridge Central Asia Forum and the GCRF-COMPASS team at the University of Cambridge very much helped me to finalize this manuscript and take important steps in further conceptualizations of power, the field I am most passionate about. I am grateful to them for their support and guidance throughout, which involved close readings of numerous chapters, long chats in Cambridge, and talks in the field.

I want to thank Douglas Northrop, the editor of the Central Eurasia in Context series, Peter Kracht, and the whole editorial team at the University of Pittsburgh Press for their advice, close reading, and generous assistance during the completion of this project. I also want to thank all three anonymous peer reviewers for their detailed reading of an earlier draft of the manuscript and for valuable comments that shaped the final version.

The book would not have been complete without the reproduction of a work of the noted Kazakh contemporary artist Askhat Akhmediyarov, *If Pain Could*

Burn Away, to be used for the book's cover. To me it represents the complex and often perplexed nature of Soviet and post-Soviet times and its effect on all people whether they reside in Europe or Asia, or in this case, whether in Latvia or in Kazakhstan. Akhmediyarov's visual and performative work ideally captures the pain and trauma, the thought process and the fight for one's own voice in these grand historical and contemporary narratives of power. He is the gift that keeps on giving. I am deeply grateful to Askhat Akhmediyarov for permission to use this work to represent the book and, most important, to represent the time we all live in. I finalized this book at a turbulent time for my own generation in Kazakhstan on the eve of the first presidential elections without the country's long-term leader Nursultan A. Nazarbayev, whose name appears throughout the pages of this book as the visual and bodily representation of the state and power itself. I want to thank my friends and arts activist community at home for their support and inspiration during this chaotic time for all of us. More work lies ahead for us as a community and society beyond nationalist and ethnic boundaries.

Over the years I have benefited from numerous grants and fieldwork support from my college in Cambridge—Trinity Hall Graduate Fund—and from my departments in Cambridge for fieldwork funds and research trips, for which I am grateful. Much research for this book was also funded by two grants from the Centre for East European Language Based Area Studies (CEELBAS), which allowed me to learn Latvian in Riga (in 2012) and to conduct my initial fieldwork in Latvia. CEELBAS also funded a grant giving me the opportunity to work in 2013 as a Researcher-in-Residence in the archives of the OSCE Secretariat in Prague. At that institution, I am indebted to Alice Nemcova and her team for their tireless support and provision of my endless requests for more archives. Months spent in Prague twice in 2013 and again in 2018 were filled with productive work that is yet to be finalized in my other writing and in most memorable discussions and quiet evenings in the company of Alice who is an excellent archivist and the provider of rich information about the creation of the European nations and their minority politics.

I also benefited from a UACES grant (2015) to conduct fieldwork in Ukraine, Kazakhstan, and Latvia. Finally, the University of Cambridge Overseas Trust provided me with a generous grant to conduct fieldwork in numerous places across the post-Soviet region, which are contextualized in the study. I am grateful to them for long-term financial and personal support of my professional development at Cambridge.

I spent numerous months researching and living in Latvia as a visiting researcher in the Department of Social Sciences of Latvian University and I am grateful to everyone for their support, advice, and networking. My dear friends across the region were my gatekeepers—especially Evija Zaca and Janis Daugavietis and all my colleagues at Latvian University who, among other things, taught me Latvian and took me to explore underground musical scenes around Riga. Thanks to Evija and Ligita, my hosts in Riga, Latvia became my second home. I also want to thank Juris Rozenvalds, Brigita Zepa, and the Baltic Institute of Social Sciences for help in identifying important sociological trends in Latvian nation-building and national politics.

I am grateful for advice and support, for extended and insightful talks with Marlène Laruelle, Erica Marat, Boram Shin, Laura Adams, Amanda Wooden, Asel Rustemova-Tutumlu, Rustamjon Urinboyev, Adrien Fauve, Karlygash Abieva, Eva-Marie Dubuisson, Filippo Costa Buranelli, Assel Doolot, Sofya Omarova du Boulay, Olga Mun, and many others. Over the years I have presented my work at a number of academic events and in discussions at the Central Eurasian Studies Society at the University of Wisconsin-Madison in 2013, at Latvia University, at George Washington University, at the University of Cambridge Department of Sociology, at Sciences Po, at the University of Oxford, and Columbia University. I am thankful to everyone who commented on earlier versions of my papers and chapters.

I want to thank my extended multicultural family in Kazakhstan for their support and encouragement during this project. I am grateful to Ibragimovs "mahalla," my brother Kuanysh Kudaibergenov and his family for support, Marzhan, Karima, Kaisar, and Mansour were always there to share a break from writing; my family in Astana—Sardarbek Abiev and Saule Abieva for hospitality and taking care of me when I was in the field.

My parents have always been my inspiration and my best supporters in life and work. I had my first "fieldwork experience" as a child falling asleep in the backseat of my father's car while he was rummaging across post-Soviet farms in Kazakhstan collecting interviews for his research in economics and training farmers. I also learned my first intercultural communication skills with my mother who took me on distant rides with her French partners and taught me about research during my early childhood. I have won a lottery ticket in life to be their child, and I thank them for everything! I dedicate this book to mom and dad, Raushan Ibragimova-Kudaibergenova and Turarbek Kudaibergenov, whose experience inspired me to become an academic and a writer.

Toward Nationalizing Regimes

INTRODUCTION

"We stood shoulder to shoulder on that square back in the beginning of the new era, in the early 1990s. . . . So brave and so united, we thought we could die for the common cause. But what for? Now, after so many years I wonder," said Laima, my Latvian host whom I met in Riga in Kengaraks raion on a freezing evening in early February 2013.[1] In Riga they say one can tell how time changes by looking at the metamorphosis of one space, Kengaraks, a predominantly Russophone neighborhood outside Riga's city center over the period from the late 1980s to the present. "Here used to be the famous [Soviet] porcelain factory," says Laima, pointing at the rubble of an old factory on the other side of the bridge. She then returns to her memories of the Soviet Union and the 1990 barricades at the central square in Riga, in front of the Milda monument to the Latvian nation. Laima is a middle-aged ethnic Latvian who speaks to me in perfect Russian—"a remnant of the *Soviet time* in me," she laughs. The fact that we both speak Russian is perhaps the only thing that unites us at the point of our first encounter. Setting us apart are a generation gap, two different citizenships that require us to obtain visas to visit each other's countries, and two completely different experiences of navigating the post-Soviet world, or rather worlds.

On top of that, my only memories of the Soviet Union are ironic and subconscious—a box of Latvian sugar-coated cranberries (*kliukva v sakhare*) brought from Moscow, a luxurious gift at a time of total deficit. A nice, very typical "Soviet" ribbon on top of the box echoes in my early childhood memory as something very alien and cruel at a time of the most heightened economic crisis in Kazakhstan. Laima's and my personal "Soviet" conceptualizations and memories clearly differ. Hers are of barricades, the Baltic Way human chain across Estonia, Latvia, and Lithuania, the communal feeling of coming together as a Latvian nation in 1990. Mine are of fading images of a strange balding elderly man with a beard, called Lenin, who is seen teaching kids how to be moral and not to lie and giving them presents in far-off Moscow. These are the things I have seen in the "Soviet" book that my older cousin threw away as an unnecessary and meaningless "remnant of the *Soviet time*" in 1995 post-Soviet Kazakhstan. Little did we know that Lenin would pop up again as an obsession of hipsters with the old time in the very late post-Soviet period.

Throughout my fieldwork in 2011 to 2019 I would see his portrait in a popular bar in Riga's downtown dance clubs; and then again at the largest Kyiv book bazaar, at Tashkent's flea market, on the streets of Baku's old town where Lenin's busts are sold at a higher price—as a "tourist attraction," says the local seller. I found Lenin again even in the public area around Astana's new bridge, where he reappeared on the old Soviet pins that are fashionable among the generation of teenagers who have a very distant idea of what "Soviet" means. As one of my respondents who was born in 2001 once said, "Soviet to me is represented through the most depressing apartment building blocks"; these are surprisingly similar everywhere, even in Kengaraks, which is so distant and yet so close to the apartment buildings in Kazakhstan, Ukraine, Azerbaijan, or any of the post-Soviet urban spaces. Remnants of the Soviet time are present in the material structure of the old residential parts of the cities.

In that sense, Laima and I find a lot more in common because we can refer to some sort of "Soviet" abstract yet meaningful language beyond just Russian. She does not need to explain to me in 2013 what the rubbles of the "Soviet factory" are or why Kengaraks is a home to a predominantly non-Latvian Russophone population who migrated here in the 1960s, 1970s, and 1980s as a Soviet labor force. But she does narrate what is ahead of us—an old automobile center "where Soviet people came to 'buy' cars after waiting in line for that event for years," she says, and then she glances at me as if to check whether I understand what it meant to "buy a car" or "wait in line" to make a big purchase in Soviet Union. "Now everyone can buy whatever they want, whenever they want, as long as they have money for it," she concludes as the old Soviet automobile center now hosts a major shopping mall for the old residents of the neighborhood. Ironically, the Soviet dream transfers into a capitalist one in the same exact space. Then what happens to the residents of Kengaraks? How did their lives change before and after Latvia became *post-Soviet* and independent?

My question brings Laima back to present reality. As her thoughts are no longer focused on the memories of the late 1980s Atmoda—the Latvian National Awakening wave and "singing revolution,"[2] she describes her sadness and despair about the "little changes" that independence brought. Her dissatisfaction is not new and is actually experienced by a lot of other people I interviewed across the post-Soviet space where "old elites" assumed power over their respective countries virtually overnight. Power struggles took place and continue to take place behind closed doors, and these processes are almost equally dominated by the power elites in democratic and nondemocratic post-Soviet societies. "I don't think my vote can change much," says Laima, as I question what brought us, two post-Soviets of very different worlds, into this very similar sociopolitical situation of our inability to change the regimes in our countries. As we walked and talked, big questions popped up in our conversation uniting what I research and what Laima lives through everyday: Where is the power? How is it exercised and who has control over it?

The answers to these questions are at the core of this book—political elites who operate on the level of nationalizing regimes, the ideational power field of meaning production, who control access to this field that in turn regulates other dimensions of power relations in the country. But why does nation-building become the most powerful space that guides political decision-making mechanisms post-1991 in such distinct places from Latvia to as far as Kazakhstan and beyond, to Russia itself? Why is further separation into distinct "nations" seen by political elites as the best legitimating principle for their political competition or for the exclusion of other parties from such competition on the basis of their centrist position, as it happens in Latvia? This question can lead to further examples of why certain regimes and politicians call for building real walls on their borders to stop what they view as "illegal immigration" or why certain political elites push for Brexit despite growing popular demand against it in the light of devastating political chaos in Britain on the never-coming eve of Brexit. Why do political elites push for constructed boundaries of difference, why do they make the exclusiveness of a certain ethnic or national group the cornerstone of their own legitimation, a source of their own power?

In this book I turn to power elites who have the most power in decision making and in determining the limits and frameworks of national ideology or ideologies to explain why and how mechanisms of nationalizing processes guide political competition. The power elites are "composed of men [and women] whose positions enable them to transcend the ordinary environments of ordinary men and women; they are in positions to make decisions having major consequences."[3] But how do these elites exercise their power under different political circumstances and systems but with similar sociodemographic conditions at the inception of their independent state-building?

My journey to understanding the mechanisms of power and decision making started with the puzzle of regime change and difference in political contexts. I selected Latvia and Kazakhstan as the most differentiated comparative case studies,[4] which allowed me to question whether "democracy" differs from a nondemocratic system when it comes to the treatment of national minorities and creation of new fundamental national ideologies on which the whole structure of states and power relations is built. It also helped me to flesh out these mechanisms of power contestations, the rules of the game in elitist fields and how these are influenced by the formula for competitive elections in Latvia and "selections" of elites by the president himself in the super-presidential republic in Kazakhstan that had almost no free elections. But most important, the contrasting study of Latvia and Kazakhstan allowed me to distinguish differences in the experiences of political elites in building the states, reviving or constructing nations after 1991 in "democracies" and "nondemocracies." It also permitted me to see how communities on the ground responded to these processes in very different, post-Soviet spaces with their distinct systems, which I term here *nationalizing regimes*.

TOWARD NATIONALIZING REGIMES

Nationalism in the post-1991 realm is power in itself because it is the source of identification, meaning-making, and control of what type of identity is defined politically, when, and for whom. Within the power field, nation-building is an instrument to acquire more power for actors because elites try to convince others that they are the ones who possess the knowledge and capacity to bring the nation, society, and country to prosperity or to focus on any other commonly shared value because this is how they gain even more power to rule. Nation-building becomes the language for this meaning-making, which is at the same time the source of power within the politically defined power field of a regime guided by control and an obsession with nationalism—the nationalizing regime.

Nationalizing regimes are formed of the most powerful elites who manage to control and impose the specific discursive and nation-building outcomes on the wider population, including ethnic minorities. The mechanism of a nationalizing regime is directly dependent on elites' consensus over the dominant discourse that usually defines the power field where elites struggle to enhance their power positions through arguing that they have more capacity to safeguard and enrich the most sacred discourse. Different nationalizing regimes pursue specific goals that are ruled by the interests of the dominant elites to stay in power and pursue their domination over the main nation-building discourse, thus circumventing political competition from other distinct discourses and potential counter-elites.

In other words, "nation" discourse dominates the competition for power in nationalizing regimes. Political elites compete to define and control this discourse that simultaneously constructs the power field and its rules of the game and closes its access to outsiders like Laima and me as well as many more people defined as society. Society is seen by these elites as "the web of interlocking fields" that nevertheless rarely forms the power field where "players try to impose the legitimacy of their particular species of capital in order to dominate the entire social order."[5]

I use the term "nationalizing" here in relation to the regime to demonstrate that in reality the dominant discourse for power struggles is defined by the search for some sort of lost national identity or nationalist distinction. The nationalizing sphere then becomes the most popular, dominant, and lucrative discourse for state builders and their competition in the wake of the collapse of the Soviet utopia, but where the framework of ideological structures and divisions on national levels remain. While the power elites try to position it as stable and deeply rooted in the history of one ethnic group that allows them to seek more domination because they represent this ethnic group, the nature of the nationalizing process is never fixed, but in constant flux due to the changing contexts within and outside the regime itself. As I will show throughout the pages of this book, in some scenarios elitist competition within the nationalizing regime itself is the main driving force of further nationalization. Power elites are simply afraid of competing discourses that drive the agenda away from the dominant national-ethnic discourse and could potentially shift the rules of the game and disempower them due to the shift in their own positions and the telos they support and safeguard. In other scenarios, the set of complex issues outside the regime influences elites' indecisiveness in defining what they imagine as a *stable* or fundamental "national identity project." This forces the regime to come up with new slogans and even new state programs in searching for this national identity. These complex issues involve either the demands of ethnic minorities if these groups are defined as more than the "titular ethnicity" or other kinds of demands, when the electorate no longer votes on national preferences but demands the provision of economic and social programs instead.

All these issues and contexts influence the formation and implementation of mechanisms of nationalizing regimes because within the power field of each nationalizing regime most dominant political elites struggle for more power by controlling the production of meaning of this most popular discourse. So how can the study of elites help us to identify power struggles and further nationalization of the political field?

Elites are crucial to the understanding of power relations because they are "tiny but powerful minorities" that are "made up of autonomous social and political actors who are interested primarily in maintaining and enhancing their power, so that their power struggles are not reducible to classes or other collectivities."[6] Elites can be defined in various ways, for example, as political elites, cultural elites, regional elites, and finally, as power elites, a group that can comprise all three groups. In most contexts, political elites are the ones who gain more power positions within nationalizing regimes and take over cultural elites who are seen as "producers of the national discourses" but, in reality, are very weak when it comes to political competition.[7]

The term "nationalizing regimes" intentionally focuses on the nature of political ordering from the elitist perspective; it directs attention toward the dichotomy of rigid political categories of being democratic or nondemocratic in the post-Soviet state definitions and blurs them. It also links formal and informal structures of power within a given state. Derived from comparative politics, which refers to regimes as "the formal and informal structure and nature of political power in the country, including the method of determining office holders and the relations between the office holders and the society at large."[8] The concept of nationalizing regimes exposes and analyzes nation-building through the internal networks and interests of those who govern such policies—the elites in comparison to those who are ruled by them—the citizens and noncitizens (in the case of Latvia) or multiple linguistic and cultural minorities (in the case of Kazakhstan).

The "nationalizing" part of this definition also focuses on the fluidity and constant repositioning of discourses as well as political elite competition to influence these discourses. This first half of the term, "nationalizing," is similar to Rogers Brubaker's idea of nationalizing states where the "nationalizing" connotation pointed to "the dynamic and processual implication of the term" suggesting "the unfinished and ongoing nature of nationalist projects."[9] The analysis in this book further enriches the term "nationalizing" by providing details about how the nationalizing regime actually works and by showing that though certain parts of the nationalizing discourse are in fact presented as finished and determined, others are intentionally kept unfinished and ambiguous to disempower minorities' leaders or other categorical groups and their agency. It is important to expand the existing framework of nation-building analysis and to address the agency and complexity of these processes through an empirical comparative study of very distinct cases. The focus reverts back to the question of "which nation" are elites talking about or trying to develop? The content of the concept of "nationalizing" in this book demonstrates the diversity of competing, coexisting, and parallel discourses of nations, to whom these nations belong, and who has the right and power to shape and control these discourses.

In the following chapters of this book I discuss the vibrant diversity of nationalizing that, although it is presented as singular—the one protecting the "core" ethnic group of Latvians or Kazakhs—in reality, it is dispersed, heterogeneous, and complex. As previous studies have demonstrated, the nationalizing process attempts to create homogeneity and it seeks its own power through controlling this homogeneity, but the nature of the process is such that by homogenizing only one core group, it inevitably creates divisions, inequalities, and differences and in the end becomes heterogeneous. Therefore, nationalizing cannot be total—it goes against complex social processes and people's own perceptions on the ground. Kazakhstan is never fully Kazakh and neither is Latvia completely Latvian or nationalized in the way its power elites imagine it. In fact, both host a number of different "nations" with their complex definitions, constructs, and identities. What the domination of the nationalizing regime as a power structure brings to the social dynamics is actually further dispersion of the meaning of "Kazakh" or "Qazaq" and division into urban and rural Kazakhs, *mankurts* and *mambets*, Russophones and Kazakh-speaking, and many other distinct identities and perceptions of what it means to be Kazakh.[10] And Latvia, too, has diverse understandings of Latvianized, Latviskii, Russkii, Russian-speaking, Russophone, ethnic Latvian, or European identities.

In this book I develop a critique of the ambiguity of contemporary post-Soviet nation-building analyses and an in-depth consideration of its weakest links, namely, Brubaker's nationalizing states. Rogers Brubaker's idea of nationalizing states has been the most dominant framework for the study of post-Soviet nation-building since the collapse of the Soviet Union. It encompasses five characteristics and domains of such a state:

> (1) the idea that the state contains a "core nation" or nationality, understood in ethnocultural terms and distinguished from the citizenry or permanent resident population of the state as a whole; (2) a claim to ownership or primacy: the state is understood as the state of and for the core nation; (3) the claim that the core nation is in a weak or unhealthy condition; (4) the claim that state action is needed to strengthen the core nation, to promote its language, cultural flourishing, demographic robustness, economic welfare or political hegemony; and (5) the claim that such action is remedial or compensatory, needed to redress previous discrimination or oppression suffered by the core nation.[11]

The nationalizing states framework is useful for identifying and capturing the prime discourses and trends in post-Soviet nationalization ab nihilo if such a context exists. It captured the importance of the relevant Soviet legacy of ethnic codification and signaled the rise of the core nation defined in the constructed categories of ethnonational codification, but it also failed to theorize further on the temporal structure of this legacy and to answer the questions of who governs. The temporal link between Soviet and post-Soviet is something that the field is still addressing, and only a few works have succeeded in identifying this problem.[12] Local Kazakh and Latvian scholars accepted the temporal linearity of Soviet and post-Soviet as a sacred divide between the "past," which was supposed to be condemned, and the "post," which was supposed to dissolve by itself sometime soon. The persistence of this post-Soviet "transitionary" form of thinking only impedes the analysis of fluidity and hybridity of these post- and past experiences. Moreover, the nationalizing states framework hints at processes of post–Soviet-type postcoloniality in the claims for remedial actions (Brubaker's points [3], [4], and [5]), but does not resolve the ongoing tension of colonialism under the Soviets.[13] It also does not resolve decolonial attempts after the post-Soviet concept eventually passes, opening spaces for new temporal and perhaps spatial concepts.[14]

Although a broad and generally good starting point, the nationalizing states framework proposed to focus on grand narratives only, without further specificity and more detailed and empirical comparisons. Most important, it is ambiguous in defining the actors who contain and reproduce the nation and national narratives in the successor states. As a result, it fails to capture the full contextual picture of nation-building processes and roles of nation-builders. Although Brubaker propagated a contingent and multifaceted approach to the study of the processes and events of nation-building, he too often implicitly assumed two- or three-way communication between the nationalizing state, its minorities, and possibly the kin state.[15]

The nationalizing regimes approach argues for a multifaceted and more nuanced perspective on these processes. Instead of being a limited two- or even three-way communication, nation-building is seen through this framework as a battlefield of ideas, interests, aspirations, discourses, and power struggles among the power elites in the country. Who influences nationalizing strategies development and who is in charge of controlling and challenging the dominant discourse? Brubaker's notion of nationalizing states acknowledged the importance of the elite agency, but similar to other nationalism studies, it simply took it for granted. Who is nationalizing? How and when does this happen? Why do nationalizations lead to different scenarios in different cases? No further explication or conceptual framework was offered for understanding mechanisms, agency, and processes of the nationalizing part, and as Brubaker himself stated, this was a limitation of the framework. Furthermore, this point of complex political developments in the world as a whole and not only in the post-Soviet space requires a critical reading of the rather ambiguously defined notion of the "state" in Brubaker's initial argument of nationalizing states.

I contend that the answer to the puzzle of elite-led projects of nation-building had to be found on the ground, within the sociopolitical systems of these states—it was tied to the regime, to the rules of the game in the power field. Throughout the book I demonstrate that in Kazakhstan the nationalizing agenda is clearly identified with the hybrid regime of one-man rule and President Nazarbayev's personalized regime. The concept of "regime" in the nationalizing regime framework was used in Kazakhstan's local discussions and political reports more often than "state" (*gosudarstvo*) or "government" (*pravitel'stvo*) to identify the ruling political and economic elites and the political discourses they were producing and guarding. In Latvia, the idea of the Latvianized regime was described more clearly by those who were outside of it—by the so-called Russian-speaking minority activists. The views of these outsiders, external to the ruling elite circle, helped me to identify some of the most important features of the nationalizing regime as the one that separates people into "national" and "alien" bodies based on the historical-legal status of their citizenship. In this complex picture of legitimating the decision to cut through almost half of the population after independence by claiming that they were part of the legacy of the "occupation" and did not legally belong to the independent prewar Latvian nation, one had to dig deeper to separate a Baltic Russian from a Russia-proper Russian or Latvian.

Legal and discursive structures of defining and separating citizens and noncitizens through the means and mechanisms of a nationalizing regime often drew physical boundaries among lifelong friends, neighbors, and even families. Passports of different colors—red for Latvian citizens and blue for non-Latvian citizens—generated insecurities, fears, lack of self-confidence, and even hostility in Latvia. Throughout my ethnography I encountered these distinct boundaries, the outcomes of the nationalizing regime face-to-face often in Kengaraks but also in other parts of Riga and Daugavpils—the second largest city in Latvia and a hub for Latvian Russians. For those outside the dividing line of being Latvian, gaining a red passport not only meant securing their jobs as school teachers, museum guards, or engineers, it also meant confidence and a feeling of fitting in and not being looked down on, even within their own family, not being separated at the airport when four family passports are red and one is blue. For most of my interviewees within the elite circle, the nature of the Latvianized regime was not questionable and became a normalizing, commonsensical discourse about *how things ought to be*. But for Russian-speaking elites and nonelites alike it was evident that the regime pushed them out of the circle due to their Otherness from the dominant discourse that is politically and ethnically Latvian.

The features of nationalizing regimes include closed and restricted frameworks of involvement in decision making. The most important attribute was that it became both an empowering and ideologically constrained field for the ruling elites, which often excludes the intelligentsia and intellectuals.[16] Elites, not states, are the main actors in these processes of nationalization. For example, my findings demonstrate that in electoral democracies elites are elected but then reselected by the ruling political elites in the nationalizing regime through various formal and informal ideological coalitions. In less democratic (in terms of elections and political appointments) regimes as in Kazakhstan, elites are *selected* before the formal elections by the ruling political elites of the nationalizing regime and precisely by the president himself.

In the nationalizing regime the elites either have to conform with the hegemonic perspectives and values dictated by the regime or engage in competition against it. As my findings regarding the Harmony and ZaRYA parties demonstrate this usually leads to the "artificial opposition" of such parties or their complete negation and disempowerment, even under democratic regimes (see chapter 3).

NATIONALIZING REGIMES AND MOST DIFFERENTIATED CASE STUDIES

The nationalizing regime is discussed here in the perspective of a power field, the space of interchangeable positions of actors involved in the process of competing for power but also as elites relating to nonelites in the state.[17] The postcommunist legacy of institutionalization, state control, and ideological training of the communist elites provided the space for diverse and hybrid political developments after independence. We can adopt a hypothesis that elite selection or election depends on democratization processes, and thus defines the openness or closedness of the nationalizing regimes and their policies. This process in turn influences the democratization of each state. Let us consider this in a theoretical perspective.

It is widely believed that a democratic regime requires open and competitive elections for "open contestation over the right to win control of the government, and this in turn requires free competitive elections, the results of which determine who governs."[18] It is also believed that authoritarian regimes function under the logic of nonrepresentative elections. In other words, elites are selected and co-opted by the court of power elites rather than by the mechanisms of open elections. And although elections are also held in nondemocratic contexts, these are often not open to wider contestation and are not free. Lisa Wedeen argued that elections in nondemocratic states served as performative politics: they "signaled that 'support' for the president, by those who admire, fear, and loathe him, could be tied to public performances of democratic openness *and* to the sense of lost opportunities such public performances made apparent."[19] Other scholars also argued that staged elections in nondemocratic postcommunist states are used for the domestic and foreign audiences and stakeholders.[20] However, democratic regimes by all means require "competitive" elections in which each citizen can technically participate; this leaves Latvia with a quarter of its population noncitizens in a rather nondemocratic context. How can one test the nature of that democracy? Charles Tilly, for example, writers that "a regime is democratic to the degree that political relations between the state and its citizens feature broad, equal, protected and mutually binding consultation. Democracy means net movement toward broader, more equal, more protected, and more binding consultation. De-democratization, obviously, then means net movement toward narrower, more unequal, less protected, less binding consultation."[21] We have already established that state- and nation-building in this context of post-Soviet politics is defined by the elites' struggle and their power in different state institutions including the government, parliament, and others. If democratization is then defined and evaluated by an "equal" and "broad" relation between the state and its citizens, then both Kazakhstan and Latvia would be considered nondemocratic for the reason that equal and broad political participation of nonelites in political development is limited in both states.

In principle, although nominally a democratic state and a member of the European Union, Latvia remains a closed ideological regime that controls the sacredness of the "immortal" Latvian nation. This means that any other political party or group that decides to challenge this dominant discourse or deviate from it to support the rights of the vast Russian-speaking minorities, will fail in the political competition. For example, the centrist party Harmony (Sarkanas) won the popular vote in the parliamentary elections in 2014 and 2011, but never managed to get even one minister in the cabinet, which is now almost by default composed of the ruling Latvianized right-leaning coalition. One of my respondents described the situation as an "artificial opposition" of the Harmony party. The party only managed to win for the charismatic Russian-speaking mayor of Riga, Nils Ušakovs, three terms in the citywide elections ruled by the popular vote of Riga's diverse bilingual residents (including ethnic Russians and ethnic Latvians) where the Russian-speaking population constitutes almost half of the residents.

Kazakhstan, the second largest post-Soviet state after Russia, is considered nondemocratic and is often described as an authoritarian state.[22] In Kazakhstan the regime is solid in composition, representing the loyal bond of pro-Nazarbayev power elites. It is distinguished in the literature as authoritarian rule that is characterized by the regime's continuous manipulation of "formal political institutions" and by the "increasingly repressive" sole leadership of "societal institutions" by a very powerful political group of elites.[23] The growing financial crisis and devaluation of the local currency (tenge), rumors about the Land Reform, and the lending of Kazakh land to the "Chinese" spurred the most recent (April–May 2016) social protests across the country. This was followed by more recent waves of mothers' protests (in winter 2019) and protests for open and fair elections (April–July 2019).

The mothers' protests were sparked by a tragedy in February 2019 in Astana when five girls in one family died in a fire while their parents were working at night to provide for the family. This event demonstrated societal unrest regarding inequality, economic and social insecurity, and overall instability. Movements such as Oyan Qazaqstan openly call for a parliamentary republic, open elections, and the right to conduct public rallies. This political-social movement calls for political freedoms as well as the economic-political changes necessary to help classes at risk and mothers. In his numerous speeches President Nazarbayev defines more challenges to Kazakhstan's "stability." These include internal Islamic terrorism threats coming from the supporters of radical Islamic movements. Growing intra-elite competition since Nazarbayev's resignation also threatened the regime's overall stability—Nazarbayev was and remains the connecting link between numerous political interest groups. Nazarbayev regime stability rests on the regime's control of regional and central elites and on control over the dominant discourse propagated by the regime to the wider population.[24] When Nursultan A. Nazarbayev, the country's first and only president, in power since 1989 and reelected numerous times for almost thirty years of Kazakhstan's independence from the Soviet Union, voluntarily resigned in March 2019, it first shocked various groups of population including those who expressed the view that they "never knew a different president."

For a short while lasting no more than twenty-four hours after Nazarbayev's voluntary resignation in a televised presidential address, there was hope for Kazakhstan's democratization. Some Western commentators even considered the start of a new era in Kazakhstan. Yet the symbolic resignation of Nazarbayev and the symbolic following of the constitutional mechanism calling for the interim president position to be held by the speaker of the Senate, who happened to be one of the most loyal elite members of Nazarbayev's regime, shattered these hopes in seconds. One of the first decisions of the interim president, and now elected second president, Kassym-Jomart Tokayev, was to rename Astana, the capital of Kazakhstan to Nur-Sultan, to reflect the historical role of Nursultan A. Nazarbayev, the *Elbasy*, translated as the Father of the Nation. The move spurred local protests.

These major changes in Kazakhstan's domestic policy only revealed the obvious—the dominant discourse in Kazakhstan is centered around the legitimacy of Nazarbayev as the sole guarantor of the miracles of development that had been accomplished and of interethnic stability in the country,[25] even after his official resignation. Any alternative discourses deviating from this presidential discourse are doomed to be marginalized and defeated, for example, the stagnant agenda of the Kazakh national-patriots, who are nevertheless taking over the agenda at the moment, or the defeated opposition.[26] The interim president, Kassym-Jomart Tokayev became the de jure second president of the country and announced elections that were already being contested by growing dissent among young urbanized groups of artistic and civil society activists demanding open and fair elections. On June 9, 2019, Kazakhstan held the first presidential elections in which Nazarbayev's name was not on the ballot for the first time, and for the first time including an oppositional candidate, Amirzhan Kosanov, who was nevertheless discredited after the elections as the pro-regime candidate. The June 2019 presidential elections also signaled the growing involvement of young activists who formed the Oyan, Qazaqstan (Wake Up, Kazakhstan) movement and volunteered as independent electoral observers at the polls, when Tokayev was elected as the second president of the country. Yet President Tokayev continues to work in the shadow of the Father of the Nation, *Elbasy.*

Even after the official departure of President Nazarbayev, the regime continues to live in the conditions of his personalized rule. Nazarbayev's positions as the lifelong chair of the Security Council and as a recently named Honorary Senator allow him to remain in power and offer his guidance to the new president, parliament, or any other political institution in the country. Time will show how long it takes for Nazarbayev's influence to continue in person, but it is clear from the outset that his resignation brought only visual changes and that the regime remained intact: the first presidential elections without Nazarbayev did not promise or deliver real political or elite changes in Kazakhstan.

The discourses that Nazarbayev was able to develop throughout decades of his personalized rule will continue to influence the nationalizing regime and its tactics in diminishing discursive and political competition in years to come. This will allow study of the development of a personalized nationalizing regime in more detail and with more nuance than just studying a cult of personality. The difference between a cult and a personalized nationalizing regime is that cults of personality are diminished or even condemned after a leader's death. But the institutionalization of the Father or the Leader of the Nation discourse into every concept of what the nation meant in the first decades of independence has a lasting effect on further nation-building processes, even after the departure or death of the leader. This happens because the remaining political elites use institutionalized discourses of the personalized rule of the Father of the Nation to build their legitimacy until they come up with new discourses and new institutionalized systems of state programs on national identities. Alternatively, personalized regimes may not survive competition from rival groups that do not support the ideas of the personalized nationalizing regimes. Thus, they either attack the Father of the Nation, defy every project he implemented, or criticize the whole system. The situation in Kazakhstan after Nazarbayev's departure is still unclear but there are signs that a young artistic community of urban activists across Kazakhstan has chosen to protest against the system with their slogans "For Fair and Free Elections," "I have a Choice," "I woke up," and "You cannot run away from Truth." And it continues to the present with a war of positions and ubiquitous new slogans and posters citing the Constitution in Roman Zakharov's artistic activism.

The hegemony of specific dominant discourses challenges pluralism in political development and political participation beyond the ethnic field in Latvia and beyond the authoritarian leadership in Kazakhstan. Throughout this book I will demonstrate that despite Nazarbayev's resignation and even after his physical death one day, he remains and will remain one of the most powerful discourses on which political elites and nationalizing regimes can build their legitimacy and political messages. This happens because the elitist discourse of the nationalizing regime was constructed so that the figure of the first president would be dominant in every positive development in the country and he would be placed at the discursive core of every ideological program or paradigm.[27]

This is what defines the personalized nationalizing regime where the dominant discourse is based not only on the notion of the sacred nation but also on the sacred Nation-Builder who creates and sustains this nation in contemporary time himself. The question for a different book would be to study how long the personalized discourse of Nazarbayev would sustain itself after almost three decades of consistent injection of his words, his historical role, and his vision into nation-building fabric that is almost comparable to the Soviet obsession with Lenin and his "physical" appearance in the daily lives of every Soviet citizen. Nursultan Nazarbayev's busts are not yet ever-present in public spaces as Lenin's busts were, but his portraits surely occupy too much space across Kazakhstan, even after his official resignation. This phenomenon problematizes the development of democratized political and public spheres.

Latvia's ideational nationalizing regime is not better than a personalized one because it also continuously cuts off pluralistic views in debates about what the nation is and how it should develop. Moreover, an ideational nationalizing regime that is stuck on defining and safeguarding a very narrow perspective of the nation, for example, a very distinct ethnic connotation of what it means to be Latvian, impedes the development of the country as a whole. The obsession with controlling what the nation is also creates difficult precedents that leave large parts of the population outside the nation, but within the state where the nation is constructed. And although non-Latvian elites have long spoken about the creation of parallel communities in that homogeneous view of the Latvian nationalizing regime, what is happening at the moment is that Latvia is a country of migrants creating their own diasporic communities away from the state of their citizenship and away from the territory of the sacred Latvian nation.

How do we make sense of these complex discourses, practices, institutionalizations, and power relations in understanding how a nationalizing regime works? In the following section I discuss the main methodological tools used in this study, including elite interviews, content and discourse analysis, and archival study.

FRAMEWORK AND METHODOLOGY USED IN STUDYING NATIONALIZING REGIMES

In the study of power and nationalizing regimes I was driven by the "performative" approach, in which my main questions including in interviews with elites were guided by the unraveling of how processes of state- and nation-building were done. The performative nature of "How is the state being done?" as well as "In what ways does the performance of politics reproduce, enable, challenge, or naturalize ideologies about the state?"[28] done through control of the national imagination about the boundaries and limits of the specific nation within the realm of the nationalizing regime required a set of different methods ranging from elite interviews and political ethnography to content and archival analysis and the study of legislation, state programs, and speeches. It was important to identify these processes and performances in historical texts, elite interviews, newspaper content analyses, and even the memoirs of politicians. The overall fieldwork for this study spanned various states beyond just Latvia and Kazakhstan and over the period from 2011 to 2019. In this process of validating the main findings when the principal decision makers were "asked to reflect upon past events" and in order for them not to "strategically misremember or revise their accounts, and likely in a way that is favorable to them,"[29] it was important to collect a larger sample of interviews and to contrast and compare the accounts of different political elites. To validate the information further I also had to evaluate the context in which each interview was conducted and collect factual and contextual data from other resources, such as the most widely read public newspapers as well as official newspapers. Part of this multifaceted research also included the study of secondary polling data, for example, from the Baltic and Eurasian Integration Barometers. Let me briefly discuss the main methodological tools used in studying nationalizing regimes.

Elite Interviews and Political Ethnography

In the study of nation-building and its ideological construction, most of the information concerning the actual construction of meanings and symbols is not part of the public discourse. To assemble particular information about actors and producers of such meanings and the ways in which they were produced, the study of nationalizing regimes relies on interviews with relevant elites.

Elite interviews are a very successful tool for contextualizing the processes of nation-building because they allow reflection on contexts, time, and decision making. Preparation for the interviews includes research on the elite field, historical comparison of the two cases, and the methodology for elite interviews in studying nationalism. Consequently, I had two or three questions that started with the introduction of my project and led to the discussion of the concept of nation and nationalism with my interviewees. Following this, I asked the interviewees to remember how post-Soviet nation-building evolved in their respective countries and explain their role in these processes at the point when they started their political careers. This varied from more senior elites such as former speakers of the first parliaments or founding fathers of specific parties (especially the National Alliance in Latvia or the post-Soviet Communist Party in Kazakhstan) to younger elites who had joined the political arena only two or three years ago. I had two of these interesting interviews—one with the Unity representative in Latvia and one with Zhanbolat Mamay, a member of the new national-patriot movement in Kazakhstan in 2013. Generational gaps of the first wave of independence politicians compared to the newcomers of the late 2000s era allowed changes to be distinguished within the elitist field and discourses that were navigated by different parties and actors. Significant historical events and periodization constructed by each of my respondents helped with mapping the initial historical development of nation-building, which I then compared suing legal documents, historiography, and archival documents. It was important for me to capture the elitist imagination of the past and its gradual development into the present to grasp elite visions of time and to balance elites' own involvement in these processes. I wanted to narrate decision making and power mechanization based on firsthand experiences.

My interview pool was selected based on their active role in envisioning and discussing national discourses in their respective countries. After the introductory questions I elaborated on the development of national projects, giving the respondent the power to prioritize his or her views on specific discourses and policies. In this way I could compare and contrast the interviews to determine what was seen as the most important set of projects and discourses among the different elites. Differences were drawn mostly between the nationalists (Kazakh and Latvian) who prioritized language, traditions, and the importance of specific historical discourses and more nonnationalist elites who focused on multifaceted approaches to nation-building, for example, politicians who also focused on economic development beyond ethnic problems. The rest of the interview focused on the processes of such decision making, for example, the selection of discourses and projects in nation-building, and the role of different power elites or other members of the regime who had more power in decision making.

The sample was balanced across the cases. In Latvia I tried to interview a sample from each political party that was present in the Saeima (Latvian Parliament) throughout its modern history from the early 1990s to the 2010s. In addition, I interviewed independent experts, opinion leaders, and intellectuals. I also focused on members of the party who had worked on specific nation-building projects. For example, I interviewed the 2013 speaker of the Latvian Parliament and prominent member of the National Alliance, Inara Murniece. She was also one of the leading authors of the post-2012 referendum Program on the Integration of Non-Latvian Minorities, an important strategic document reflecting the ruling coalition's approach to Russian-speakers in Latvia. This interview proved to be very fruitful as Murniece was very open and went into a detailed explanation of what the project of building the Latvian nation meant to her, her colleagues, and Latvian politicians in general. She also talked about the changes made to the law on referendums provide stricter conditions for organizing new referendums after the 2012 referendum on the status of Russian as the second official language in Latvia, which was nevertheless unsuccessful. She further explained in detail different categories of belonging and identification (variations of nation, people, citizens, and so on) in the integration program she had worked on. These types of interviews when collected in a large sample and in greater detail allow us compare and contrast narratives across different players, while also shedding more light on decision making at the critical moments of Latvian parliamentary crises.

These interviews with political elites are very useful because they "give access to information about respondents' experiences and motivations that may not be available in the public or documentary record; they allow us to understand opinions and thought processes with a granularity that surveys rarely achieve; and they can add micro-foundations to events or patterns observed at the macro level."[30]

The sample in Latvia included advocates of different views regarding how the nation should develop further—by becoming a political nation, ethnode-mocracy, or some alternative. This selection ranged across different parties, and even the Unity party had advocates for more open and inclusive versions of nation-building. In my sample there was a large selection of pro-Russian activists from Riga and Daugavpils, from the former PCTVL and ZaRYA and other local Russian movements. The setting of the interviews varied a lot but was embedded in the urban structure—near or inside the buildings of political institutions, in special parks such as the World War II memorial site in Daugavpils or the Monument of Independence in Riga. This provided an interesting setting that further contextualized my respondents' historical, cultural, and social references. They offered brief explanations on a specific building, especially for example, when we passed the Saiema, near the monument to the heroes of the 1990s barricades located near the parliament, or the contested monument to World War II Soviet liberators that pro-Latvian elites proposed to demolish almost every year closer to the Victory Day celebration. I collected around two hundred interviews with political elites, cultural elites involved in political processes and regime programs, oppositional leaders, and opinion leaders of the new youth movements.

Nonrandom sampling was chosen as a technique to identify respondents based on their position and power. I prioritized four–five specific groups of elites. The sample is divided into four different layers. The first layer was aimed at the ruling elite members and the "ideological gatekeepers": political and nonpolitical members who had direct access to the "political" formation of national symbols, identification, and culture. These interviews provided firsthand experience and knowledge of the field. The people interviewed here had been involved in sym-bolic formation at the first stage of national constructions in the late 1980s and early 1990s. I used snowball sampling to find most of my respondents.

The second layer represented major political forces—members of political parties and movements both progovernmental (more visible in Kazakhstan's case) and oppositional. Here I was interested to see the evolution of the national symbolic narrative over the change of the regime and political party in power, which may change the symbolic content of the national ideology.

The third layer of respondents was represented by the so-called cultural elite—public intellectuals, writers, artists who either work for the ruling elite in the construction of state ideology,[31] work for the opposition, or form a neutral, third side of observant and "objective opinion." This set of respondents consists of opinion leaders for different social groups (intelligentsia, ethnic minorities, indigenous nationalists, etc.) who either have power or strive for it. Although they are not key figures in the decision-making process over nation-building, they are strong players in the field of content provision for such projects. So it was important to determine their vision of national development and further ethnicization, especially among indigenous intellectuals who usually become guardians of purity of the "national" culture in Soviet vocabulary.

The fourth layer consisted of ordinary citizens, most of whom represented so-called ethnic minorities, Russian–speakers, and non-Latvians or non-Kazakhs. A large part of the fourth layer included numerous interviews and ethnographic data among the minority groups in large cities of Kazakhstan and Latvia.

Political Ethnography

My use and understanding of political ethnography spanned far beyond the initial boundaries of the first days of fieldwork in snowy Riga in March 2012 on the famous Lomonosova Street when the door opened to a slightly different understanding of post-Soviet *time* through discussions with local residents and local institutionalized knowledge.

This method allowed me to become immersed in political discussions in the ministerial offices and endless corridors of power in Astana, Almaty, Daugavpils, and Riga, but also helped me contextualize power from below—from the perspectives of the everyday lives of ordinary people, citizens of each respective state and nationalizing regime. The pages of this book often introduce readers to these narratives of nation-builders and ordinary people—through the ways many of my interviews divided these two groups, through the eyes of Laima and her circle of family and friends further divided into citizens and noncitizens, often not just based on legal or ethnic lines but on social statuses and their own identifications.

These identifications also included categories of time—Soviet and post-Soviet, the urban and rural divisions I have already mentioned, including *mambets, kolkhozniks,* and urban dwellers, *korennoi zhitel' goroda,* a native resident of the city. While my political ethnography continues in the realm of empowerment from below—from grassroots art-activist movements across Central Asia or national-cultural revivals that grant certain social actors unexpected empowerment in conditions of further state ordering[32]—the nationalizing regime framework benefits from these ethnographic findings and contextualization from within the field, through the active process of becoming local but also foreign at the same time.

Content Analysis and Archival Research

The study of major newspapers during the more than twenty-year-time span from the late 1989s to the 2010s was designed to help identify the main ideological narratives used by political elites over the course of change through elections. The study of newspapers enabled me to identify the main discourses and public debates prevailing at specific times.

In Kazakhstan I conducted a bilingual search focusing on the official newspaper, *Kazakhstanskaia Pravda* (in Russian), the more nationalist *Ana Tili* (in Kazakh) and *Qazaq Adebieti* (in Kazakh). I also analyzed the publications (2012–2014) of the *Central Asia Monitor,* a newspaper that targeted the urban middle class and intellectuals. This newspaper initiated a heated central discussion about the absence of a stable national ideology and the necessity of creating more feasible identification markers, defined by respondents as a *concrete ideological framework.* Each issue in this series of discussions, published over about two years, featured a major opinion leader, politician, or political analyst and in-depth analysis of the situation. The selection of these interviews and discussions serves as a backdrop for detailed content analysis focusing on the discussions around nation and nation-building in Kazakhstan. In Latvia I focused on the Latvian *Diena* and the Russian-language newspapers *Telegraf* and *Chas,* the most influential and popular newspapers in both communities since independence.

The choice of such media sources is explained by the fact that newspapers, especially government–sponsored papers such as *Kazahstankaia Pravda,* were among the main ideological and informational outlets created by the Soviets to transmit information and meaning to the respective populations in these republics. Immediately after the collapse of the Soviet Union, most of the newly independent republics were unable to construct informational systems anew, so the remaining Soviet-type outlets were transformed into informational channels

for new regimes and elites. In some countries, the Soviet legacy in the informational and ideological fields still prevails.[33]

I focused on the following categories for the selection of articles: (1) the
discourse of independence; (2) the discourse of the "Other," for example, the
Russian minority or Russia both in positive and negative connotations as the
symbol of Soviet "Occupation" in Latvia; and (3) the discourse of the political
elites in power, for example, the role and figure of the president or prime minister. These three categories were chosen to test and explain the nature of the
"independence" symbol that is important in these nations.

The discourse of the "Other" or othering was the simplest technique for identity construction and self-imagination. Finally, the latter category helped identify
some of the main actors behind these policies and the public's reaction to them.
Content analysis aims to identify the main symbolic fields in which national
symbols and ideas formed throughout the twenty years of independence. Some
examples of keyword searches in newspapers are: Latvian/Kazakh/Kazakhstani
"nation," "occupation"–"colonialism," "nationalists," "national memory," "Russians," "ethnic minority," and "national identity"; additional searches included
dates of celebrations of state official and unofficial commemorations, for example, the controversial March 16 and May 9 in Latvia—days of remembrance
of Latvian legionnaires and Russian-Soviet soldiers who fought during World
War II; and the image of third parties—"Russia," "European Union," "Customs
Union," "Estonia," "Belarus," and others.

I also focused on particular opinions and debates in the public space about
initial national projects on national symbols, laws (on language and citizenship),
addresses of the dominant ruling elite, and opinions of the opposition. The analysis of newspaper content thus provided a very fruitful background for my discussion of national discourse in both countries (further discussed in chapter 2).

Finally, in late 2013 I was able to conduct archival research in the office of
the Organization for Security and Co-operation (OSCE) in Europe in Prague
where I collected data on the OSCE Mission to Latvia and reports of the High
Commissioner on National Minorities. This important mission monitored minority rights and interrelations with the Latvian majority during the turbulent
periods of the main policy decisions on citizenship and language laws. These
data provided a significant background for the analysis of external influence and
Europeanization in Latvia.

As part of the research I also analyzed data across the cases and focused
on the more limited involvement of the OSCE in Kazakhstan and finally,

Kazakhstan's chairmanship of the OSCE in 2010 and the importance of the de-mocratization agenda and pressures on Kazakhstan. Most of these findings are covered in chapter 4 where I discuss the creation of national minorities in both nationalizing regimes.

PLAN OF THE BOOK

This book is built on historical, contextual, and empirical accounts of the post-Soviet world and its nationalizing regimes as a whole. It also addresses the Latvian and Kazakh cases in more detail to conceptualize the mechanisms of those who rule meaning-making and how they do it. Chapter 1 provides more detail on why these two divergent case studies help shed more light on the mechanization of nationalizing regimes. The aim is not only to study the nature of post-Soviet nation-building but also to flesh out the power struggles within the nationalizing regime. For this reason, it requires the comparison of a nominally and structurally democratic regime and a nondemocratic one. The chapter includes methodological and theoretical discussions of nationalizing regimes and how to study them. I first address the main concepts used in this study—nationalizing regimes, elites, states, and nations. Then I discuss differ-ent types of elite structures and differences that can be formed in nationalizing regimes. In this chapter I also address the most recent developments of President Nazarbayev's resignation and analyze how changes from outside and within the regime affect its nature.

The chapters 2–5 focus on the mechanization of nationalizing regimes through understanding how they construct and dominate discourses over the time of independence (chapter 2), how elites contest power within nationalizing regimes and why and how democratic and nondemocratic contexts shape this competition (chapter 3). Then I discuss (chapter 4) how groups outside nation-alizing regimes—those constructed as national minorities—respond to these power discourses and power contestations. In chapter 4 I also discuss further the most recent developments of protest movements in Kazakhstan.

In chapter 5, I demonstrate how political electoral participation declined equally in Latvia and Kazakhstan throughout the end of the 1990s and mid-2000s because both electorates felt unable to change the established structure of their regimes. These regimes must be understood as formal and informal structures guiding and forming governments and political institutions based on the interests of the ruling elites at the time; the chapter clearly deconstructs the effects of these interests and actions. Chapter 5 sheds light on societal feedback through elections and popular responses to nationalizing regimes. Finally, in the Conclusion I draw on the major aspects of nationalizing regimes and their different types, discuss the development of post-Soviet nation-building, and discuss further avenues of research in this field.

1

NATIONALIZING REGIMES

THE STUDY OF POWER FIELDS AND
THE REIMAGINATION OF THE STATE

How can we conceptualize power and nationalism in postcommunist states where the dictates of the formerly dominant ideology of the Communist Party provided the space and institutional memory of "concrete" ideological structures but denied even the use of "ideology" in the new time? What can one understand methodologically and conceptually from the comparison of two completely different cases that do not have common borders, that have contrasting geopolitical realities united only by the pressures of globalization and the looming "geographical" presence of the Russian Federation on the map as well as the legacy of the former dominant political structure it represents now, that of the Soviet Union?

Conventionally the collapse of the Soviet Union brought about a brief moment of fragmented territorialities—Moscow stopped being the common capital of the fourteen union republics (except for Russia for which it actually remained the capital) and there was no longer an enormous pink splash showing the country's borders uniting the Baltic Sea with the other end of the Soviet territory on the border with China. Rapid changes, painful breakups, fears of civil wars and actual outbreaks of civil war, ethnic conflicts, and territorial disputes across this vast region that continued to depend on the existing links and in some places even on the existing ruble currency and Soviet passports defined the long post-Soviet time.

The temporal subjectivity of the Soviet collapse was not a linear or homogeneous experience for all its former people, and it was not felt in the same way across this vast space. As it was simply put by one of the respondents in Central Asia, "The Soviet Union was a mess and its collapse was a messier mess." So how does one make sense of these complex realities when trying to disentangle the very recent concept of post-Soviet state-building and nationalism? How do we measure the differences in forms, genres, structures, and actors who are actually building both the states and nations or, sometimes only states or only partially nations?

There is an abundant methodological literature to guide one's choices in investigating and finding answers to many research questions, but there is no one recipe or magical mix when it comes to the choice of case studies. In searching for answers to my questions I did not turn to Kazakhstan or Central Asia merely because I am a native of the "region" that only came to conceptual existence recently. In fact, over years of research spent in different borderlands, hours of recorded interviews, translations, archival work, and political ethnography in parliaments, with state officials and in state-owned enterprises, my understanding of the region became even more complicated just as it is in the perplexed reality of contemporary time in the post-Soviet space itself. Is there a region called "Central Asia"? Are the borders between five, seven, or more states, which are characterized by different forces as Central Asia or Central Eurasia, real and stable? Or is the Central Asia and Kazakhstan formula that follows the Soviet categorization of the region still applied, wherein Central Asia consists of the four post-Soviet states of Uzbekistan, Turkmenistan, Kyrgyzstan, and Tajikistan plus Kazakhstan? These explorations stemming from wider fieldwork in Eurasia led me to the question where is Central Asia in general?[1] This inevitably leads to the discussion of who *we* are, the post-Soviets of the world in this complex picture beyond simplistic territorial demarcations on maps, in museums, and in censuses.[2]

The realization that my position as a local in Latvia to the extent that most people spoke to me in Latvian and my position as a local in Kazakhstan, but where some of my respondents were surprised at having to explain what they meant by "distinctly *our* realities," raises many of the questions about post-Sovietness that I discuss in this chapter.

In this chapter I provide further explanations regarding why I chose Latvia and Kazakhstan as the comparative basis for conceptualizing nationalizing regimes and how these two nations developed under Soviet rule. I expand on the understanding of post-Soviet worlds, post-Soviet temporal subjectivities in nationalistic perceptions, and I theorize about post-Soviet processes of nation-building by discussing post-Soviet state structures. These are the key conceptual and methodological threads that constitute this book and its theoretical arguments.

DECIPHERING THE MOST DIFFERENTIATED CASE STUDIES OF KAZAKHS, RUSSIANS, AND THE BALTICS

Post-Soviet Latvia and Kazakhstan were the only two post-Soviet states in which ethnic Russians and those closely identified with Russian ethnic or linguistic identity were close in number to the titular ethnic groups before independence (see tables 1 and 2). [3] After 1991 both states were represented by their respective elites as dual-community states in which identity overlapped with ethnic identification, language proficiency, citizenship, and cultural belonging. In reality, this meant that many long-term citizens found themselves in the position of ethnic minorities practically overnight, many lost their citizenship as well as political and cultural rights, and they were cut off from electoral participation due to either their citizenship status or their lack of democratization and access to political participation and mobility. The drastic change was rooted in the new nationalistic policies that were controlled by the elites. These elites claimed legitimacy for nationalization through historical injustices, unlawfulness, and comparisons of Soviet policies to colonial practices. [4]

Unlike Kazakhstan, Latvia, was incorporated into the Soviet Union only in 1945, after World War II, and in the process of what was then termed by the Latvian diaspora and postindependence politicians as the "Soviet Occupation." [5] Latvian interwar and pre-Soviet independence legally and historically justified the state's ferocious primordial nation-building policies post-1991: jus sanguinis citizenship policies, a Language Inspectorate and fines for non-Latvian speakers, and no provision of political rights for noncitizens, most of whom were ethnic Russians and so-called Russian-speaking communities. [6] Latvian citizenship policies based on jus sanguinis and legal continuity allowed only the descendants of prewar Latvia (up to 1943), residents and citizens and their descendants to gain automatic citizenship after independence in 1991. This policy covered most of the ethnic Latvian population and some of prewar minorities but circumvented "Soviet-era migrants," many of whom were ethnic Russians and other Slavs who were Russian-speaking minorities. After independence Latvia declared Latvian

Table 1. Ethnic composition in Kazakhstan from 1979 to 2009

	1979	1989	1990	1994	1999	2009
Total number	14,688,300	16,464,400	16,451,700	16,870,600	14,953,100	16,442,000
Kazakhs (%)	36.0	39.7	40.3	44.3	53.4	63.1
Russians (%)	40.8	37.8	37.6	35.8	30	23.7
Germans (%)	6.1	5.8	5.5	3.6	2.4	1.1
Ukrainians (%)	6.1	5.4	5.4	5.1	3.6	2.1
Tatars (%)	2.1	2.0	2.0	2.0	1.7	1.3

Sources: Itogi Vsesoiuznoi perepisi naseleniia 1979 goda, in A. N. Alekseenko, Respublika Kazakhstan v zerkale perepisei naseleniia Informatsyonnyi biulleten' Tsentra demografii i ekologii cheloveka Instituta narodnokhozaistvennogo prognozirovaniia RAN 2000, No. 47. Based on Kratkie itogi Vsesoiuznoi perepisi naseleniia 1989 goda po Kazakhskoi SSR, Alma-Ata, 1990, pp. 7–9. Predvaritel'nie itogi perepisi naseleniia 1999 goda v Respublike Kazakhstan, Almaty, 2000 in Dinamika chislennosti i sostava naseleniia Kazakhstana vo vtoroi polovide XX veka, E. Zimovina 2003. Analytical Report "Results of the 2009 National population census of the Republic of Kazakhstan," ed. A. A. Smailov, Astana, 2011, Agency on Statistics of the Republic of Kazakhstan, p. 19.

Table 2. Ethnic composition of population in Latvia from 1920 to 2009

	1920	1935	1959	1989	2011
Total number (millions)	1.86	1.91	2.08	2.67	2.06
Latvians (%)	72.6	75.5	62.0	52.0	62.1
Russians (%)	5.7	10.6	26.6	34.0	26.9
Byelorussians (%)	4.1	1.4	2.9	4.5	3.3
Ukrainians (%)	0.0	0.1	1.4	3.5	2.21
Germans (%)	3.6	3.2	0.1	0.1	0.1
Jews (%)	5.0	4.8	1.7	0.9	0.3
Poles (%)	3.3	2.5	2.9	2.3	2.3
Lithuanians (%)	4.0	1.2	1.5	1.3	2.7

Source: Latvijas Statistikas—Latvian Statistics.

the only official language in the country and introduced a special Language Inspectorate for all state employees (including minority schoolteachers) to monitor Latvian language proficiency levels among them. The Language Inspectorate also functioned to impose substantive fines and even to dismiss employees for poor knowledge of the official language.[7] Latvian language acquisition became key for safeguarding Latvian citizenship, which left many non-Latvians in a rather disadvantageous position.

These "Soviet-era migrants" were allowed to naturalize only with the implementation of the 1994 Citizenship Law and a quota-based system (chapters 2 and 3) and draconian naturalization rules. Initially the quota-based system was age-based and prioritized those who were born in Latvia, but it prescribed no citizenship status for children of noncitizens. Until its abolition in 1998, the naturalization quota system of the Latvian Citizenship Law was severely criticized by the European Union (EU).[8] However, none of these criticisms, including reports of the Organization for Security and Co-operation in Europe (OSCE) High Commissioner on National Minorities, which mentioned the undemocratic nature of noncitizen status that practically excludes noncitizens from all levels of political participation, including municipal elections had a lasting effect on changing the dominant discourse in Latvian elite-led political discussions. Until the 1998 abolition of the quota-based naturalization rule, the Russian-speaking minorities had almost no political voice in the Latvian parliament, where new laws on citizenship, state language, and naturalization were decided. In 2011 almost a quarter of the population in Latvia has noncitizen status (see table 3). And although there is a centrist party in the Latvian parliament at the moment, there are still very few political mechanisms for non-Latvian minorities to represent themselves politically within the structures of the Latvian state.

The Republic of Kazakhstan gained its independence in December 1991, after seventy years of Soviet history and only a short-lived independent movement before that. Nomadic groups, known as the Kazakh Khanate, were colonized by tsarist Russia from the late eighteenth to the beginning of the twentieth century.[9] The local intelligentsia became engaged in the process of "imagining community" and common national cause for the "Kazakh people" in the late nineteenth and early twentieth centuries,[10] but was defeated by the Soviet communists and perished in the Stalinist terror in 1937.

After the 1991 independence, laws in Kazakhstan granted citizenship to all pre-1991 residents but declared Kazakh, a language of the Kazakhs—the ethnic "minority" in their own land—a state language.[11] The problem with the linguistic divide persists in contemporary Kazakhstan even today. The latest available report (2009) on Kazakh language proficiency demonstrates that Kazakhstan's Russian-speakers of Slavic origin never managed to raise their overall proficiency in the state language, even to reach a 10 percent threshold, but many ethnic Kazakhs who reside in urban areas remain predominantly Russified as well.[12]

Table 3. Citizenship composition in regions of Latvia based on the 2011 census

	Latvia	Riga region	Pieriga region	Vidzeme region	Kurzeme region	Zemgale region	Latgale region
Total population	2,067,887	657,424	369,638	211,233	270,168	255,200	304,224
%	100	100	100	100	100	100	100
Citizens of Latvia	1,732,880	488,760	323,243	199,469	234,916	222,371	264,121
%	83.7	74	87	94.4	86.9	87	86.8
Noncitizens of Latvia	290,660	146,964	41,032	10,801	28,146	30,338	33,379
%	14	22	11	0.5	10.4	11	10.9
Citizens of Russian Federation	31,394	15,032	3,359	497	5,781	1,630	5,095
%	0.15	0.22	0.09	0.02	0.2	0.06	0.16
Citizens of Ukraine	2,468	1,301	381	70	297	158	261
%	0.11	0.019	0.01	0.003	0.001	0.006	0.085
Stateless	188	70	40	13	27	10	28
%	0.009	0.001	0.001	0.0006	0.0009	0.003	0.009

Source: Latvijas Statistikas—Latvian Statistics.

This explains the duality of language use in Kazakhstan. But it also threatens the regime's stability and one of its main discourses of interethnic harmony when natural Kazakhification of the public sphere threatens the balanced use of Russian and Kazakh skillfully used by the first president Nursultan A. Nazarbayev to legitimate his rule.

After two decades of independence, the Kazakh language is still largely marginalized, a situation that continues to raise concerns in the growing nationalist rhetoric of Kazakhified social movements and leaders (Mukhtar Shakhanov, Mukhtar Taizhan, Berik Abdygaliev, and Zher (land protests) movements). Kazakh is still the official language of public administration.[13] In addition, the most rapidly growing segment of primary and secondary schooling in Kazakhstan is predominantly monolingually Kazakh.[14] Nevertheless, state language policy is weak and disorganized. The introduction of a Latinized alphabet for Kazakh language further creates confusion among the sociolinguistic communities that are catching up with learning Kazakh and, furthermore, with a lack of professional literature or a body of experts on Latinized Kazakh. This complex situation leads to an unbalanced use of Kazakh language by Russified groups who do not have access or further incentive to learn the Kazakh language.

Every state policy on Kazakh language introduced since 1991 failed to implement the goals of making Kazakh more widely spoken or attracting non-Kazakh speakers (among them urban ethnic Kazakhs as well) to gain fluency in the state language. These failures lead to potential sociolingual divisions and increased the rural–urban divide in the country.[15] But these linguistic divisions also allowed the regime to combine the pro-Russian/cosmopolitan and pro-Kazakh/nationalist agenda in presidential addresses, which meant that many of the citizens who are not fluent in Kazakh were potentially unaware of the growing but contextual nationalization proposed by the former president Nursultan Nazarbayev in his annual addresses to the nation (see chapter 3).

This brief context sheds light on the divisions and heterogeneous processes that nationalism leads to in trying to define an exclusivist approach to identity, which is fluid and complex as well as hard to pin down. Categories such as citizenship and language do create a certain order and level of separation in the understanding of belonging and identifications. These too are fluid because one person can possess more than one citizenship, even if illegally, or have citizenship in the Russian Federation and a noncitizen passport, but linguistically have a more Ukrainian background as the member of a family that came to Latvia from Ukraine during the Soviet period. Or take the example of a Russophone Kazakh person who ethnically identifies as Kazakh, lives in Kazakhstan, and has a Kazakh passport but who is not fluent in Kazakh. Where does this person belong?

In contexts of recent state-building and even in contexts of countries and states with prolonged periods of nation-building, there is always a question of belonging—territorially, culturally, spiritually and religiously, gender-wise, linguistically, and so forth. The purpose of meaning-making is to confront all these questions and puzzles. But who has the power and authority to decide that meaning? Who essentially drives these processes of defining and authorizing the different categories described above? Does this process differ in democratic and nondemocratic regimes? To test these questions and to analyze the structures of power under very different political systems, it was important to find two or more cases that had similar historical and demographic contexts that influenced their challenges in nation-building in the same way, but differed in their political development. Latvia and Kazakhstan, two states that faced the burden of post-Soviet nation rebuilding with complex ethnolinguistic divisions inside their own borders and that, in essence, represent textbook examples of "democratic" and "autocratic" regimes, served as ideal comparative cases for exposing power structures and strategies in nation-building processes.

The post-Soviet space provided an ideal testing ground for that because all

fifteen states approached the Soviet legacy of simultaneous ethnic institutionalization and Sovietization or depoliticization of ethnicity on almost the same level
as a negative aspect that required *rebuilding* their nations. The main question
in this remedial nation-building concerned history: protecting the sovereign
and often disputed borders of the new states and establishing the dominant
ethno-state language and ethnic history and authority of one ethnic group over
the whole nation-building process. The mechanisms of these processes worked
through the incorporation of dominant ethnicized discourses in political regimes, post-Soviet nationalizing regimes.

The notion of a nationalizing regime is at the heart of post-Soviet nationalism. It is inevitable because nationalism as an ideology and as a system of highly
emotive beliefs was already historically built-in with "identifiable frames of reference that are recognizable and transposable, even under conditions dramatically
different from those under which nationalism originated."[16] As Ernest Gellner
has pointed out nations are only identified as such if people belonging to the
nation "recognize each other as belonging to the same nation."[17] What binds a
nation together as a political community of citizens and permanent residents is
an overarching idea of belonging to a specific country, a political-territorial unit
with a distinct identification, shared values, and multiplicity of cultures but also a
unified understanding of that specific cultural and national belonging. But what
categories do these people use to feel that they are part of the same nation and
who is in charge of creating and controlling these categories for the larger parts
of the population? According to Ronald Grigor Suny: "The practice of fixing
nationality in each citizen's internal passport on the basis of parentage rendered
an inherently liquid identity into a solid commitment to a single ethnocultural
group. Young people with parents who had different national designations on
their passports were forced to choose one or the other nationality, which then
became a claim to inclusion or an invitation to exclusion in a given republic. In
some cases, people could opportunistically change their nationality officially, or
change their names, to ease their situation in the national republics."[18] The Soviet
experience of nation-building and national delineation in Kazakhstan and then
Latvia's incorporation into the Soviet Union resulted in the "solid" codification
of the ethnicity. The Soviet Union and its Nationalities Policy "helped create
powerful and distinct indigenous national identities," and also simultaneously
helped "remake local gender practices," which involved more women in active
social processes.[19] Soviet Nationalities Policy molded the Latvian peasant nation
and Kazakh nomadic society into a set of Soviet republics with clearly defined

territorial-ethnic political units. Territory became the constitutional "political frame" for nationhood in both the Soviet and post-Soviet contexts. For example, as Valerie A. Kivelson and Ronald Grigor Suny conclude in their study on nations and empires:

> Nations in the modern sense exist within this discourse of the nation. They are political communities that imagine themselves in a particular way that became possible only with the coincidence of the idea that cultural communities ought to become political communities and that the ordinary people within those communities ought to be able to rule themselves or at least choose those that govern them. This moral imperative to self-rule often pairs with ideas of citizenship, of the people as bearers of political rights and ultimately as an electorate or site of political choice. Finally, the modern sense of nation articulates a community of people, citizens, that is separate from and grants legitimacy to the state but is not to be conflated with the state. The nation is the imagined political community, while the *modern state is the set of institutions legitimized by the nation.* The nation's destiny, as prophesied by the discourse of the nation, is to form a state, or take over an existing state, and become a nation-state.[20]

It is important to note that many discourses of the post-Soviet or post-imperial political community stem from the legacy of Russian imperial and Soviet national codification. The Soviet experiment is particularly crucial for determining what led Latvian and Kazakh nationalizing regimes to choose sets of nationalizing discourses and techniques in their post-1991 nation-building policies and discourses. Elites wrap the post-Soviet "state" into nations that they imagine and construct through their own discourses and policies.

During the incorporation of both nations into the Soviet Union, in 1945 and 1918, respectively, they underwent a Marxist typology of society in order to be fit into the corresponding tier of modernization and communization. For communists there were five stages of societal development: "the primitive-communal, [tribal] slave-owning, feudal, capitalist, and finally socialist and communist."[21] Latvia was already an independent capitalist state on the eve of World War II and did not create a problem for Stalinist incorporation of the Baltic states into the Soviet Union. Whereas the Baltic states served as a more developed industrial hub, sort of a "near abroad" within Soviet borders, Kazakh nomadic nationhood was a greater problem. Nomads were perceived as "tribal" and thus "backward" but where did they belong on the five-stage arrangement of societal development?

Pastoral nomadism was a way of life for Kazakhs since the inception of their type of political community in the fifteenth century.[22] This presented "a problem for Marxism which is just as fundamental, if less immediate[ly] conspicuous."[23] The Soviets did not consider nomadism within the framework of modernity but, on the contrary, believed it had to be dismantled both physically and in the minds of the new Kazakh Soviet subjects as something archaic and requiring modernization[24]

The nomads, among them Kazakhs, were arranged into a "rough formula." The "social organization of nomads is this: communal ownership of pasture, [firm] ownership of herds."[25] Soviet ethnographers long debated nomadic communal organization and ownership of pastures. The nomadic community was organized on tribal and kinship ties. Land was tenured to specific tribes and hordes where the territory was distributed among three hordes based on the geographical placement of horde's tribes. "The ownership of animals" in nomadic society was distributed by tribal leaders but it was technically communal. Wealthier tribesmen had to help their poorest kinsmen, and when this order was neglected it spurred discontent.[26]

The problems with Soviet categorizations of nomadic societies went even further because "what state formation and social stratification" there was seemed "to be ephemeral and unstable and elusive."[27] According to Gellner, the debate on the nature and categorization of the nomadic Eurasian steppes in the Soviet Union continued to the end of perestroika. One thing was clear, the Soviets perceived nomads as backward and feudal. Nomadic feudalism technically implied the existence of sedentarization, which was practically absent before the advent of Sovietization in the steppe.[28] Thus, nomads had to be developed in order to fit the Soviet ethnographic categorization,[29] and then to the heights of building communism, even though they suffered devastating human losses because of sedentarization and Sovietization.[30]

Through the active but ill-informed policies of rapid modernization under the Soviets, the steppe was transformed into sedentary urban and rural, "consolidated" and dependent (kolkhoz) "farmsteads," a more or less cohesive and structured map of stable socioeconomic units.[31] Nomadic culture was almost entirely destroyed by the sedentarization and collectivization that led, in 1932–1933, to a major famine within the Soviet borders and claimed one-third of the Kazakh nomadic population.[32] With the introduction of the Cultural Revolution in the late 1920s and 1930s, Kazakh language and official culture were unified under the categorization set by Soviet ideology, and dissident voices were repressed as members of the Kazakh national intelligentsia were persecuted during the Stalinist Terror of 1937.[33] By the end of this period, Kazakhstan also became a partial nation-state just as Latvia had during the interwar period—a stable territorial and administrative unit but within the Soviet ethno-federation and under Soviet totalitarian rule.

By the time of independence in 1991, both Kazakhstan and Latvia were well-informed, well-structured post-Soviet republics characterized by "pervasively institutionalized social and cultural forms" of embedded notions of ethnicity and ethnic entitlement to the titular republics.[34] For example, Latvians became the bearers of Latvian statehood and Kazakhs served the same role in Kazakhstan. With the dismantling of the Soviet Union as a result of growing nationalist movements in the Western part of the Soviet empire and, marginally, also in Central Asia, where the December 1986 revolt in Kazakhstan had still not been forgotten, new nation-states emerged to replace and reset the map of the Soviet Union. These states, also called successor states, remained within the defined borders—apart from territorial insurgencies in Georgia and Ukraine, annexation of Crimea, and older conflicts in Moldova and Karabakh between Armenia and Azerbaijan—established under the Soviet Union, and largely reproduced the former republican national elites, many of whom still bore the birthmarks of the Soviet communist regime. These new old elites at first applied the existing vocabulary of national imagined communities—either the pre-Soviet, prewar memories of the Latvian authoritarian state of Karlis Ulmanis or the Kazakh imagined past as written in Kazakh Soviet literature.[35] Nation-building at first followed a very standard scenario of ascribing history, territory, and culture to the dominant ethnic group and rooting its achievements as far back in history as possible because:

> The *longue durée* of the past also gives this particular form of imagined community a potent claim to territory, the "homeland," which the people constituted as nation argues that it held first. The national history is one of continuity, antiquity of origins, heroism and past greatness, martyrdom and sacrifice, victimization and overcoming of trauma. It is a story of the empowerment of the people, the realization of the ideals of popular sovereignty. While in some cases national history is seen as development toward realization, in others it is imagined as decline and degeneration away from proper development. In either case an interpretation of history with a proper trajectory is implied.[36]

When considering how a political imagined community is constructed, one must pay equal attention to the power of the constructed discourses and the ways in which they are operated, controlled, and sometimes manipulated by those in power. The new historicity and historical myth-making for selective discourse creation and appropriation become the main tools of nationalizing regimes in the post-Soviet space.[37] In other words, elites who are in charge of selecting and controlling the dominant discourse insert their power into selected historical discourses depending on the context and scope of elite competition within the nationalizing regime.

I discuss this mechanism in detail in the chapters 2 and 3, but first it is important to conceptualize the different types of nationalizing regimes and how power relations constitute the outcomes resulting from nationalizing regimes. Before that I discuss temporal understandings of post-Soviet regimes and the processes of their ideological "making of the new nations."

TWO POST-SOVIET WORLDS

A large graffiti sign on one of the Soviet apartment buildings near my home in Riga displays a quote from the 1990s Russian film *Brat* (Brother): "What is power, Brother? Language is power, Brother" (*V chem sila, brat? Sila v iazike, brat*). I find myself standing in front of this wall with my Latvian colleague who also speaks Russian. "What do they mean by language [*iazik*] here?" I ask her.[38] Is it about Russian language in contemporary Latvia and the fact that Russian-language schools are diminishing even in cities where more than half the local population speaks Russian? Is there a specific reason that this quote from an iconic post-Soviet film about order and disorder appears on a wall in Kengaraks? "I don't know, maybe they meant *iazik* as a tongue? So, power is in the tongue,"[39] laughs my Latvian friend and colleague Astrida, who herself grew up in the neighborhood and cites her "excellent Russian" as an advantage in multilingual and now globalized Riga.

This discussion about differences in how we understand language as a meaningful container goes beyond the initial joke full of cultural connotations about *iazik*, whether language or tongue. Like Laima, my friend Astrida shares a common language beyond Russian with me, a sort of Soviet and post-Soviet language of cultural, social, and political connotations. We were born at almost the same time, we share memories of Sovietness as in our parents' generation, but we also grew up in very distinct post-Soviet times. Astrida attended the only Latvian-language school in her neighborhood but excelled in Russian due to the urban surroundings of the predominantly Russophone working-class area, a place where Russian ethnicity is not yet totalized by the ambiguity of the "Russian-speaking" category that seems to be in place to diminish the ethnic Slavic boundaries between "ethnic Russians" and "ethnic Ukrainians" or "ethnic Byelorussians." "Russian-speaking" identity becomes an ambiguous and disempowering nonethnic category for many of my non-Latvian respondents. In other words, Russian-speaking identity draws on a linguistic identity in contrast to the dominant ethnopolitical and clearly defined identity of the titular group of "Latvians." There is almost never a "Russian-speaking Latvian" identity for Astrida who is ethnically Latvian and bilingually both Latvian and Russian but also English-speaking. There is also no "Russian-speaking Latvian" for someone who is ethnically non-Latvian but linguistically equally bilingual in Latvian and Russian. Thus, *iazik*, which means both language and tongue, as the communication power or disempowerment instrument and almost a physical deethnicized part of the body proper of the noncitizen (almost always the Russian-speaking minority) became the dividing line between the powerful and the disempowered. It is the dividing line between Latvian nationalist elites and deethnicized sociolinguistic and marginalized minority groups. More often "Russian-speaking" identity is already marred by an unfortunate *nepilsoni status* (Latvian: noncitizen). So the power is in the "language" of defining and controlling someone down to their physical and sociolinguistic identities in not being able to claim full citizenship status in Latvia.

On the other hand, in contrast to Astrida's realities in post-Soviet worlds, I attended one of the first Kazakh-language schools in my neighborhood, which quickly opened in post-Soviet Kazakhstan, and I grew up bilingual in a place that was constantly reminded of its symbolic role in the Russian Empire's conquest of Central Asia. Yet in our encounters and discussions we spoke of similar books, music, films, and cartoons that bore the labels of Soviet and post-Soviet. Our experiences were very similar to what Diana Ibañez-Tirado described as "alternative temporalities" and disassociations when considering the temporal and categorical break between Soviet and post-Soviet.[40] Her research in Kulob in Tajikistan demonstrated that instead of clear-cut perspectives on Soviet and post-Soviet, people "tended to mark the passage of time using categories 'before' (*pesh*) and 'after' (*ba'd*)."[41]

In Latvia too all my respondents located past and present beyond just the post-Soviet, and for most of them the sense of nationalism started not just in the post-Soviet period but clearly during the second or third independence—depending on their temporal position with respect to 1918, 1920, 1990, or 1991. More far-right-leaning nationalist party members counted many more "crucial" periods of Latvian independence associated with specific moments in the nation's uninterrupted discourse that they imagined and sustained, including what they call the Soviet Occupation. In their imagination Latvia was hundreds of years old. I experienced a similar temporal narrative in Kazakhstan, where one of my respondents immediately created a temporal grid of fourteen post-Soviet republics, slicing and lumping them into what he understood as colonial and historical regions—with the Baltic states separate from the rest "because they were incorporated into the Soviet Union later"; the Caucasus united, despite a "difficult historical path"; Central Asia with five states but Kazakhstan separate with its own "nomadic path"; and Ukraine, Belarus, and Moldova closer to Eastern Europe. The post-Soviet paradigm rarely entered this temporal imagination—both Latvian nationalists and Kazakhstan's highest officials, elites who were in control of nation-building discourses in the two states *after* the collapse of the Soviet Union, disassociated this temporal break from the bigger story of the state-building that they were directly involved in.

Only in their later discussions they often embodied state-building with themselves. They did this by inverting the "state" into themselves, which is what they meant by "us, the nation-builders." In doing so they also diverted the time of the collapse into the temporal frame of their own actions as if they owned time and its change:

> The perestroika period is all about Gorbachev, that's 1985–1991 but it really finished by 1987–1988; it exhausted itself by that period if we speak in a strictly scientific and chronological manner. What happened in 1991 was not perestroika at all, it was independence [*eto nezavisimost'*]. One cannot apply this terminology [of perestroika] after December 9 or 21 [1991] because what happened here [in Kazakhstan] by then was already de facto gaining independence and establishing it in all sorts of different forms. You can call this [independence] period perestroika too [perestroika is literally translated as restructuring] when not used by the late Soviet period because for sure, *we were engaged in rebuilding everything*. And while there were no conventional terms of revolutionary change—there were no barricades here (in Kazakhstan) *but everything was different already*. [At that time] you already lived in a different country because you [as a state] were responsible for your actions on your own [*potomu chto ty sam za sebia samostoiatel'no otvechaesh*].[42]

In this temporal-spatial complexity of the establishment of independence as a process, elites also construct a very strong separation between themselves and the people. Elites clearly view the state as themselves in Kazakhstan and people as "ordinary people" or "commoners"—*obyvateli*. The elites see the "state" as a living body of institutions guided by elites who take control and become "engaged in rebuilding everything." Elites view the people on the ground, ordinary citizens, as consumers of this order, which is created for their daily existence within a system that the elites safeguard through tireless work. In another interview, for example, this issue of tireless work came up when one of the politicians of the early Nazarbayev era mentioned how the president worked day and night with almost no sleep for the good of the people of Kazakhstan, "*tirelessly* making decisions about the future of the country."[43] The clear spatial separation and embodiment of the state by the elites, and the everyday routine on the ground by the people, is clearly seen in the discourse of the time change from Soviet to post-Soviet in Kazakhstan, as seen and analyzed by these elites two decades later:

> The vast majority of citizens did not feel this change [from Sovietness to independence], they did not feel that we as a country, gained independence, that something has changed in our lives; an ordinary person or a common man [*obyvatel ili prostoi chelovek*] thinks simply—what is the change if the sun is shining, trams continue to arrive on time, your surroundings are the same. But [independence] was a different reality. Maybe on the level of ordinary citizens and routine life of ordinary folks it was also ordinary but for *those who were in charge* of the state[-building], who had to be accountable for it [post-independent state-building]—there was an enormous level of responsibility on *our* shoulders and a colossal level of intellectual weight.[44]

This quote, along with many other interviews I conducted with political elites both in Kazakhstan and Latvia as well as in the wider post-Soviet region, demonstrates the elitist imagination of nation-making. It describes their active engagement in something that is cut off from the people for whom this nation is constructed. My position as a young researcher almost two decades *after* the initial establishment of each nationalizing regime allowed me to gather this discourse of elites' agency in these processes as well as their appropriation of the whole dominant discourse of the nationalizing regime. In other words, and as I will show in the remaining chapters, the nationalizing regime is able to continue functioning and gathering power and control over the polity or society only by the means of consolidating the main discourse that it aims to safeguard. In Latvia this is the discourse of the sacred Latvian nation whereas in Kazakhstan it is the dominant belief and shared telos among the power elites themselves that only they are accountable and powerful enough to ensure the state's functioning, the nation's existence, and the country's development. During President Nazarbayev's official thirty-year tenure,[45] the shared telos within Kazakhstan's nationalizing regime was also about the president's own power above all of the elite's individual powers. He was the one who had full control over decision making on national discourses and major state-building programs and visions, as I discuss in the following section.

Elites continuously play a crucial role in establishing and sustaining nationalizing regimes. In this regard, their typology is guided by different strategies toward the dominant discourse that keeps regimes together. Regimes that choose a defining nationalist agenda that satisfies their interests and often their personal and ideological views, will continuously support this idea and find ways to generate more popular support in different parts of the electorate, as in the case of Latvia.

The dominance of this type of nationalist discourse would open up restricted competition among political parties and players who consider this an agenda for driving their own interests and political survival. This agenda might also provide a scenario in which other strong contenders for political power simply may not comply with the limits of the dominant discourse and thus, unless they are capable of changing the dominant discourse, they will continuously lose in the political power-sharing game (see chapter 3). For the remaining players this means that the political shuffling will not entirely change, and each election will allow key players and their parties to sustain their shares in the parliament, the Cabinet of Ministers, or other key institutions of state power, as has been the case in the development of the Latvian political field since the collapse of the Soviet Union.

For elites whose interests depend on the strong competition within the elitist field guided not by the dominant nationalist discourse but by loyalty to the leader, their survival depends on the leader's position and his belief in their loyalty. This is the case in Kazakhstan's personalized nationalizing regime, where loyalty to the first president, Nursultan Nazarbayev and his interests guaranteed elites a place in any state institution—from regional bodies to higher stakes in the central decision-making bodies, primarily as part of a ministry or the president's administration.

This is why in Kazakhstan, unlike Latvia, the composition of the elite is much more solid than that of the party or its main ideological divisions. In Latvia, political party lines are stable and continuous as members of these parties and their political representatives change regularly over two or three terms in parliament.

In Kazakhstan political parties exist to create a sense of democratic performance or, in the case of the pro-Nazarbayev Nur Otan party, to consolidate and order the nationalizing regime at its mid- and lower-range member level. The party accounts for almost a million members, most of whom are employed in the public sector, and it has regional offices in each major city and all regions of the country.[46] Major elite members are often reshuffled back into the party structure after fulfilling a term in a major political post, as in the case of the former prime minister Bakytzhan Sagintayev, who recently became the mayor of Almaty, replacing Bauyrzhan Baibek who returned to the Nur Otan party as deputy chairman.

The current chairman of the Nur Otan party is the former president Nazarbayev himself whose figure continues to cause a stir. At the Eighteenth Party Congress in February 2019, members of the Nur Otan party made news when they lined up after Nazarbayev had left, and had their pictures taken near the chair in which he had been sitting.[47] At the end of June 2019 news agencies in Kazakhstan reported that a young Kazakh composer, the son of a Nur Otan party member, proposed to the Astana Opera a work dedicated to *Elbasy*, the Father of the Nation, Nursultan A. Nazarbayev.[48] Later Astana Opera denied the news and the opera was not staged. Nursultan A. Nazarbayev was continuously cited in the proposed opera as the "destined" Father of the Nation and the builder of Kazakhstan's bright future.

The difference between the "first Fathers of the Nation" and people of the first post-Soviet generation to which Astrida and I belong involves the conception of the Soviet collapse itself. Through my interviews with activists, political commentators, and the rare parliamentarian of my generation across the post-Soviet space over the course of fieldwork from 2011 to 2019, I understood that *our*, first post-Soviet generation continues to view the Soviet Union as something that was not supposed to last, and that its collapse was logical. The Soviet Union was and remains a temporal process of something that emerged to disturb the continuous process of development of the land now called Latvia, Kazakhstan, or any other post-Soviet state—a completely contemporary thought, constructed in the nationalist discourse of the post-Soviet era and its tireless elites.

In this temporal imagination, post-Soviet is not so much a break as the logical finale of a system that had to end. Seeing this temporal process from the perspectives of different people everywhere in the former Soviet space has great value in this study. This is because, as the post-Soviet state continues to disintegrate, its paths of development diverge even within the limits of one region (such as the very distinct political developments in Central Asia at the moment). It is thus important to evaluate the way the legacy of what was Soviet mutates differently in two completely divergent spaces that used to be one.

As I sat across from a rising star of Latvian politics who was just few years older than I, he shared a view the same as that of Diana Ibañez-Tirado's respondent in Tajik Kulob: "I am not post-Soviet at all!" he protested though he could not entirely argue that it was because he was never Soviet.[49] Ibañez-Tirado's respondent who claimed that she could not be "post-Soviet" because she "was never Soviet" based on historical time—not having been born during the chronological existence of the Soviet Union, which officially ended in December 1991; my Latvian respondent was Soviet because he was born in Soviet Latvia and possibly even went through the last Soviet school system that collapsed in the early 1990s. But this did not stop him from engaging in a long discussion about why he views this temporal perspective as he does—that neither Latvia nor he are post-Soviet at all.

> How would you say the pre-Soviet and post-Soviet was different in Latvia and would you say these were two different nations or is it still some type of continuation that a lot of policymakers try to connect? There is continuation of course. I want to stress that the identifications of the nation changed, the language changed. There are some letters that were used in the 1930s and that are not used today. But it is not very crucial because, for example, during the interwar period, there was even an alphabet change. Until the early 1920s, I think it was early 1921, the year after the War of Liberation, but before that the Gothic font was used and it was changed to the Latin font later. The language was dilemmic all the time. We don't know the words that were used 100 years ago, and I believe you also don't know them [in the Kazakh language]. So, the same with culture. It's only my opinion that the culture changes as well. We cannot compare Latvian culture 100 years ago and Latvian culture today.[50]

The time imagination here is distinctive because it was rare to hear mentions of "culture" in my interviews with political elites unless it involved the martyring of national culture perceived in very strict notions of ethnically Latvian culture, including its language, traditions, and even food, which were believed to be repressed or actually were repressed during the Soviet period. And though my respondent was and still is a member of a more right-leaning party, which is a continuous trend in all Latvian post-Soviet politics, he did not engage in the martyr of Latvian culture but continued to view it as the dominant culture intrinsically connected with or even born out of the Latvian state (*Latvijas valsts*). In these times the term "post-Soviet" remains a dividing line for those who view it nostalgically (the older generation), those who are curious about how it actually felt (the new generation), and those who believe time cannot be turned back. But the temporal aspect of the post-Soviet remains highly nationalized and controlled by the ruling elites nevertheless:

> Today, I am sorry, but globalization takes place everywhere. Even in the small pond here, in Latvia. This issue of globalization and historical immigration and emigration mainly I would say today the question is also about the clash of generations. My generation mostly doesn't have very strong direct memories from the Soviet past, many of them who are younger don't even know anything [about it]. In some cases, they are wearing pink glasses on all young [Soviet years] of their parents because my parents recognize it as great time as well. Some people are wearing black [dark] glasses on the same issues [of Soviet history in general]. So, understanding [this Soviet time] is very important for its overall misunderstanding in society.[51]

The discussion of "Soviet time" in the Latvian case, however, remained within the restricted terms of "bad" and "acceptable," which continuously divide the political and public sphere alike. Celebrations of the Latvian Legion and May 9, "Soviet" Victory Day, two events intrinsically connected to World War II, Soviet legacy, and the contemporary Latvianized nationalizing regime, are the most telling examples of this division wherein the regime attempts to silence and erase the former while pro-Russian activists continue to highlight Victory Day as an important part of local history and national imagination in the present. Though these tensions are less clear in Kazakhstan where the nationalizing regime continues to co-opt the Victory Day celebration and highlight the "ethnic" part of the celebration by stressing the heroism of Kazakh soldiers in World War II, these divisions are present in debates about using St. George's Ribbon on Victory Day. St. George's Ribbon was replaced by a blue ribbon with a Kazakh ornament on it in yellow symbolizing Kazakhstan's flag. After the annexation of Crimea, St. George's Ribbon is seen by many national patriots, for example, as a symbol of the colonial Russian past, something that does not correlate to Kazakhstan's contemporary state or its independence. It is not completely gone and has not been replaced, as many, among them ethnic Russians, continue to use it as a symbol of the World War II victory of the Soviet Union and Kazakhstan alike.

BUILDING NATIONS AND STATES IN ETHNIC DEMOCRACY AND PLURAL AUTHORITARIANISM

The nature of the state and the emergence of fifteen successor states of the Soviet Union—Russia being the most peculiar case of postimperial state formation— begs for further explanation. For example, it is largely believed that Kazakhstan was an "accidental state," which was "born by default" because its independence "was neither the result of secessionist demands *by its leadership*, nor a national liberation movement." On the contrary, it is believed that "it resulted from the decision by Moscow to withdraw its maintenance of the Soviet edifice."[52] Whereas in Latvia, independent statehood was not only expected and fought for but also was seen as a "normalizing discourse" of the way of life and especially the historical development of the Latvian nation.[53] In post-Soviet Latvia, for some "normality entailed the restoration of the social order that existed before [Eastern European] states were drawn into the Soviet orbit" whereas others associated it with Western Europe.[54] State formation, which also coincided with the creation of exclusivist, ethnically defined nations, was key to these processes.

State formation is defined here as "elite competition over the authority to create the structural framework through which policies are made and enforced."[55] In the postcommunist context, elite competition is crucial for state- and nation-formation (or *nation-building*), processes of envisioning state and nation, and construction led by the elites. Although a very simple idea of elite domination over political life, suggested by a Gramscian historical blocs framework, it remains overshadowed by the ambiguities of state-led formulations of nation-building in the postcommunist space, where the state is defined as an independent actor and not in terms of the elite formation of the nation. The state's capacity might be shaped by internal factors (e.g., legitimacy and state provision of security or welfare to the population) or by external factors (e.g., international pressure, threats, and war). In this book I discuss elitist regimes as actors within and beyond state institutions, borders, and frameworks.

The question addressed in this book involves the nature of diverse forms of political development in line with varied forms of power acquisition and domination and their influence on democratization and, most important, the voices and rights of nonelites. Despite the existing citizenship restrictions for "Soviet occupants" via the historical and legal continuity of the interwar Latvian independent republic and jus sanguinis based on citizenship categories of the 1938 law, the Latvian regime is still perceived as democratic by virtue of being a transparent electoral democracy and by the existence of a civil society.[56] The Kazakh regime remains relatively open and pluralistic regarding the inclusion of its ethnic minorities but very exclusive concerning elite selection and closed political contestation within the regime. In the end, as this study will demonstrate, both the Latvian and Kazakh regimes represent much more political diversity in identifying regimes along the grid of democratic or less democratic political entities. These hybrid regimes technically observe various characteristics of democratic regimes in terms of plurality of views and identities but an exclusivist monopoly over decision making in nation-building, citizenship, and access to elections. However, my findings demonstrate that both regimes pursue and control ethnically defined differences regarding group and individual identities of their citizens and noncitizens.

The Latvian ethnic electoral democracy may be seen as a more democratic regime than, for example, the Kazakh regime, by virtue of its free press and open (but not always competitive) elections. But in Kazakhstan, unlike in Latvia, ethnic minority groups are not deprived of political rights based on restrictive policies of citizenship by descent, but competition for political power is closed and no fair elections are technically possible under the present regime. The most recent presidential elections in 2019, the first without the long-term leader, Nursultan A. Nazarbayev, are a case in point.[57] The Kazakhstan's elite composition is a case of selection rather than elections—new members of elite groups are chosen and *selected* by the remaining power elites.

This is partially explained by an arrangement whereby Latvian post-independence elites were "renewed" in 1993, in the first open and democratic elections since the mid-1930s. Communist elites were largely replaced by "liberals" and, although the country's power elites did not change for almost ten years (with the reign of the Latvian Way party and coalition), these groups were far more diverse and had very distinct neoliberal interests even compared to the leaders of the revolutionary Popular Front (1989–1993) who were "crushed" in their first reelection bid. In Kazakhstan, elite renewal also happened in 1989, but this was a nomenclature renewal. The young and charismatic Kazakh leader Nursultan A. Nazarbayev adapted the content of his policies to the changing context of Soviet state transformation and liberalized its agenda. However, the form of elite composition remained the same as it was in the late communist regime, where "the growing awareness among socialist leaders that elite turnover invariably destabilized politics and thereby posed a threat to their own tenure and possibly the system itself" led to adaptation of the elite and durability of the regime.[58]

Elite composition within each regime—either through election and careful and durable coalition building (Latvia) or through elite selection by the power elites for similar but closed coalition building (Kazakhstan)—led to differences not only in their political development but also in the ways these nationalizing regimes were formed. The logic of each regime composition provided that the elites had to consent about the major discourse constituting the overall nation-building agenda, provide legitimacy to the regime and ruling elites, and establish the "rules of the game" within the political field. The defining discourse of Latvian ethnic and historical primacy for Latvian nation- and state-building, for example, formed prepolitical consensus in Latvia and virtually excluded non-Latvian discourses or parties from active participation in the power struggle. As I demonstrate in chapter 4, the so-called Russian parties and movements managed to voice an alternative agenda of the political nation and Russian language inclusion. This even led to the 2012 Referendum on State Language that proposed to amend the constitution and make Russian the second official language, given that almost 40 percent of the country's population claimed Russian as their native language bringing the debate back to the power of the *iazik*, language. This empowerment of the Russian agenda, however, only led to the rise of the conservative-right coalition and amendments to the constitution regarding the quota of signatures collected for a referendum. Although this quota was lifted, which impeded democratic processes, in June 2014 the conservative-right majority in the Latvian Saiema (parliament) also voted for significant symbolic changes to the preamble of the constitution turning it into a more "ethnicized version," which says:

> The State of Latvia, proclaimed on 18 November 1918, has been established by uniting historical Latvian lands and on the basis of the unwavering will of the Latvian nation to have its own State and its inalienable right of self-determination in order to guarantee the existence and development of the Latvian nation, its language and culture throughout the centuries, to ensure freedom and promote welfare of the people of Latvia and each individual. The people of Latvia won their State in the War of Liberation. They consolidated the system of government and adopted the Constitution in a freely elected Constitutional Assembly. The people of Latvia did

not recognize the occupation regimes, resisted them and regained their freedom by restoring national independence on 4 May 1990 on the basis of continuity of the State. They honour their freedom fighters, commemorate victims of foreign powers, condemn the Communist and Nazi totalitarian regimes and their crimes.

This was followed by an even stronger assertion:

Since ancient times, the identity of Latvia in the European cultural space has been shaped by Latvian and Liv traditions, Latvian folk wisdom, the Latvian language, universal human and Christian values. Loyalty to Latvia, the Latvian language as the only official language, freedom, equality, solidarity, justice, honesty, work ethic and family are the foundations of a cohesive society. Each individual takes care of oneself, one's relatives and the common good of society by acting responsibly toward other people, future generations, the environment and nature.[59]

These changes to the Latvian Constitution completely "silenced" the non-Latvian population of the country. There was no mention of the historical Russian population of the Eastern parts of Latvia, many of whom were official citizens of interwar Latvia and thus their descendants were also granted automatic Latvian citizenship after 1991. The clause on "nonrecognition" of the "Occupation"— meaning the Soviet period in Latvian history from 1945 to 1991—also left third of the country's population with the official status of "Soviet-era migrants," a rather stigmatized and problematic category. But many Russian-speaking noncitizens and citizens alike expressed their dissatisfaction with the existing identity politics in Latvia. Afraid of losing their visa-free status to the Russian Federation—a discussion spurred most recently in the Russian media—many Latvian noncitizens fear remaining in political limbo where their rights are absent and their representation does not depend on any state whatsoever. The citizenship issue or rather its absence and the cultivation of the dangerous discourse of "Soviet occupants" leave almost a third of this European democratic country in an insecure position.

Finally, the decision of the Latvian parliament in September 2016 that proposed to prohibit all non-Latvians from specifying or changing the "nationality" on their passports to "Latvian"—meaning that Latvian status was now completely ethnicized and the ruling coalition had moved farther right on the spectrum of its agenda. This dangerous rhetoric already caused problems for refugees—Latvia established a quota that accepted only five hundred refugees a year. These refugees were paid less than minimum subsistence levels but were required to gain obligatory proficiency in Latvian language in order to secure even the lowest entry-level jobs in Latvia.

The regime in Kazakhstan depends on its stability and on the former president Nazarbayev himself who balanced the elite field. In this case, the term "authoritarian regime" was usually used to define the "the combination of limited pluralism and possibilities for political participation with the existence of a more or less free economic space and successful market reforms."[60] The nature of the regime in Kazakhstan is still much more complex since it is responding to social turmoil and demands. The regime's legitimation in Kazakhstan is not based on open and competitive elections, but rather on control and the provisions of the major discourses of societal demands, for example, economic and interethnic stability. So the regime in Kazakhstan is in an insecure position with regard to social and popular support for its policies. These policies are also directly connected to elite members: for example, the new president Kassym-Jomart Tokayev, the prime minister, and respective regional leaders (*akims*) are directly accountable to the provisions of the regime's promises of stability and prosperity. So when at-risk social groups organize protests, such as the mothers' marches, they protest directly to President Tokayev, and often also to *Elbasy* Nursultan A. Nazarbayev.

The regime in Kazakhstan does not observe most aspects of consolidated democracy such as fair and free elections,[61] wider pluralism, and competition. More constraints are imposed on the growing civil society through blocking and censoring oppositional media,[62] which demonstrates its nondemocratic nature. However, until recent financial and social crises it was relatively stable, and President Nazarbayev successfully claimed legitimacy for his policies and the regime itself. Morever, Nazarbayev's regime is defined by limited political pluralism and "political apathy and demobilization of the population or limited or controlled mobilizations"[63], where major changes in social movement formations are nevertheless taking place. Growing dissatisfaction with social security and welfare, along with housing problems for internal migrants in the country's major cities continuously shake the regime's "stability" paradigm. This "authoritarian" nature of the regime, however, does not explain the durability and relative popularity of Nazarbayev in wider society even after his departure as president in March 2019.

Kazakhstan's first president, Nazarbayev, was famous for his promises of development for the whole country. However, these promises played out only for a limited number of those in elitist circles closest to the president himself, and developmentalist visions represented in the architecture of major cities[64] and the capital Astana, state programs,[65] or parliamentary discussions did not materialize further. This created a space for growing discontent and social insecurity for lower-income families, including mothers with many children (*mnogodetnie materi*) who started staging multiple protests after the February 2019 tragedy in Astana where five young children from one family died in a fire in their temporarily built home while both parents were working at night to provide for the family. This tragedy sparked "mothers' protest movements" across major cities in Kazakhstan where protestors demanded the provision of stable housing and the wiping out of their bank and mortgage debts. In June 2019 a group of mothers protested right in front of the Ak Orda presidential palace demanding welfare provisions from the president himself. Finally, an arms depot blast in the southern town of Arys prompted the mass evacuation of the local population (44,000 people) to the nearby major city of Shymkent at the end of June 2019. This emphasized problems with social inequality, low living standards, housing insecurity, and economic hardship and exposed the unmet promises of Nazarbayev's regime to guarantee economic development, prosperity, and stability for all. The new president Kassym-Jomart Tokayev eventually had to visit the Arys survivors at different relocation centers in Shymkent with promises to pay off their debts and provide better living conditions.

Until these tragedies revealed the growing problems in society and challenges for the regime in Kazakhstan, the political field was defined by the hybrid conditions of formal coercion, legal obstacles to mass gatherings and demonstrations, and a lack of considerable political opposition, but with growing social mobilization. The year 2019 promises to be a dividing line in Kazakhstan's political history not only due to the unexpected resignation of Nazarbayev, its first and only president of the independent republic, but also due to the popular rise of political rallies and new social movements, including those of impoverished mothers and the young generation of opposition forces (such as the Oyan Qazaqstan movement). In the longer term and in historical comparison, this raises the questions: To what extent does Kazakhstan's nondemocratic regime enjoy legitimacy? Moreover, if it did so before these events, why was this the case?

In his explanation of regime stability in the Soviet Union, Juan Linz has established that it was the ideology, "the 'wooden language' of the regime that had become a mentality for the apparatchiks and even citizens, which survives today in the new democracies."[66] This ideology determined the regime's stability in times of severe economic crises but caused its collapse when regional elites in union republics dismantled belief in it. Kazakhstan is still significantly influenced by the Soviet legacy in terms of institution-building and political culture, and I argue that primarily the role of semi-ideological and power-centered discourses around President Nazarbayev that sustained the regime's stability.

In the historical span, President Nazarbayev's gradual consolidation of power has resulted in the dismissals of two parliaments from 1993 to 1995, and a change in the constitution in 1995, which extended presidential powers and lengthened the term in office from four years to seven. The June 2000 Law on the First President of the Republic Kazakhstan—the Leader of the Nation gave Nazarbayev almost lifetime immunity. It also gave him guaranteed membership in Kazakhstan's Security Council and other important state institutions, and further consolidated his authoritarian rule to the point of "personification" of power. In 2010 the same law was amended to give Nazarbayev even more privileges—for example, lifetime immunity from prosecution for him personally or his assets, a lifetime right to advise on the most important domestic and foreign policy issues, along with the title *Elbasy*—the Leader, Father of the Nation (in Kazakh). More amendments all concerning the role and status of the first President of the Republic of Kazakhstan were also proposed. For example, Article 44 of the Constitution was amended to allow the president to schedule regular and extraordinary elections of the parliament. These amendments were unanimously supported by both chambers of the parliament and then-prime minister Karim Masimov, the speaker of the Senate Kassym-Jomart Tokayev, and the speaker of the parliament Ural Mukhamedzhanov, which gave the law more "legitimacy" as the discourse spread in the media.

When Nazarbayev resigned in March 2019, the transition to the next leader legally followed the constitutional clause providing that the speaker of the Senate, Kassym-Jomart Tokayev, who had occupied this position for six years, became the interim president. On June 9, 2019, Tokayev was elected as the new president of the country. At the same time, Nursultan A. Nazarbayev remains active and present in the political and public sphere in Kazakhstan as the chairman of the Security Council. He has an official office, duties, apparatus, and even a salary. *Elbasy* Nazarbayev holds regular meetings with political representatives including President Tokayev and continues to "advise" the regime. Due to the nature of the personalized nationalizing regime in Kazakhstan, Nazarbayev's power, name, and legacy will continue to influence the policies and discourses of the regime until the competing elite groups within the regime decide to change the "rules of the game."

Although there is a vast discrepancy between elite formations in the context of an elective democracy and elites in the context of more controlled elections, like those of Latvia and Kazakhstan, both fields of power elites represent similar levels of high competition and mobility. In the words of Wright Mills,

> Despite their social similarity and psychological affinities, the members of the power elite do not constitute a club having a permanent membership with fixed and formal boundaries. It is of the nature of the power elite that within it there is a good deal of shifting about, and that it thus does not consist of one small set of the same men in the same positions in the same hierarchies. Because men know each other personally does not mean that among them there is a unity of policy; and because they do not know each other personally does not mean that among them there is disunity. The conception of the power elite does not rest ... primarily upon personal friendship.[67]

I stress that the power elites within the nationalizing regime unite or disintegrate based on their views on national politics and policies, but the group is defined by a desire and ability to impose hegemony over such decisions. By creating and imposing this hegemonic framework, within it the elites also frame their competition and continuity of the nationalizing regime and its interests. I further explore this framework on the example of the historical development of Kazakhstan and Latvia since 1991.

ON STATE-NATIONS AND NATION-STATES

On June 15, 1993, President Nazarbayev gathered renowned intellectuals, writers, policy advisers, and lawyers in the capital city of Almaty to form a national committee for state policy. This mighty institution later became the ideological hub of domestic politics in the presidential administration, although in time it required further restructuring, shifts in members, chairmen, and elites who were deeply involved in the regime's nation-building policy. At the first meeting in summer 1993, the president's main agenda was: "Where are we going and how are we building our independent state?" During the time of turbulent transition to "unexpected" independence, and at a time when former Communist Party cadres hastily formed committees to choose new national symbols for the new state, Nazarbayev posed the following crucial question before the "ideological" committee: "In our [first] Constitution we declared that we are building a democratic state with the rule of law and social and market economy. What is it [all about]? What do we mean under the 'democratic state' in Kazakhstan's context, in our conditions of unprepared people [narod], unprepared masses?"[68] In this speech as in earlier programs in 1992 directed toward a search for state ideology, Nazarbayev stressed the need to address two crucial issues at the time of early independence: building a strong and democratic state and sustaining interethnic harmony in the wake of the collapse of the Soviet order in Kazakhstan and growing instability in the whole post-Soviet region. These were the earliest attempts of Kazakhstan's elites in "making" the new nation and building a strong presidential state in the aftermath of "decades of living under the harsh conditions of the totalitarian [Soviet] system."[69] Unlike Latvia, where legal and state-building frameworks were reestablished, independence was renewed after the proclaimed "Soviet occupation," and where Latvian elites who came into power immediately after the collapse of the Soviet Union accepted the legal continuity of the 1938 Latvian Constitution, Kazakhstan's elites shared the opinion that they had to start their state-building processes almost from scratch and with strong presidential power. It was President Nazarbayev who posed the crucial questions that later influenced the country's political development for decades: "What is a democratic state in Kazakhstan's context, [in a country] that knows no practice, has no previous experience of such state-building? What values [should] such a state be built on? What are we proposing [in terms of new state values]? Where are we leading our people [narod]?"[70] At the time of heightened debates about Kazakhstan's first Constitution that was adopted on January 28, 1993, and replaced by the second Constitution accepted on August 30, 1995, President Nazarbayev gathered the top ideological elites under the auspices of the presidential ideological committee with one goal—to form a "fixed" institution to define state- and nation-building policies, which was to follow a top-down approach of decision making. This institution had to monitor socioethnic relations, problems of ethnoterritorial conflicts, including potential Russian secession movements in the northern and eastern parts of Kazakhstan,[71] and meet regularly to discuss the situation and report directly to the president.

This institutional directorate was later dispersed into the Assembly of People of Kazakhstan and into separate institutions and committees under the Administration of the President of Kazakhstan, partially shared its role with the secretary of state, the prime minister's office, and various parliamentary groups dealing with domestic policy (vnutrenniaia politika). It was one of the first attempts to address state- and nation-building policies at the top political level and it did not take into consideration any nonpolitical and nonelite actors or provide for any citizen discussions or the participation of opposition or civil society groups apart from the involvement of writers and the so-called intelligentsia. Writers and the intelligentsia were the first post-Soviet surrogates of a form of "civil society" acceptable to the regime. Many writers of non-Kazakh descent, such as Moris Simashko and Gerold Belger, were honored invitees to many presidential meetings on national issues and were used by the regime for two reasons.[72] The first reason aimed at a symbolic representation of non-Kazakh cultural elites in the official decision-making body. Photos of famous writers next to President Nazarbayev occupied significant space in republican newspapers next to news about another "strategic" meeting in regard to nation-building. The presence of non-Kazakh elites in important discussions of mechanical approaches to nation-building such as the consideration of presidential programs justified the regime's idea of multiethnic policy.

Famous Soviet writers who now entered the realm of political decision making also served as nonpolitical actors at first. This was the second goal of the regime in involving cultural elites in some decision making—they provided the space for supposedly civil engagement and democratization. In reality, however, all decision-making institutions were formed directly by the decision of President Nazarbayev and based on his understanding of the present situation and "challenges of the current time." At the meeting of the same national committee for state policy on September 29, 1993, predominantly the voice and vision of President Nazarbayev was heard concerning the grand idea of the "state ideology" and development path:

> We do not have a strong party or strong parties that could produce ideology, parties that could take on the task of ideational consolidation of Kazakhstan's society. [Our parties] are still too weak, but the task of the ideational consolidation of society is clearly evident to us. As of today, there is no one in Kazakhstan to whom we can redirect this issue; naturally, power [*vlast*] and state [*gosudarstvo*] have to take this task onto their own shoulders whether we call it the party of power or the state ideology. In any case, someone has to deal with this issue and for sure, there is no one else right now apart from the state [who can do it].[73]

In the early 1990s Kazakh elites conceptualized ideology as something that "gives a sense of perspective," but its development further highlighted its role as a guiding principle of the ruling regime's legitimation. Institutional building and making sense of the new independent reality transformed the meaning of the words power (*vlast*) and state (*gosudarstvo*) to represent the ruling regime and its goals rather than commonly shared values. Exactly the same criticism was echoed by activists in 2019 when in a political podcast, the Kazakh journalist Gulnara Bazhkenova bitterly concluded that the people of Kazakhstan view *gosudarstvo*, the state, as a group of individuals close to the Nazarbayev regime and not as a set of institutions they should have control over.[74] By the time President Nazarbayev resigned in March 2019 it was clear that the institutional building and compartmentalized ideology (discussed in chapter 3) that the regime had pursued since the early 1990s had succeeded in establishing an order that was completely dependent on Nazarbayev.

The regime's compartmentalized ideology created a system of discourses and experiences, ways of thinking and imagining oneself only within the framework provided by the nondemocratic regime itself. Because the regime is fixated on a balance of interethnic stability and guaranteed powers of the president, the important ethnolingual divide is politicized to the level of national identities within the provided frameworks guided only by the regime. In this way the regime is able to legitimate itself to many audiences by providing them with the desired discourses and representations as projected within nation-building, clearly dividing the identification and agenda of each audience. Because these discourses are aimed at providing a differentiated and not "socially shared," "fundamental," unifying, and most important, stable discourse, they do not form viable and lasting effects of self-identification and a meaningful and constructive belief system in the same way that ideologies do.[75] Compartmentalized and dividing mechanisms are crucial for the regime's own stability in its nation-building policies and in attempts to stabilize the ethnolingual situation but not in solving the problem of the growing gap between these two communities. In this way political elites' power is centered in the discourse of the nation and on the actors who control this discourse to safeguard their own positions within this power field. In other words, mechanisms of acquiring power in post-communist states depend on the power to control the dominant discourse, the "dominant values and myths" of the society that are centered on ideas of nation.

Nationalist ideologies in these states replaced the dominant ideology of communism and continue to play an integral role in defining elitist competition to the same extent that attainment of communist ideology did in the Soviet period. Even in nondemocratic cases defined by a lack of, or limited, political pluralism that "are based on political apathy and demobilization of the population or limited and controlled mobilizations" nationalistic discourses continue to occupy the dominant space for contestations and heated debates.[76] Nationalism thus becomes the cultural hegemony of the nationalizing regime.

But the regime's fixation on interethnic stability in Kazakhstan as one of the major provisions of regime stability from below required further institutionalization and control of ethnic relations. And over time the initial national committee for state policy, the ideological hub controlled directly by President Nazarbayev, had to grow, divide, and spread within the state structure. New institutions and new hubs of decision making and control were formed while political parties outside presidential control were continuously weakened and ethnic identity was further codified and routinized in political policies, programs, and institutions. One of the main state organs for facilitating further ethnic relations was the Assembly of People of Kazakhstan envisioned by President Nazarbayev since the early years of independence and brought forward by the national committee for state policy in the mid-1990s.

The Assembly of People of Kazakhstan (APK, or ANK in Russian) was formed in 1995 and became a presidential device for providing and promoting the multiethnic and multicultural democratic process of nation-building in Kazakhstan. Today it unites more than eight hundred different ethnocultural organizations all over Kazakhstan. Its administrative network is represented in each region and has special offices in two major cities of Kazakhstan, Astana and Almaty. In 2007 a constitutional amendment granted the the APK the political right to elect nine deputies to the parliament from a separate list. However, the APK's role remained marginal and more symbolic in Kazakhstan's political system. Recent ethnic disputes between ethnic Armenians and Kazakhs in Karaganda in early January 2019 or ethnic tensions in 2015 in Bostandyk village in southern Kazakhstan demonstrated that the APK had no legitimacy or real power in intervening or mediating these conflicts.[77] The fact that the APK did not comment on interethnic clashes in Karaganda until the official response from the Ak Orda presidential office, demonstrated the APK's pure symbolic role in dealing with interethnic issues. The APK has no real power or independent response mechanisms when it comes to a real crisis situation.[78]

The APK's failures to mitigate real ethnic conflicts is in part explained by the absence of real power within this institution. Created as a symbolic hub for presidential discourses of interethnic stability, it was able to grant certain "minority" politicians positions and marginal representation in the parliament or regional organizations. One of its main goals was the continuous separation of Kazakhstan's population into distinct ethnic groups, which numbered 130 ethnic groups according to the regime itself. This initial move toward the establishment of a committee on monitoring and policy advising under the president was a continuation of late Soviet-type committees that monitored sociological perceptions of interethnic conflict in Kazakhstan post-1986.[79] The political language of this new post-Soviet regime later refrained from using the tainted concept of "ideology"[80] but continued to operate within the Soviet institutionalized and codified notion of "ethnicity" (*natsional'nost'*) and "friendship of peoples" (*druzhba narodov*), which distinctively defined the Nazarbayev regime's confusion regarding the changing socioethnic and sociolinguistic makeup of Kazakhstan's society, in which many ethnic Kazakhs are still Russified and many of those considered "ethnic minorities" have embraced one of the two dominant sociolinguistic groups—"Kazakh" or "Russian." But the Soviet codification and institutionalization of "ethnicity" continued to "constitute basic categories of political understandings," form "central parameters of political rhetoric" and "specific types of political interest[s]" as well as influencing "fundamental forms of political identity" from the elites' perspectives.[81]

On the one hand, separation into ethnic compartments, sociolinguistic groups, and divisions on regional levels gave these groups institutionalized distinctiveness, but on the other hand, the separation and division into often artificial groups based on fluid "ethnicity," belonging, and often unquestionable multilingualism also depoliticized these groups. Most conflicts of "ethnic background" that APK has been unable to deal with in recent years concern either extremely nationalist issues, such as when a member of one ethnic group attacks or discriminates against a member of the titular group (Kazakhs), or serious economic problems. For example, clashes between foreign contractors and the local population in Western Kazakhstan are often portrayed as a "national question" whereas in reality they also are part of a much longer conflict concerning the provision of economic rights and better working conditions for local industrial workers who are citizens of Kazakhstan and, although they identify predominantly with Kazakh ethnicity, also have diverse non-Kazakh backgrounds.

The continuous aim of the nationalizing regime in Kazakhstan to divide and depoliticize any resistance to the regime based on contrasting ethnic or political instability agenda. And it is done through the use of compartmentalized ideology. Compartmentalized ideology itself demonstrates weaknesses of the regime in its inability to come up with newer discourses or to deliver on the promises of development and prosperity for all or at least for the provision of economic conditions for majority of the population.

Nazarbayev's constant emphasis on developmentalist state agenda issues without delivering any major outcomes on his promises has created an ideological crisis, insofar as the population no longer believes in discourses without results. This raises questions as to how these mechanisms of elite control over crucial nation-building processes develop over time and what the logic of these regime developments is under different political and ideological contexts and circumstances.

TYPES OF ELITE STRUCTURES AND NATIONALIZING REGIMES

Nationalizing regimes are usually composed of political and co-opted cultural elites, but there is a clear hierarchical distinction with the power elite. It is their possession of decision-making power that makes elites significant, even when they decide not to act: "The power elite is composed of men whose positions enable them to transcend the ordinary environments of ordinary men and women; they are in positions to make decisions having major consequences. Whether they do or do not make such decisions is less important than the fact that they do occupy such pivotal positions: their failure to act, their failure to make decisions, is itself an act that is often of greater consequence than the decisions they do make, for they are in command of the major hierarchies and organizations of modern society."[82] In the post-Soviet space, political elites are both elected and chosen by their populations, through voting or by internal elite networks that eventually lobby, promote, and appoint particular members of an elite group to higher political positions, as ministers, prime ministers, and so on. In the Soviet period the formal structure of institutions such as the party, the Communist Youth League (Komsomol), and local *obkoms* (committees) determined the selection and promotion of elites and transformed ordinary party practitioners into powerful political elites. After independence this formal structure of the Communist Party and its various adjunct bodies that provided such channels was broken.[83]

A crackdown on the system was already evident during the late perestroika period. With the advent of glasnost and democratization a trend toward demystification and the condemnation of Stalinist atrocities spread throughout the Soviet borders and dissent accumulated among republic populations. At the same time, "power shifted from the center to the republics" and for the first time open elections were held for the Supreme Soviet to which many nationalist and anticommunist forces were elected in the same year.[84] Even in Kazakhstan there were enough nationalist movements for democratization and by the beginning of 1990–1991, movements and unofficial parties such as Alash, Azat, and Zheltoqsan, Nevada-Semipalatinsk already existed.[85] In Latvia, the Popular Front of Latvia's call for "ideas of national awakening and national consciousness, and civic responsibility for the sovereign state" had "consolidated the Latvian population."[86] According to David Lane, "these developments reflected major conflicts in ideology and aspirations among the governing elites about how reform should proceed. The political leadership in the republics—now constituted largely from politicians with authority in their Supreme Soviets—sought independence and the dissolution of the USSR. Nationalism became a unifying ideology of dissent."[87] This was only partially the case in Kazakhstan, where in the turbulent context of the dismantling of the Soviet Union, President Nazarbayev sought to keep the federative union of sovereign republics intact. However, by December 16, 1991, all illusions of further unification were lost and Nazarbayev declared the independence of Kazakhstan, the last republic to leave an already nonexistent Soviet Union.[88] The Commonwealth of Independent States was formed on December 8, 1991, without the membership of the three Baltic states, which were already looking for opportunities to rejoin the West on their way to "normalizing" the political and social life of their respective nations after the so-called Occupation.

The turbulent new political reality also meant new challenges and opportunities for the sovereign elites of the newly established and reestablished republics. The new realities of the proposed democratic system had changed and diminished the linkages of former elite composition and channels of competition. How were the elites chosen under the new circumstances and what influenced their logic of development? As further discussion will demonstrate, partial Latvian electoral democracy provided different scenarios for the development of nationalizing regimes that both depended on elite composition and influenced the power field of elite composition.

What influences elite composition and elite circulation is the elite's ability to join the power field and be upwardly mobile in that field. This mobility required a telos or some shared consensus among the elites who wee setting the rules of the game. Prepolitical consensus relies on agreement among the elites, even before independence or the building of the state and power field along with it. This idea of consensus has influenced variations in both elections and the transformation of the political regime and nation-building policies in post-Soviet Kazakhstan and Latvia. Whereas in Latvia elite consensus is found in the preservation of the Latvian nation, in Kazakhstan it is the preservation of the nondemocratic personalized regime of President Nazarbayev's strong and solid leadership, which the nationalizing regime defines as development.

In Latvia the formal discourse of the Latvian nation was closely envisioned by the ruling elites of the nationalizing regime as "returning to Europe." This return to *normalcy* could only have been achieved through the means of legitimate democratic development as defined by the West. This was also defined by denial and condemnation of the Soviet past and legacy (discussed in chapter 2).

In Kazakhstan before independence, power and legitimacy were already in the hands of the charismatic bilingual leader Nursultan A. Nazarbayev. But the political consensus among the elites was consolidated only in August 1995 with the new constitution that cemented Nazarbayev's sole role and power in further political transformations. The growing role and legitimacy of this personified rule created conditions in Kazakhstan's politics that centered decisions on the president himself. Thus, prepolitical consensus differed before and after independence in these varying regimes. It was a template for consolidating power with a broader scope (as in the parliamentary republic of Latvia) or for concentrating major decision-making power and authority with a narrower scope in the president and his close elite circle (as in the presidential republic of Kazakhstan).

The outcome of such consensus over power sharing or power concentration largely influenced the practices that formed and transformed nationalizing regimes in Latvia and Kazakhstan. Both regimes were led and influenced by the immediate conditions of the postindependence order: instability, economic crisis, growing social uncertainty, and vast competition in the face of the remaining Russian-speaking minority. This immediate sociopolitical context created fruitful ground for variations in the nationalizing regimes (see fig. 2). In Latvia, where democracy required open political competition and, thus, higher probabilities that non-Latvians would win elections, it was necessary to restrict the power field by imposing legitimate historical-legal regulations. Citizenship law became this restricting and dividing line. It was governed by concepts of Latvian descent in order to exclude non-Latvians by means of political selection but also perceived legal and historical injustices imposed by the "colonizing empire" that many Latvian political elites envisioned in the face of the former Soviet Union. Kazakhstan, where democratization was formally proclaimed but elite competition was largely influenced by elite desire to sustain and stabilize its power within the regime, chose the framework of elite selection based on loyalty to the regime/figure of the president. The pressures of stability on an ethnosocial level (in light of Baltic syndrome hysteria in the 1990s) also influenced the choice of overall open competition in formal and informal levels of elite selection.[89] This resulted in more balanced ethnolingual representation among the formal and informal political players.

Figure 2 reveals the way in which the elitist composition transformed the nationalizing regimes in Latvia and Kazakhstan. Where elites were divided on prepolitical consensus about the nature of the Latvian nation-state, Latvia represents both a divided elite regime and a very stable ideocratic nationalizing regime. The stability of the Latvian nationalizing regime is explained by the remaining political marginalization of the consensus of Russian elites and Latvian elites over the dominant ethnicized ideology of Latvian primacy in the state—this consensus defines the ideocratic nationalizing regime.

Even with the postnaturalization advent of parties and movements such as Harmony and PCTVL, their participation in the main decision making and thus their access to actual political power was still very limited and marginalized. This situation is fruitful for pro-Latvian elites who are united on the nationalizing agenda and divide their power in the parliament and in the government based on this shared telos regarding the main narrative of Latvian politics—the stable building of the Latvian nation-state with the minimal participation of non-Latvians. This type of nationalizing regime is only possible under specific conditions of internal (elite formation and consensus building) and external (geopolitical and historical positioning) factors. Pre-independent political actors in Latvia shared consensus on building an exclusive nation-state of ethnic Latvians. The telos was limited to one socioethnic group and ethnic competition among the elites within the Latvian group alone.

Anticommunist rhetoric and Soviet occupational discourses framed and legitimized this development of the Latvian nationalizing regime. Although John Higley and Gyorgy Lengyel identified such regimes as sultanistic and authoritarian (see fig. 2), I contend that a new category could be made—one of ethnic democracy with legitimate legal claims on elite divisions and exclusions based on citizenship (jus sanguinis) due to the Soviet occupation. Historical justifications apart from Soviet or any other occupation can also be examples, such as diverse forms of colonization, direct rule, or the historical traumas of previous political contexts. In Latvia it was the preestablished elite consensus on Soviet occupation that became the guiding principle for discursive formation within the regime due to processes that were already happening in the political sphere in Latvia and outside, within the diaspora and the Western world's support for Baltic independence. The study of other nationalizing regimes also reveals the

Figure 2. Types of nationalizing regimes. *Source*: Adapted from Higley and Lengyel, *Elites after State Socialism*, 7.

Classic Circulation	Reproduction Circulation
scope: wide & deep	scope: narrow & shallow
mode: gradual & peaceful	mode: gradual & peaceful

ELITE UNITY

Strong	*Weak*
CONSENSUAL ELITE	FRAGMENTED ELITE
ethos of "unity in diversity"	weak or no shared ethos: *multiple discourses on nation but weak ethos in general*
norms of restrained partisanship	reciprocal distrust and suspicion
Wide compromise	*Deep elite fragmentation*
networks dense and interconnected	networks dense and segmented
Regime: consolidated democracy	Regime: unconsolidated democracy
	Nationalizing regime: Kazakhstan

ELITE DIFFERENTIATION

IDEOCRATIC ELITE	DIVIDED ELITE
single belief system	deeply opposed beliefs
	Russian world opposed to the Latvian post-occupied nation
networks run through *narrow* highly centralized party or movement	networks confined to opposing camps, one of which dominates
	Pro-Latvian camp dominates
Regimes: totalitarian or post-totalitarian	Regimes: authoritarian or sultanistic
	Nationalizing regime: Latvia

Replacement Circulation	Quasi-Replacement Circulation
scope: wide & deep	scope: narrow & shallow
mode: sudden & enforced	mode: sudden & enforced

use of selective powerful discourses from the past as well, for example, unfinished processes of nationhood formations that were interrupted by the advent of Soviet power in the region or Stalinist purges (the case of Ukrainian and Azeri claims for such national legitimacy in the past are particularly interesting in this regard). Overall, the elites are divided due to their differentiated positions on the nationalizing regime's agenda before and after independence. However, even Russian elites might be co-opted by the ruling bloc within the nationalizing regime if such elites fully conform with the provided telos. Such is the example of the Harmony Party's partial acceptance of the Latvian nationalizing regime's agenda (see chapters 3 and 4).

The Kazakh case is represented in this chapter by the fragmented elite—the shared telos within the nationalizing regime is either weak/ambiguous or absent. The Nazarbayev regime is only partially nationalizing insofar as the telos is intentionally fragmented into two distinct sociolinguistic groups within the electorate. Those elites conformed to the status quo post-independence, that is, an ambiguous national discourse, united under the personalized rule of President Nazarbayev. Their competition and political survival were determined by the stability of the regime and its ability to support both the sociolingual communities it had artificially created within the electorate. Elite division under this ambiguous nationalizing regime is defined by the deeper elites' fragmentation into several power groups or clans, their growing distrust and competition. The elite networks are dense and separated into divisions united by individual or multiple leadership of each clan, exemplified by the former mayor of Astana and Almaty, Imangali Tasmagambetov.

To sum up, elite composition and competition follow different scenarios and logics in Kazakhstan and Latvia. Kazakh elite selection until recently was not entirely influenced by ethnic criteria, although several influential groups or clans do express their nationalistic plans. The logic of selection in Kazakhstan is followed by elites' economic and political interests and members of elite groups are chosen based on the criterion for achieving these goals and interests. A unifying ethos is absent because beliefs in democracy are blurred and not very popular either at the elite or mass levels (see chapter 5) and the political field is represented by multiple discourses and messages. One coherent structure uniting propresidential political elites and public servants is that of Nazarbayev as the first Kazakh president (charismatic legitimacy) and his Nur Otan party.

In Latvia the dominant ethos of ethnic democracy has divided elites and counterelites based on ethnolingual identification and divisions. The

Russian-speaking parties and electorate are highly marginalized, and deeply opposite belief systems exist based on this ethnolingual divide. Election after election, Latvian parties and Latvian elites dominate the political field, but there is no coherence in political organization as powerful parties (like the Latvian Way) fall out and cease to exist, and other competitive forces and elites swap places without affecting the dominant ethos. The interchangeability of elites in Kazakhstan does not depend on formal elections or change of ethos. It is dependent on the personal views and opinions of the most powerful elites in the clan elite structure.

Tables 4 and 5 show the evolution of the Kazakh and Latvian elite regime and the current disposition of power elites in Latvia and Kazakhstan based on ideological affiliation with different signifiers in the regime—nation-ideology or leader-led ideology.[90]

As we can see from figure 3 on elite fragmentation and tables 4 and 5 there was a great deal of variation and elite disposition in the Kazakh case, but it also had the highest number of powerful elites—the president himself, key names such as the current Kazakh president Kassym-Jomart Tokayev, Karim Masimov, Nurtay Abykayev, Umirzak Shukeev, Bulat Utemuratov, Asylbek Dzhaksybekov, and Marat Tazhin remained powerful although their positions were shifting in the official domain and within the regime itself. However, the key power elites in Kazakhstan remained stable and dependent on the strongest figure in the regime—Nursultan A. Nazarbayev, even today. Latvian elites saw greater fluctuation, although the power elite struggle was also defined by a similar set of names and faces throughout the first decade of independence—the top party representatives of Latvian Way, Prime Minister Andris Šķēle's group, and several members of the conservatives and nationalists who were able to compete within the coalition; and in the second decade of independence—with the rise of the Unity party, its former leader and prime minister Valdis Dombrovskis's circle, and nationalists within the coalition who continued their conservative nationalist-leaning agenda after the departure of each prime minister. The Unity party provided three prime ministerial positions after the 2009 corruption crisis in the Latvian Parliament when Valdis Dombrovskis became the interim prime Minister and was elected to the same leadership position twice: from November 2010 to October 2011 and from late October 2011 to late January 2014. He had to resign in November 2013 following the tragic event of the Zolitude shopping mall roof collapse, which left fifty-four people dead and was seen in Latvia as an act of severe neglect. This had a lasting effect on security and

Table 4. Political elite composition in Kazakhstan

Hierarchy of Political Elites in 1990–1995

President's circle	President Nursultan Nazarbayev Vice President Eric Asanbayev (position abolished in 1993) Tulegen Zhukeev Oleg Soskovets (in 1993 already migrated to Russia, vice-prime minister in Chernomyrdin's government 1994–1995) Marat Tazhin (from 1993 to 1994)
Political financial elites	Akezhan Kazhegeldin Nurtai Abykaev Sergei Tereshenko Zamanbek Nurkadilov Sarybay Kalmurzayev Aleksandr Mashkevich and Trio of Tycoons from the Eurasia group
Regional elites	Nurlan Balgymbayev Zamanbek Nurkadilov (Almaty) Galymzhan Zhakiyanov
Parliamentary elites	Abish Kekilbayev Sandzhar Dzhandosov (deceased in 1995) Serikbolsyn Abdildin Daulet Sembayev Petr Svoik Uraz Dzandossov
Party and movement elites, cultural elites	Olzhas Suleimenov Murat Auezov Mukhtar Shakhanov Nurlan Orazalin Sergey Duvanov

Hierarchy in Political Elites in 1996–2006

President's circle	President Nazarbayev Marat Tazhin Karim Masimov Yermukhamet Yertysbayev Bulat Utemuratov
Political financial elites	Nurlan Balgymbayev Rakhat Aliev Nurtay Abykayev Umirzak Shukeev Timur Kulibayev
Regional elites	Zamanbek Nurkadilov Imangali Tasmagambetov Victor Khrapunov Umirzak Shukeev Shalbai Kulmakhanov
Parliamentary elites	Zharmakhan Tuyakbay Marat Ospanov Abish Kekilbayev Kassym-Jomart Tokayev Oraz Dzhandossov Dariga Nazarbayeva

Hierarchy in Political Elites in 1996–2006, continued

Party and movement elites, cultural elites	Olzhas Suleimenov Mukhtar Shakhanov Dispersed artistic elites: Kzyl Traktor, underground Almaty art movement
Opposition	Akezhan Kazhegeldin DVK Group: Altynbek Sarsenbayev, Uraz Dzandossov, Mukhtar Ablyazov, Galymzhan Zhakiyanov, Bulat Abilov, Tulegen Zhukeev, Alikhan Baymenov. Independent: Evgeniy Zhovtis Sergey Duvanov

Hierarchy of Political Elites in 2006–2014

President's circle Strongest groups	President Nazarbayev Aslan Musin Karim Masimov Timur Kulibayev U. Shukeev Nurtai Abykayev Imangali Tasmagambetov Kairat Kelimbetov Asset Issekeshev Marat Tazhin Asylbek Djaksybekov *Nur Otan* Party
Political financial elites	Nazarbayev clan Bulat Utemuratov Karim Masimov and Timur Kulibayev Umirzak Shukeev Western Kazakhstan (Musin) Imangali Tasmagambetov Asylbek Djaksybekov, Dariga Nazarbayeva
Regional elites	Southern Kazakhstan Umirzak Shukeev Western Kazakhstan Ryskaliyev clan Akhmetzhan Esimov Almaty clan
Parliamentary elites	*Nur Otan* Party Dariga Nazarbayeva Azat Peruashev and post-2006 *Ak Zhol*
Party and movement elites	Altynbek Sarsenbayev (deceased 2006) Zamanbek Nurkadilov (deceased 2005) Tulegen Zhukeev Alikhan Baymenov Mukhtar Shakhanov Aidos Sarym Mukhtar Taizhan, Rysbek Sarsembay, Sofy Smatayev
Opposition	OSDP Azat: Zharmakhan Tuyakbay, Amirzhan Kosanov, Bulat Abilov.

Table 5. Political elite composition in Latvia

Period of the parliamentary elections	Leading party	Prime minister	Other leading elites
1990–1993	Popular Front	Ivars Godmanis (PF) May 1990–August 1993	Anatolij Gorbunovs Dainis Ivans
1993–1995	Latvian Way	Valdis Birkavs (Latvian Way) August 1993–September 1994 Maris Gaillis (Latvian Way) September 1994–December 1995	Latvian Way party members
1995–1998	Democratic Party *Samnieks*	Andris Šķēle December 1995–August 1997 Guntar Krasts (TB-LNNK) August 1997–November 1998 Villis Krishtopans (Latvian Way) November 1998–July 1999	
1998–2002	TP Popular Party Latvian Way	Andris Šķēle (People's Party) July 1999–May 2000 Andris Berzinsh (Latvian Way) May 2000–November 2002	Latvian Way Lembergs Shkele Repshe
2002–2006	The New Era PCTVL (pro-Russian party)	Einars Repshe (New Era) November 2002–March 2004 Indulis Emsis (Greens) March–December 2004	
2006–2010	The People's Party Union of Greens and Farmers The New Era Harmony Centre (currently Harmony) TB-LNNK	Aigars Kalvitis December 2004–December 2007 Ivars Godmanis (Latvian Way) December 2007–March 2009 Valdis Dombrovskis (The New Era) March 2009–November 2010	Kavitis Godmanis/Dombrovskis Ushakovs/Tsilevich
2010–2011	Vienotiba Harmony Union of Greens and Farmers TB-LNNK	Valdis Dombrovskis (Vienotiba) November 2010-January 2014	S. Aboltina Berzins
2011–2016	Vienotiba Harmony Union of Greens and Farmers TB-LNNK	Laimdota Straujuma (Vienotiba) January 2014–February 2016 Maris Kuchinskis (Liepaja Party) February 2016–present	I. Dzintars I. Murniece S. Aboltina N. Ushakovs

safety violations. After this disastrous event, Dombrovskis resigned, citing the need for strong leadership in times of crises. He was followed by another Unity politician, Laimdota Straujuma, who was prime minister position from early 2014 to November 2014 and then again from November 2014 to February 2016. The Latvian power elite, however, is more vulnerable to competition and its

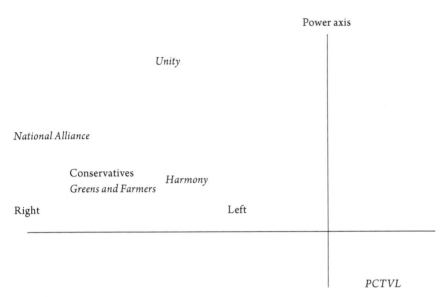

Figure 3. Power elite composition in Latvia 2010–2016.

fluctuation—the rise and fall of individual politicians is much more volatile than in Kazakhstan. This is partially explained by the democratic context in which the nationalizing regime is inevitably placed, but is also a result of fierce elite competition where, unlike in Kazakhstan, the situation is not stable or balanced by a single powerful figure and the elite much more fragmented on the individual level.

These conditions of elite competition are discussed in more detail in chapter 3, but it is important to specify that the most important transformations leading to these conditions took place in the late 1980s (precisely in September 1989). The introduction of competitive electoral democracy in the Soviet system led to further democratization in both Latvia and Kazakhstan, but it also led to the rise of key figures in Kazakhstan who remained in power afterward—a key example being Nursultan A. Nazarbayev's legitimacy as the Kazakh leader.

PRE-INDEPENDENT CONDITIONS FOR ELITE COMPETITION

Despite the practice of nonparty selections to the councils, in the 1990 Soviet elections more than a quarter of the deputies to the Supreme Councils within each republic were to be elected from organizations other than the Communist Party.[91] This was seen as a "liberation" wave in both Kazakhstan and Latvia.

It had also spurred the development of various movements and public orga-nizations (*obshchestvennie organizatsii*) and the active involvement of the intelli-gentsia (cultural elites) in the political process. Olzhas Suleimenov, a prominent Kazakh-Soviet writer, was elected from Kazakhstan's Soviet Writers' Union. Timur Suleimenov, another renowned member of the Kazakh intelligentsia, art-ist, architect, and designer,[92] was also elected. He later recalled, "During this new transition period my friends and I [Kazakh-Soviet urban intelligentsia] ended up in the parliament (1990), where we initiated our ideas [for democratic reforms], for the first time in our country's history.[93] The intelligentsia movements in Kazakhstan and Latvia (especially the Popular Front) failed to form a viable and strong political force because they neither possessed the skills for building a political network nor were taken seriously as important players. However, democratization of the electoral process influenced the fruitful development of the political parties that formed in great numbers in Kazakhstan and Latvia pre- and post-1991 independence. The 1989 list of public organizations and move-ments in Latvia (compiled by the Academy of Sciences of the USSR, Institute of Ethnography) included eight organizations but the elections of 1990 saw only two competing parties—the Latvian Popular Front (total 65 percent of votes) and the Latvian Communist Party and Interfront combined (total 27.3 percent of the votes).[94] In the following elections of June 1993, a total of twenty-three Latvian political parties ran for election (the winning party Latvian Way se-cured 36 percent of the vote), nineteen parties in 1995 (Saimnieks winning with 15 percent), and twenty-one parties in 1998 (Popular Party winning with 21.30 percent), clearly indicating not only the growth of the political parties but also the complexity of political networking among the parties (see tables 23–30 in the appendix on the results of elections in Latvia from 1993 to 2014).

Several important organizations emerged during that period in Kazakh-stan as well. These were the Green Front of Kazakhstan (June 1988), Nevada-Semipalatinsk (February 1989), and the December 1986 investigation commis-sion (July 1989).[95] Most of the active political parties and movements formed in Kazakhstan in just three months, from April 1990 to May 1990. These included the Alash party, Social-Democratic Party, and National-Democratic Party, Zhel-toqsan. In the summer of the same year the national movement Azat was formed; it later developed into a full-fledged political party. The party had a "strong leadership who had a managerial grip and strong links with the establishment;

successful slogans; balanced position; and left orientation with a national character"; "Although there were five official leaders of the party (co-chairmen) there were mainly three leaders who all expressed different positions—Mikhail Isinaliev, professional politician, former minister of foreign affairs, brilliant orator and traditionalist [conservative]; Marat Chormanov, subtle tactician and former functionary of the Communist Party (KPSS) of the highest rank, a very knowledgeable and intelligent politician, a centrist; Sabetkazy Akataev, PhD who taught the history of the Communist Party at some point, one of the leaders of the *Zhas Tulpar* movement which was covered with a notion of romantic-nostalgic ideas, a populist."[96] The context of independence was an important factor in the formation of these movements, parties, and networks in Kazakhstan. Traditional communists were removed from the political scene either by force of law (Latvia) or by the will of the new establishment (Kazakhstan). The situation varied in the two cases. Whereas Eastern European postcommunist regimes found themselves victims of a vast postcommunist witch hunt, which turned politics into a dichotomy of communist and noncommunist (which subsequently led to a deficit of elites who were not involved in communist organizations and the party before 1991), Kazakhstan's case refined the remaining communist network and kept it. Many postcommunist elites remained within the circle of important regional elites, for example, local oblast governors or *akims*. President Nazarbayev was instrumental in the approach that excluded the remnants of the Communist Party—the post-Soviet Communist Party under the strong and charismatic leadership of Serikbolsyn Abdildin, who until 1994 was a strong rival of President Nazarbayev. The communist regime and the legacy of the creation of the communist network continued during the selection of the Kazakh independent elites because "traditional forms of informal political relations and behavior developed during communist rule, combining with Soviet bureaucracy to create a *form* of patrimonial communism."[97]

It is important to mention that apart from the Communist Party remaining under the leadership of Serikbolsyn Abdildin, Zhasaral Kuanyshalin, and Gaziz Aldamzharov, there was another Communist People's Party of Kazakhstan. This alternative communist party was led by Vladimir Kosarev and is now led by a trio of party secretaries—Dmitry Legkiy, Aikyn Konurov, and the 2019 presidential candidate, Zhambyl Akhmetbekov. It is currently the third largest party in the parliament. In the 2012 parliamentary elections the Communist People's Party of Kazakhstan gained the threshold of 7.19 percent of votes to guarantee seven seats in the Parliament where the vast majority of seats are occupied by the Nur

Otan party. In the June 2019 presidential elections, Zhambyl Akhmetbekov, the candidate from the Communist People's Party of Kazakhstan gained only 3 percent of the votes. Gaziz Aldamzharov's Communist Party of Kazakhstan is in opposition to the Nazarbayev regime and has remained so since the very beginning of post-Soviet political development in Kazakhstan.[98] It emerged out of Abdildin's "old" Communist Party and was registered in 2004. It is are an unofficial propresidential party and currently remains in the parliament along with the major propresidential party, Nur Otan, and Ak Zhol of Azat Peruashev.

In Latvia, Article 25 of the 1994 Citizenship Law banned former communist party leaders and supporters from citizenship, naturalization, and any involvement in political activity. A majority of the "old" Russian activists who, for example, were actively involved in the protest movement against initiating the law on 60 percent Latvian education in minority high schools, do not possess citizenship and are technically are prevented from exercising their political rights. However, there were many exceptions to the rule where, Anatolijs Gorbunovs and Ivars Godmanis, former communists became the new leaders of the regime even after the 1993 elections.

What were the historical contexts in which nationalizing regimes in Latvia and Kazakhstan constructed their respective dominant discourses? How did these discourses influence further elitist competition within the regime? Dominant discourses of nationalization guide the development and stability of the nationalizing regime, but these also exclude other elite and nonelite members from wider political discussions and participation. In certain contexts, discourse dominates over political decision making and thus defines the capacity of power. In chapter 2 I discuss these main national discourses and narratives that the emerging nationalizing regimes were able to produce after independence.

2

THE ARCHAEOLOGY OF
NATIONALIZING REGIMES

NARRATIVES, ELITES, AND MINORITIES

> Identities, then, are always formed within broad discourses, universes of available
> meanings, and are related to the historic positioning of the subjects involved,
> which are themselves constituted and given meaning by the identity makers.
>
> —Ronald Grigor Suny

The aim of the nationalizing regime in Latvia and Kazakhstan is to impose hegemony over the national imagination, to provide a stable yet very limited framework for understanding and identifying with the given nation. It is also a stable discursive field that is controlled by the ruling elites within these nationalizing regimes. It is a specific political *doxa* that guards and guides the selection and behavior of elites in the nation-building process. In other words, the important difference between the nationalizing regime and other structures of political and national decision making is that it defines and governs the decisions made by political players within the specific nationalistic and ideational framework that it represents. The nationalizing regime is also a power field.

What defines power in the post-Soviet context is the regime's ability to wield its decision-making capacity in a more influential way. The power within the nationalizing regime is exercised not so much by coercion as "by the construction of meaning on the basis of the discourses through which social actors guide their action."[1] To demonstrate this argument, this chapter analyzes the main set of powerful discourses about nation in Latvia and Kazakhstan. These are the dominant and recurrent discourses that I traced and found both in the official discursive field (the constitution; the official ideological narratives of the dominant political parties) and in recurrent narratives and discourses of the popular, official, and oppositional bilingual media. The analysis also uses data collected from interviews with political elites and members of the opposition from 2012 to 2015.

I argue that in Latvia a discourse of Latvianization dominates and rules over elite competition; thus, this discourse is restated and enhanced over time regardless of elite circulation. In Kazakhstan, the discursive field of the nationalizing regime is dominated by a small group of people, mainly from the presidential administration; it structures the actions and decisions of elites within the regime on the basis of loyalty to the president, regardless of the discourse the regime is propagating. Unlike in Latvia, where the discourse dominates the elites, in Kazakhstan selected elites dominate the discourse.

THE NATURE OF NATIONALIZING REGIMES IN THE POST-SOVIET SPACE

One important characteristic of the nationalizing regime is that it was in place before formal independence from the Soviet Union was achieved in both Latvia and Kazakhstan. In Latvia, the nationalizing regime was formed on the wave of intellectual resistance and dissidence against Soviet domination and the so-called Soviet occupation (1945–1991). By 1989 it had become a part of the larger Baltic resistance movement, and by the 1990 elections the Popular Front, the main intellectual force behind the resistance movement, became a winning political party.

Kazakhstan's nationalizing regime differs substantially from Latvia's because, since the inception of the post-Soviet regime, it has been controlled primarily by the remaining Communist political elites. The Communist political elite in power was more consolidated and stronger than the voices of charismatic yet powerless intellectuals, yesterday's leaders of the Popular Fronts. United around the charismatic and popular figure of the young Nursultan A. Nazarbayev, the nomenklatura in pre-independence Kazakhstan was solid and acted accordingly,[2] in response to the challenges of transition, "without unnecessary emotions and nationalist sentiments," as one of the former power elite members recounted in one of our numerous interviews.[3]

The first president, Nazarbayev, who until late independence remained a politician who was "national in form but socialist in content,"[4] did not allow broad-based nationalist movements to emerge as he extended his control over Russian and Kazakh ethnonationalists in the country. This was achieved despite the political geography and varying demographic concentrations in Kazakhstan as in Latvia. In Latvia, ethnic Russians mainly reside in the major urban centers and Latvian capital, Riga, and in the eastern transborder region of Latgale. In Kazakhstan, too, the majority of ethnic Russians reside mainly in the urban centers, such as Almaty, but also in the northern transborder regions along the frontier with Russia.[5]

The overall characteristic of the nationalizing regime is a process and framework of ideational and managerial nation-building that is governed by the interests and ideas of the ruling group, including economic elites who also try to exercise control over political decision making. It rests on a Gramscian notion of hegemony, a form of state control and value production by a specific ruling group whose legitimacy is built on moral and intellectual leadership and guidance that is embedded in social and institutional structures of the society.[6] As Andrew March has put it:

> A war position suggests the overall strategy of appealing to, co-opting, synthesizing with, the multiplicity of non-class social groups in the process of giving meaning to social relations, defining interests and identities, structuring the political and creating a "common conception of the world." It involves the construction, or transformation, of popular consciousness through intellectual and moral reform as well as the appeal to (and invariably the formation of) "common sense." Wars of position establish the political terrain—who is included and excluded, what are the assumptions of the political system, which questions are open, and which are not even regarded as questions. From the standpoint of a ruling hegemonic class, the war of position involves making the claim to universality, common sense and inevitability, and excluding counter-narratives not only from the realm of practical politics but from the realm of the imaginable.[7]

In my analysis of post-Soviet nation-building processes, I rely specifically on this notion of the appropriation of hegemonic discourses on the nation and national belonging by a specific political ruling group. I argue that, even though cultural elites have largely contributed to the creation and legitimation of a "popular consciousness" and ideational common sense of national ideologies in Kazakhstan and Latvia, their power within and outside the nationalizing regime was highly marginalized. In the words of one of the first nation-builders in Kazakhstan, for example, intellectuals were too emotive and simply could not adapt to this highly responsible and historical mission of state-building. As one former member of the presidential administration in Kazakhstan puts it:

In Kazakhstan there was a different situation, different context. Having 7,500 km of border with Russia and around 40 percent of the whole population in the northern regions (every year 200–300 thousands of ethnic Russians would leave) and we had only 42 percent of Kazakhs [in the total population of independent Kazakhstan], with all these factors we followed a very correct [strategic] position. There were no shocking acts [*nikakogo roda epatazhnykh deistvii ne bylo*] with demonstrations (a demonstration may please you, but it is not a strategic move, because we could have aggravated our economic conditions, being so dependent on Russia), so we chose a very rational way of development. Maybe it wasn't as brave as in the Baltics—there is a different situation there; they have the sea [access], they do not need to transport their goods via railway that is located on foreign territory and so on.... In our situation, when you were in the realpolitik, when you were responsible for 17 million people and you have economic crisis, your pseudo-heroic nationalistic escapades could have been provocative and incite your neighbors, you had to realize that it could have turned into a catastrophe.[8]

The "war of position" in Latvia and Kazakhstan established the rule of one ideology (Latvia) or one man (Kazakhstan), and excluded all alternative views from the ideological and political domain by framing them as either unimportant or threatening to the nation's development. The exclusion of minorities from the sociolingual public sphere (mostly Latvia), followed by exclusion from political participation (both in Kazakhstan and Latvia) are also results of these wars of positions in which ethnic minorities have lost. It was especially severe in the Latvian case, where further Latvianization of the nationalizing regime also meant diminishing competition from non-Latvians.[9] After all, the whole discourse of the quota-based naturalization of non-Latvian noncitizens was dictated by the fear of Latvian elites, and especially the Latvian far-right movements, of allowing the Russian language to compete with the Latvianized content of the new hegemonic rule.[10]

The crucial question in understanding a nationalizing regime is not only its operational capacity (the creation and control of the hegemonic discourses, which is discussed in chapter 3) but also the discourses that allow elites to establish hegemony.

Below I discuss the evolution of the dominant discourses and describe how the nationalizing regimes have controlled and reproduced the same discourses over the years of independence. The logic of this discourse creation and accommodation lies in the ability of the ruling elites to sustain the limits of the allowed discursive field needed for the preservation of their own interests and goals. In this way, the more nationalizing regime in Latvia focuses on the primacy of an ideational Latvianized discourse in citizenship and language policies and sustains this discourse to limit non-Latvian political competition and to be more secure. In Kazakhstan the personalized nationalizing regime, on the contrary, uses its ability to control the ambiguous and binary notion of national discourses in order to feed both of its sociolingual communities (Kazakh and Russian) and sustain the power of the remaining nomenclature under the umbrella of "the friendship of peoples" (*druzhba narodov*), presidential stability, and the authority of Nursultan Nazarbayev, who has remained the dominant player in political and elite life even after his voluntary resignation in March 2019.

MAJOR POSTINDEPENDENCE DISCOURSES ON NATION-BUILDING AND MINORITIES IN LATVIA

Latvia's main claims for national legitimacy were built on notions of restoring its pre-Soviet independent republic, of becoming a democratic and European state. It also built its legitimacy on the process of overcoming its Soviet legacy of domination in demography and cultural reconfiguration. This was the hegemonic discourse of postindependent Latvia throughout the 1990s and early 2000s when voices of the "Other"—non-Latvian Russian-speaking minorities—were silenced due to their noncitizen status in contrast to the active Latvian elites. After independence Latvian became the only official language, which led to the political and linguistic alienation of many predominantly Russian-speaking minorities. Latvian was the sole language of political discussions in the Parliament on the key issues of citizenship and language laws, laws on aliens (noncitizens), and education reforms concerning the further Latvianization of minority schools.

For non-Latvian minorities to participate in the dialogue, they had to acquire language and political rights by naturalizing in the Latvian state and nation. For the dominant Latvian elites, it was important not only to circumvent competition from the major Other—the so-called Russian-speaking population—but also to appropriate the nation by restricting the boundaries of its official representation to the views of the nationalizing regime.

Latvian Citizenship for the Loyal and the Offended

The process of naturalization officially began in 1996 with the first "window" of naturalization opening for candidates between the ages of sixteen and twenty. At the time, 28 percent of the population, or 686,027 people, were noncitizens, and 469,053 of them had to wait for naturalization until the early or mid-2000s. The quota-based naturalization prioritized those born in Latvia over those who migrated to Latvia and was an age-based naturalization quota system that prioritized younger people first and then their parents.[11] However, after the adoption of the citizenship laws in 1994, the naturalization rates were very low: only 500 youngsters aged sixteen to mid-twenties applied for naturalization in the first year.[12]

This initially raised alarm among international observers such as the Organization for Security and Co-operation in Europe (OSCE) Mission and the European Union (EU) but did not occasion a major debate in the Latvian Parliament. On the contrary, Latvian parliamentarians and power elites alike were reluctant to make any changes at this stage. The majority of these political elites expressed the view that only the most loyal non-Latvian residents should be granted Latvian citizenship. The definition of loyalty was expressed in terms of fluency in Latvian; respect for the Latvian state, national history, and symbols; and support for Latvia's independent (from Russia) democratic development.

The *Baltic Barometer* survey data from the same year demonstrated that those loyal Latvian Russian-speaking populations were very numerous despite the suspicions of Latvian politicians. More than half of the respondents among the Russian-speakers agreed that all residents should learn the national language (Latvian) and 40 percent said that this should usually be the case. Only 1 percent disagreed with the statement. In addition, 69 percent of Russian-speakers agreed that residents should respect the national flag. The majority of the Russian-speaking respondents also supported Latvians' political rights in local elections (38 percent chose "definitely" and 33 percent—"usually") and in national elections (34 percent chose "definitely" and 29 percent—"usually"), although 23 percent thought it was unimportant.[13]

Throughout most of the 1990s non-Latvians (most of whom were deprived of citizenship) felt shock and resentment and experienced "moments of despair, disorganization and astonishment" in the aftermath of the 1993 Saeima elections, 1994 Citizenship Law, and other reforms that "cut them off from political competition in Latvia for years to come."[14] However, by the end of the first decade of independence, Latvian Russian political elites became more prominent. In a situation where the major ruling parties, such as Latvian Way, were unable to present a viable and strong program for the ethnopolitical divide, and the small attempts made by other parties, such as the Samnieks, to take on the issues of noncitizens and non-Latvians had failed, pro-Russian politicians like Tatjana

Zhdanoka, Boris Tsilevitch, the centrist Janis Urbanovich, and others, saw an opportunity to address these issues. The opinions and preferences of the elector-ate on both sides of the ethnolingual divide who expressed discontent with the nationalist division also provided the space for alternative non-Latvian parties. This division was revealed in the sociological data of the *Baltic Barometer* and in the public discussions that occupied the media and public sphere at the time.[15]

By the end of July 1997, the leading newspaper, *Diena*, began publishing a special section dedicated to the issues of citizenship and naturalization for ethnic non-Latvians. The section shed light on the other side of the coin—those offend-ed (*obizhennie*) and betrayed Russian-speakers who had supported the ideals of Latvia's independence and who perceived Latvia as their home. The main purpose of the section and its writers was to popularize the idea of naturalization as well as to give voice to readers' letters. At the time, this was probably the only public space where many noncitizens could openly express to the public and the government their feelings of discontent and having been betrayed.

The newspaper section became very popular and, unsurprisingly, revealed growing resentment among the noncitizens who perceived Latvia as their home-land. Letters also revealed that many noncitizens felt they were being insulted, that they were being treated unfairly by being made to "wait in line" for Latvian citizenship "against their will." The newspaper section became one of the few grounds for bilateral discussions between those imposing naturalization (Lat-vians) and those needing to pass the naturalization test (Russians). In August 1997, Iveta Pelshe from the Board of Examination Committee for Naturalization addressed these issues and accusations concerning the language and history tests for naturalization: "It is not an exam, we are not 'examining' in the schooling sense but trying to find out whether a person can integrate in the society."[16] Al-though the passing rate for Latvian language skills was usually at 93–94 percent in the mid-1990s and at 95–96 percent after the abolition of the quota system (1998–2000s),[17] the history test was the main concern of the OSCE monitoring Mission and commissioner on National Minorities as well as of the minorities themselves. This complicated version of historic-political aspects of Latvia was seen as challenging even for ethnic Latvians. This was reflected among those Latvianized Russian-speakers who saw the exam system as irrelevant to their status as long-term residents, some of whom had been born in Latvia in the first place. There were also disputes over naturalization rules and procedures. The language-test waiver for the graduates of minority schools who had already passed a similar language test upon graduation was one of the most problematic issues. Other issues included relatively high application fees for naturalization (above the average monthly wage in Latvia in the 1990s) and the granting of automatic citizenship to children born to noncitizen families in Latvia post-1991.[18]

The reluctance of the majority of Latvian political elites to amend some of the strictest aspects of the citizenship law relied on very powerful discourses: too many non-Latvians were becoming citizens in a very short time without properly learning or understanding the culture and language, and this would endanger the Latvian culture and nation.[19] The centrist and liberal political elites at the time feared that the "wrong" electorate might obtain citizenship, which they believed only those loyal to the Latvian state should be granted. Many politicians believed that most loyal non-Latvians would not mind facing the challenges posed by the quota system's waiting period for naturalization, the bureaucratic application process, and the examinations. The inflated belief in the danger that Latvia would become a "settler nation" due to the remaining and symbolic presence of Russian language in the public and private spheres impeded further harmonization in the ethnopolitical field. Even though the quota system was abolished in 1998, which resulted in an increase number of naturalization applications (more than 15,000 in 1999 alone compared to the total of 8,500 in the first three years of the naturalization quota),[20] the debate was far from over.

Language Policy

It was the restrictive language law (first version adopted in 1992 and then amended in 1997) that largely sustained these debates. The main criticism from international observers was that the law was too restrictive concerning the use of other languages in the private sector.[21] There were also serious concerns about the implication of the law and fines collected for speaking in any language other than Latvian in official governmental communications, in state-financed institutions, or even in the central governmental district in heavily Russian-speaking Riga.

In July 1992 the government introduced a Language Inspectorate. Its prime goal was to monitor knowledge of the state language in public institutions such as schools, hospitals, and police stations. The first wave of "language examinations" and fines spurred a series of scandals reflected in both the Latvian and Russian media. These included minority schoolteachers' mass protests over being fined or losing their jobs for insufficient knowledge of the state language.

The language discourse became a very sensitive issue for both Latvian- and Russian-speaking communities. A sense of insecurity was expressed by many non-Latvians (mostly noncitizens, see chapters 4 and 5) who were not able to secure better jobs or even operate in central parts of Riga or any big cities because of language inspectorates, fines, and other dividing factors in bilingual spaces, mostly urban centers. On the Latvian side there was a strong sense of resentment: "Look at this girl [working in a café in the parliamentary district in Riga]. She has to be bilingual and speak equally well in both Russian and Latvian because this customer [my respondent points to a Russian-speaking middle-aged man] came and ordered in Russian. Why is this so if this is Latvia? Everyone should speak Latvian, and the waitress should reply to this customer in English if he doesn't speak Latvian!"[22] This quote is from a leading political and academic figure in the Latvian Saeima from the ruling party Unity during our interview in May 2013. The one nation-one language view was dominant, despite the opposite view shared by both the Latvian-speaking (76 percent) and Russian-speaking (73 percent) electorate,[23] who agreed that children should be educated in the language of their parents, which may not always be Latvian. That discussion took place at the time amendments to the language law were being debated in the Parliament (1997).

Language discussions and domination of the Latvian language were also important for the discourse on education reform. The reform of minority schools had been planned in the early postindependence period. As one of my respondents at the Latvian University explained, "The school reform required 60 percent of Latvian instructed classes from the ninth to twelfth grades and it was planned for a gradual, step-by-step implementation by 2004."[24] This decision had created a conflict between two communities—the pro-Latvian and pro-Russian supporters who were practically divided into two distinct sociopolitical communities.

Nation, Latvian or Latviiski?

"I am not Latvian [ethnically] but I am *Latviika* [a female citizen of Latvia]!" This is how one of the letters ended in a citizenship debate in the Latvian newspaper *Diena* in the late 1990s. The discourse of two Motherlands had been constructed by the mid-1990s. The two Motherlands were the territorial nation of ethnic Latvians (the ethnic nation) and the Latvian Republic for all those who may or may not be ethnic Latvians but who equally identify with the state via state and civic self-identification. Although this case falls into an ethnic–civic dichotomy of nationalisms,[25] these are ideal types of nationalisms and are "categories of 'practice' alone" but not "fundamental categories for social-scientific analysis."[26] This implies that nations, or rather nationalizing regimes and elites, are engaged in either "good" projects of civic nationalism that depoliticize ethnicity and construct a political community of citizens (without an ethnic, racial, or national specification), or "bad" ethnic nationalisms that base membership in the nation on a specific selected ethnicity.[27]

In Latvia, there are two conflicting discourses: the Latvianized (with an ethnoculturally Latvian core) and universalist *Latviiskii* (accommodating ethnic minorities and, most important, the cultural and political interests of Russian-speaking groups) identities. The Latvianized discourse is the hegemonic discourse proposed and appropriated by the Latvian elites since 1989, preceding the declaration of independence. Talks on the exclusive framework of citizenship and restoration of independence did not take a strong universalist approach at the time, as many non-Latvians (Russian-speaking or bilingual residents) supported the ideals of independence before 1991. Among these ideals were democracy and freedom, which for many meant acknowledging the political rights of all and not just citizens of the interwar republic and their descendants.

The indignation and betrayal discourse of noncitizens stems directly from the change of this discourse post-1991. Russian activists of the ZaPCHEL (PCTVL) political movement (For Human Rights in a United Latvia), many of whom were members of the last Supreme Council of Latvia (1990–1993) and active supporters of the Popular Front, recalled during our interviews that at the time there was no discussion of restricted citizenship and universal freedoms and rights were "common sense." That is why the remaining communists and members of the Interfront who called for "saving" the Soviet Union and "keeping Latvia's place" in the Union were not as popular as their political opponents of the Popular Front.[28]

By the mid-1990s, media discourse in Latvia was already discussing the possibility of forming a two-commune nation in the Latvian Republic. According to local political analysts, renowned sociologists, well-known journalists, and even external experts (e.g., political representatives from Denmark, Sweden, the OSCE), there was a call for describing Latvia as a two-commune nation.[29] By this they meant two separate socioethnic and ethnopolitical communities of people within the Latvian Republic who perceived political reality differently. This difference was based on the bilingual community already in place in the major Latvian cities. Furthermore, differences between the interests of citizens and noncitizens in their political choices expanded this divide. The term "political nation," which aimed to describe this divide, had already emerged right after independence. However, it only became popular in the late 1990s with the gradual involvement of "Russian" parties like PCTVL in parliamentary discussions.[30]

The evolution of the "political nation" concept in Latvian politics is quite remarkable. At first it was addressed by the liberals (e.g., Samnieks party) who called for a partial citizenship provision for all 1991 pre-independence residents of Latvia. By the late 1990s and under pressure from the EU, the OSCE, and the Council of Europe (Russian foreign policy notwithstanding), the Latvian political field had to accommodate its goals to join the EU with a pressing need to harmonize its policy toward minorities, which entailed substantial amendments to the citizenship law. The term "political nation" then meant the community of people who, regardless of their ethnic or cultural identity, shared universal patriotism and loyalty to the Latvian state. Some liberal proponents of the idea also called for accommodation of the cultural and educational interests of minorities, by leaving space to develop their native languages, Russian, for example.

In the late 2000s, when Latvia had successfully joined the EU, and the main external, European pressure on the Latvianized nationalizing regime had disappeared, the "political nation" became an ideal type, a political unicorn. In 2004, a quarter of Latvia's population still remained in the status of noncitizens—an issue that continues to influence the ongoing political crisis of the dominant right-leaning parties and coalitions. This political crisis also endangers Latvia's further democratization.

A decade after the 1991 independence, Latvian far-right parties and groups continuously called for further Latvianization of the nation (see the amendments to the preamble to the constitution that call for acknowledging the territorial nation of [ethnic] Latvians). At the same time, there was still a group aspiring to a political nation project. By 2005, a group of centrist and center-left parties united under the umbrella of the Harmony Centre (now simply Harmony) party to successfully occupy this niche.

The Soviet Legacy

The most recent history of Latvia's forced incorporation into the Soviet Union and post-1986 struggle for independence formed the discourse of the Soviet legacy. In the official media it was defined in terms of a "decolonization" of historical and popular discourses and was primarily conducted through the discourse of Soviet occupation (domination, mass deportations, and abuse of ethnic Latvians, their culture and language). The dominant discourse that was cultivated for years by cultural and political elites represented the Soviet period as having only a negative impact on the development of the Latvian nation, society, and economy. The notion that "we would have been another Finland by now" was especially important in the 1990s, at a time when the country was going through a difficult economic transition. Other important themes of Latvia's de-Sovietization were (1) discourses of national survival, (2) Russia's imperial ambitions, and (3) domination by Moscow elites during the Soviet period.

The post-Soviet legacy included the problem of Soviet nostalgia, which the Latvian discourse portrayed as hollow but nonetheless threatening for the new national awakening of the Latvian nation. There were controversies over the remaining retired Soviet militia and army pensioners and an ongoing debate about the role and involvement of Latvian soldiers in the SS division of the German military during World War II. All these issues were widely discussed in public with various justifications for crimes committed during World War II and their seriousness. For example, some discussions involved justifying and granting presumption of innocence to several figures who had possibly collaborated with the Nazis. An interesting discourse emerged around the controversy about the Holocaust and Latvian participation in collaboration with the Nazis; it was argued that many testimonies given by Latvian soldiers were not genuine and had been extracted under KGB torture during the Soviet occupation right after the end of World War II. Article 15 of the Citizenship Law of 1994 introduced a clause providing for former KGB workers or informants, and people who had worked against Latvian independence, to be excluded forever from applying for naturalization.

Many nationalist parties and groups framed the presence of the non-Latvian noncitizens in Latvian borderlands as the primary legacy of the Soviet period. This discourse argued that migration was uncontrolled and unaccounted for by the Soviet Latvian elites and were even used to advance the process of Russification of Latvia. The vast majority of noncitizens did migrate to Latvia in the so-called Occupation period and thus were unofficially termed Soviet-era migrants.

Finally, the presumably backward Soviet system was frequently contrasted with the post-Soviet neoliberal transformations in Latvia.[31] Post-Soviet independent development in Latvia was usually viewed more positively; opinion polls from the *Baltic Barometer*, for example, showed positive support for the new system and not for the Soviet regime. In discussions of the Soviet-era welfare state and universal citizenship, the discourse stressed the complete absence of political rights and the provision of welfare opportunities in return for political loyalty. The growing dissatisfaction with and distrust of the political elites led to comparisons with oligarchs, and they were associated with corruption, artificial coalitions, and having lost touch with their electorate; there were increasing comparisons to the closed regime of the Soviet Union. Similar discourses were also observed among the top elites of the post-Soviet state of Kazakhstan, who shared identical fears of Soviet nostalgia and decided to build a new state-nation by forgetting and juxtaposing the Soviet past.[32] However, this process was fully achieved in the political discourse only in 1995 with the adoption of the second constitution in Kazakhstan.

IN SEARCH OF A NATIONAL IDEOLOGY IN KAZAKHSTAN BETWEEN POLITICAL COMPETITION AND GUARANTEES OF STABILITY

The first and second post-Soviet constitutions (1993 and 1995) of Kazakhstan became sacred focal points of discourse for elite legitimacy and contestation in Kazakhstan. For many counterelites, including Kazakh nationalists, the second 1995 constitution (which is still in place) was a tool of legitimation that the ruling elites used as an instrument for exercising control. The first constitution, which was pivotal in the discourse of political development, was adopted on January 28, 1993. Its opening paragraph was allegedly the reason for the constitutional change in 1995:[33] "We, the people [narod] of Kazakhstan, who are part of the world community, based on the inviolability of Kazakh statehood [gosudarstvennost'], acknowledging the priority of human rights and freedom, are determined to create a democratic society and rule of law, and desiring to ensure civil peace and interethnic harmony, and a decent life for ourselves and our descendants, declare . . . the Republic of Kazakhstan as a form of self-determined state for the Kazakh nation providing equal rights to all its citizens."[34] This constitution assigned more powers to the parliament than to the president and in general was very liberal. For example, the 1993 constitution allowed multiple citizenships (Part 2, Article 4),[35] and (in contrast to the Latvia's restrictive language law of 1996, which gave priority to the Latvian language alone) provided for plurality and freedom for the development of other minority languages, while preserving the Russian language's status as the language of interethnic dialogue—practically a second official language. However, talks about the "self-determination of the Kazakh nation" spurred further discussions on the matter and, with subsequent amendments to the preamble as well as further empowerment of the president's role,[36] the new constitution was adopted in the all-republican referendum of August 1995.

The preamble of the second constitution adopted on August 30, 1995, did not, however, change in regard to its national priorities: "We, the people of Kazakhstan, united by a common historical destiny, creating a state on the *indigenous Kazakh land*, considering ourselves as a peaceful civil society dedicated to ideals of freedom, equality, and harmony, desiring to take a noteworthy place in the world community, realizing our great responsibility toward present and future generations, based on our sovereign right, we adopt this Constitution."[37] Both constitutions reflected the civic ideal of equality and respect for human rights as well as other democratic state values. The ethnic backing of statehood was also an important point in both preambles; however, the majority of the Kazakh national-patriot respondents I interviewed perceived the second preamble as less nationalistically determined, but still claimed: "It is clearly written in the Constitution that this is the primordial land of the Kazakh people and it should be like that, no one should doubt it. . . . Each "guest" [ethnic minorities in Kazakhstan] needs to know in whose house [he/she] is at present, and [he/she] needs to respect the traditions and owners of this house. If every guest imposes his or her rules and says this house is as much mine as it is yours, this will lead to a very conflictual situation. The Kazakh [population] would not agree to that."[38]

Another Kazakh national-patriot movement leader, Aidos Sarym, compared the regime in Kazakhstan with a "firefighter" attempting to fight the fire of rising problems in national politics in the absence of a clear agenda for a national identity project for Kazakh- and Russian-speaking parts of the Kazakh society.[39] Nevertheless, the ruling elites attempted to construct an *ethicized* political agenda by occupying the political space with Kazakh ethnic content and politicians. This was achieved by the same type of discourse, framed around Kazakhstan's status as a postcolonial state, as in Latvia, but with a more cautious approach.[40] It was built on producing parallel symbolic spaces for Kazakh and Russophone civic audiences for which the regime constructed two narratives of nationalism.

The regime codified ethnicity as a "politicized social action, a process whereby elements of real, actual, lived cultural differences are politicized in the context of intensive group interaction" separately for two different audiences (socioethnic communities),[41] and proposed various levels of cultural and social persuasion and perception of the nation. The Russophone sphere, defined not only as Slavs but all those who did not possess knowledge of the Kazakh state language and were thus perceived by the regime as less inclined toward an ethnonationalistic vision of the Kazakh state, were fed the idea that interethnic and political stability was crucial for the country's further development and modernization.

The ideals of equality, multilingualism, and freedom of choice for education in any of the republic's three most popular languages (English, Russian, and Kazakh) or in minority languages (at the school level) constituted this widely accepted civic notion of Kazakh nation-building. However, the degree to which Kazakh ethnonationalism formed the framework for the Nazarbayev regime's nation-building in Kazakhstan cannot be underestimated.

Despite the vague political development of the Kazakh language in the 1990s, it was the official state language, and Kazakh heritage and history defined the nation-building and legitimacy proposed by the new-old elites in this post-Soviet country. President Nazarbayev evoked both constitutional preambles and the recurrent narrative of "the land of indigenous Kazakhs" in his annual addresses to the nation since 1998 and even earlier in many public speeches where he emphasized the discourse of the "ownership" and "primacy" of Kazakh ethnicity over the new state.[42] According to one of my interviewees:

> The language policy in this sense is a somewhat sacred place for the whole regime. Practically speaking, the language policy is not executed de facto the way it is written de jure (we all know what happens with language regulations and development—a very ambiguous issue for Kazakh language, for example). But its [Kazakh language's] sacred aspect is a very important point for the whole feudal system [of the present regime], maybe even the most pivotal aspect for the regime. Although the practical statehood [*gosudarstvennost'*] of the Kazakh language is lacking, this ideologem (let's put it like that) is written in the Constitution, is the pivotal part of the Constitution, is its heart. This [ideologem] is realized practically through ethnicization of power and ethnicization of business. [The state language discourse] is thus this sacred place where strangers are not allowed, and that is why any attempts of questioning this discourse create such an explosion of incomprehension; if you are allowed in that sacred place, you have to behave accordingly. If you're a woman, cover your head and pray and where necessary bow, but never ever try to question this sacral symbol or try to say that behind gilding there's only alabaster.[43]

The power of defining discursive "sacred" space of national imagination or national ideology is crucial for any elite legitimation—from the economic (who can gain from all types of privatization and restructuring) to the political.

The situation with a discursive framework of nation-building is not unique to any nondemocratic state. The nation is still framed around a particular, usually indigenous, ethnic group, its history and heritage, but in a more ambiguous and contextually framed manner. One of the best examples of such a policy is the promotion of the Kazakh language in Kazakhstan. As William Fierman demonstrated in his analysis, the strategic ambiguity that separated Kazakh nationalists and the proponents of the civic multiculturalism paradigm also blurred and contradicted the lines in promoting the status of Kazakh as the official language.

> Because of the complexity of Kazakhstan's national identity, the proclamation of Kazakh as the only state language has been accompanied by concessions to the recognized status of Russian. The 1989 language law, adopted at a time when no one expected that the collapse of the Soviet Union was so near, reserved many specific functions for Russian; perhaps the most important was its designation as the language of "cross-national communication" (*iazyk mezhnatsional'nogo obshcheniia*). This was accompanied by the guarantee that it would be used "on a par" with the state language. This designation "cross-national" was preserved in the 1990 Kazakhstan language program, as well as the first (1993) constitution of independent Kazakhstan.[44]

Moreover, "Kazakhstan practiced lingual pluralism at the expense of the Kazakh language," according to the famous Kazakh public figure and politician Berik Abdigaliev.[45] "There is still a lack of conditions for the development of the Kazakh state language and its wider implementation" while "many official organs of administration still do not use state language in their work."[46] Without a less ambiguous and opposing orientation to the "complex national identity,"[47] the regime focused on building and protecting the legitimacy of the first president, Nazarbayev, who was envisioned as a guarantor of stability and thus stable modernization.[48]

In multiethnic Kazakhstan, the idea of stability promulgated by the regime since the early 1990s, after the eruption of conflicts in Nagorno-Karabakh, the Fergana Valley, and Osh in the neighboring countries of Azerbaijan, Uzbekistan, and Kyrgyzstan, respectively, has helped to build a discourse of stability. The regime created a discourse of a much-needed interethnic stability in Kazakhstan that was only possible given (1) the population's consensus on the need for this interethnic harmony, and (2) strong state leadership that was able to oversee such stability. The legitimation of Nazarbayev under the paradigm of strong leadership that could and should guarantee stability and development built on that stability crystallized in the late 1990s and became a base both for the majority of population and for the majority of elites in power.

In a nondemocratic political context, the power to define the specific concepts of the ideology belongs to either a dominant leader or a group of elites. Such a system provides divergent outcomes in the nation-building framework. The national discourse is restricted but pluralistic and may focus mainly on the fusion of values (e.g., interethnic stability), the existence of which is presented as based solely on the personalized leadership of the president or prime minister. On the other hand, the dominant group of elites in a more democratic political setting may provide the same result—restrictive frameworks for the nationalist imagination—depending on the internal context of each specific case. In other words, other power struggle domains may structure the context of a nation-building framework, depending on the sociopolitical situation. For example, in Latvia, the dominant elites saw the presence of the Russian-speaking minority as a threat, while in Kazakhstan the presence of the Russian-speaking elites and specialists was seen as something desirable. This may be seen in the restrictive citizenship policies where "the indigenous Baltic elites saw repatriation [of large Russophone migrant communities] as the best solution."[49]

On the elite level, however, the nation-building process in Kazakhstan was very much contested in the early 1990s, and the dissolution of the parliament prior to the adoption of the new constitution in 1995 indicates that the political field was highly competitive and polarized on many issues. Growing Kazakh nationalism in post-2005 Kazakhstan shows that the consensus on nation-building has not been easily resolved and is still being contested. The regime in Kazakhstan was relatively successful in building a nation with two communities, balancing ideas of stability and modernization on the one side and more "Kazakhified" national ideals on the other. This was achievable largely because the language barrier between the two communities remains an open issue, allowing the regime to address different narratives in the two languages, depending on the context and pressures from both communities. It is important to consider the two competing discourses—the dominant presidential discourse and the marginalized yet present and persistent Kazakh national-patriotic discourse, discussed in the following two sections.

Presidential Discourse

The role of the strong and charismatic leader that President Nazarbayev represented was the core discourse in Kazakhstan. Practically all the various discussions on the nature of national development in Kazakhstan have centered on the figure of the charismatic and strong president and the regime's quasi-ideology,[50] with *natsionalizm* (nationalism) framed as both dangerous to stability and narrow-minded in most debates and political competitions.

The discourses of peace, stability, and harmony along with standard proclamations of the importance of the indigenous heritage of Kazakhs, are shuffled in the narratives presented by the president and the regime in the two languages, depending on the context of the political crisis, for example, the 2001 and 2005 oppositional insurgencies from within the ruling elite.[51] By stoking fears of bloody ethnic conflicts, the regime was able to convince the population of the need for peaceful and harmonious coexistence that could lead to stable, prosperous development in Kazakhstan.

The triangle of stability–prosperity–power was constructed as a substitute for the missing ideology in 1989 and it has endured throughout Nazarbayev's rule. It surfaced even in the address to the nation in January 2012 after the tragic events in Zhanaozen.[52] The regime envisioned this triangle as a very flexible discursive net to direct popular support for sociopolitical and economic changes. The triangle of stability–power–prosperity was framed much like the previous Soviet ideological frameworks for achieving one stage of development at a time or sacrificing one path for a brighter future of communism in the next decade. Thus, the Nazarbayev regime sacrificed democratic development during the transition period of the 1990s by consolidating power in the president and claiming the importance of a strong leader to ensure sociopolitical stability and the lasting development that depends on that stability.

Strong presidential power was portrayed as a guarantee for linked stability and economic prosperity. Even in the post-transition period, when the key goals of stability and economic development had been achieved, the regime insisted that a strong presidency was still needed. Earlier challenges were replaced with new goals and development projects, such as the "Kazakhstan-2030" program of 1997, later phased into shorter programs of "Kazakhstan-2010" and "Kazakhstan-2020," to achieve faster, well-planned development. The presidential elite's visions of rapid development growth were also visually inscribed in the official media (*Khabar, Kazakhstanskaya Pravda*) and in the cityscapes of the new, fast-growing capital city of Astana.[53]

Despite evolution of the contexts within which the ideology is framed and reframed every year, a sociolingual divide persists in the messages addressed to the Russian- and Kazakh-speaking audiences. Still, many of the older approaches of this framework remain. Although Eurasianism was one of the discourses within compartmentalized ideology,[54] I would nevertheless argue that currently it has become a tool to gain legitimacy outside the domestic domain.

Kazakh National-Patriots and an Unchanged Agenda on Kazakh Language

The Kazakh nationalist discourse was labeled "national-patriotic" in Kazakhstan, and the regime framed it as a narrow-minded, undemocratic, and unattainable scenario for Kazakh nation-state development with the prevalence of the Kazakh language. The protection of cultural values, the ethnic identity of Kazakhs, and their main cultural value—the language—were seen as the main goals of several nationalistic movements throughout the 1990s and 2000s. Kazakh national-patriots are the ones calling for protective and remedial actions for the cultural core of the Kazakhs after waves of perceived colonization and oppression by the Russian and Soviet empires. Post-2006 developments in the national-patriotic movement, with the emergence of Kazakh public figures and intellectuals, such as Aidos Sarym, Rasul Zhumaly, Berik Abdigaliev, Erlan Karin, and Mukhtar Taizhan, whose popularity is growing and whose ability to convey their messages fluently in both Kazakh and Russian continues to develop, have shifted the regime's approach to them. As one leader of the national-patriotic movement revealed in our interview, "I know I am not able to connect with all the people of Kazakhstan because our territoriality and regional communication is so disintegrated." In his public speeches and addresses, however, he believes he is able "to communicate these ideas to the ruling elites and I know many of them are listening and even sharing our views."[55] Yet other nationalists are not as encouraged by the regime as he is.

> It is clear that the regime [*bilik, vlast'*] will not allow the Kazakh field, the Kazakh part of the society to politicize, to form appropriately strong political parties. For the regime this is an unknown land, an uncomfortable format [for dialogue]. Again, they would have to speak to someone [national-patriots] in the Kazakh language. For the [current] nomenklatura this is a big challenge. Nevertheless, the Kazakh field exists and will continue to exist. It is able to facilitate interesting ideas and many new spheres of discussions emerge. This demonstrates that the Kazakh agenda will continue forming until there is a way to institutionalize it. But the present situation in the world [civil war in Ukraine, for example] remains as the impeding factor. After all, the majority of Kazakh nationalists are statists. For them the importance of the state is above and beyond everything else. So, there is no

reason to expect any threatening clashes with the ruling regime unless catastrophes were to occur.[56]

The national-patriotic movement is far from forming a united front or being able to institutionalize its role in a more feasible form. One of the main criticisms of the movement concerns its rigid agenda toward the language issue and empowerment of the Kazakh language. Other problems include variations on the ecological theme concerning a series of accidents at Baikonur that were related to the Russian Federation's irresponsible policy in ecological matters,[57] and the resistance to Kazakhstan's membership in the Customs Union and the Eurasian Union. Kazakh nationalists are also far from being united and providing new alternatives to the regime's "clear failures in nation-building".[58]

The field of being *Kazakh* became an important factor for consideration in the regime's gaining legitimacy that is acknowledged by a majority of leading national-patriots. Their opinions regarding the regime are fragmented. In our interview, one of the leaders of this movement, for example, stated: "If the current regime were to decide tomorrow to promote Kazakh language on an adequate level and provide for the Kazakh people, for its own people, I would openly support this regime."[59] Other opinion leaders, namely, Rasul Zhumaly and Aidos Sarym, express open political opposition to the regime and its failures in nation-building, and yet others, Erlan Karin, for example, have been co-opted by the regime. The instability and disunity of the national-patriotic movement puts it in the position of an attractive field that could be used interchangeably by different political actors "who would like to 'step-in[to]' the Kazakh field and Kazakh agenda and use them for their own political gain."[60] The convergence of the liberal Kazakh opposition and especially the National Social Democratic (OSDP) Azat (Freedom) party in 2005–2009 is an example of such manipulation in the counter-elite field in Kazakhstan.[61]

This chapter's main aim has been to demonstrate the evolution of the different narratives and symbols of the nationalizing regimes in Kazakhstan and Latvia. My analysis of the structures of the regimes and the nationalizing narratives they produced and controlled has demonstrated that the Latvian regime is narrower in selection of its elites and political parties based on the given ethnic dichotomy of power elite selection. Ethnicity, or rather the dominant Latvianized notions of ethnicity, *nationness*, and, thus, the political agenda of nation-building, excludes potential elites and parties from competition in the stable Latvianized political

field of its strict nationalizing regime. I argued that the Latvian political discourse on nation-building and the guiding principles of the political field of elites
had formed in a more solid and more ideological way, sharpening the principal
concept of Latvian state-building for and in the name of ethnic Latvian only.

In Kazakhstan, the nationalizing regime followed similar lines of development in terms of controlling and narrowing down the participation of elites
and counter-elites, but the defining role of their participation depended on the
shared values of the personalized regime of President Nazarbayev rather than a
unifying national ideology. In this way, the nationalizing regime in Kazakhstan
is more pluralistic in its choices of various narratives related to nation-building,
but also more ambiguous in defining one or another plan of development. This
strategy was a sustainable approach for the regime's stability and popularity,
but the ever-growing dissatisfactions and possible competition from the Kazakh
national-patriot movement and nationalizing opposition might provide a new
space or avenue for the regime's instability and prove to be a challenge.

What keeps the nationalizing regime in place are the elites who participate in
the process of producing and reproducing the same narratives of the ethnicized
and hegemonic frameworks of national domination of one group over another.
Post-Soviet nationalism is not only an ideology but a field of intensified elite
competition for resources, power, legitimacy, and support. Even those elites
who may not be called the most genuine protectors of the national culture and
language engage with a step into the nationalistic field defined by power struggles. The nationalizing regime, I argue, is in place as the main controlling entity
in defining discourses and power positions. I discuss the mechanisms of these
power struggles within the nationalizing regime in chapter 3.

3

APPROPRIATING AND
CONTESTING THE NATION

POWER STRUGGLES IN NATIONALIZING REGIMES

The desire to convert ambiguous and controversial ideas about the nation and nationhood into a coherent or strategically ambiguous and multilayered discursive system in the post-Soviet region went hand in hand with the interests of political power elites. The type of the regime structures the outcomes of the exclusion of different ethnic groups. This was based either on the legal continuity and legitimation of nationhood (Latvia) or the symbolic co-optation of ethnic minorities whose categories were highly objectified in the political language and rhetoric of state-led multiculturalism (Kazakhstan). I argue that competition from the substantial ethnic Russian (Slavic) minority group was a greater political challenge for Latvianized democratic development than for the continuous Sovietized regime in Kazakhstan. These trends were seen in Latvia as early as 1991 where local political commentators noted that,

> Now despite a steady growth in Russian residents and the corresponding decline in indigenous ethnic voters, the past three years in Latvia have witnessed increasing ethnic Russian support at the ballot box for what would be traditionally considered ethnic Latvian demands, including independence. Consequently, Latvia has been slowly charting a course away from the ascendancy of the Soviet Union, Russia, and the Commonwealth of Independent States. And Russian residents of Latvia

appear to be posing a challenge to the traditional concept of a greater Russian nationalism.

For example, considering the ethnic balance in the republic, only a sizable block of Russian votes could have yielded a Latvian majority in the Parliament.[1]

The different approach to the Slavic community in Kazakhstan was dependent on the Sovietized nation-building legacy, for example, through the concept of the friendship of peoples (*druzhba narodov*).[2] The political transition period in Kazakhstan did not allow the elites to form a widely shared consensus on nation-building similar to the consensus built in Latvia before independence. With decision-making power concentrated in the closed presidential circle, in Kazakhstan's nationalizing regime elite views remained fragmented regarding national development in Kazakhstan only on questions of further Kazakhification.

The Kazakh and Latvian cases represent very different logics of development within the elite field. The control exerted on the Latvian gatekeepers is more widespread within the Latvian power coalition, which I discuss later in this chapter, but the consensus about Latvian national development is already cemented even before new coalitions are formed. These coalitions are based on democratically renewed political elites and parties. The nationalizing discourse in Latvia is stable and it is also perceived as natural and based on common sense, whereas in Kazakhstan the legitimacy of the less democratic and more autocratic regime depends on the sustainability of strategic ambiguity in nation-building and the political field in general. In other words, the Latvian nationalizing regime narrows competition in the political field by stabilizing the core national narrative and discourses. These discourses significantly limit non-Latvian parties and individual political actors.

Dominant pro-Latvian coalitions transform their temporal competitors a given parliamentary term or election by supporting parties based on their approach to this dominant discourse. In the case discussed in this chapter, based on this logic, the Harmony party further includes pro-Latvian values and symbols. Non-Latvian parties are also pushed further into the Latvianized nationalizing regime in order to keep winning against the competition already in the parliament while addressing their preelectoral campaign to both Latvian- and Russian-speaking audiences.

The Kazakh case represents a very narrow and closed circle of elites, where competition is mainly on the level of established informal and formal political networks (parties and "clans"). Today counter-elites are active in the Kazakh

national-patriot field rather than in the weak political opposition. Even during
the events of 2019 in Kazakhstan, marked by the resignation of President
Nazarbayev, the voice and agency of the political opposition was almost nonexistent. In other words, elites in Kazakhstan are "selected" and their mobility
and competition within the power field depends on their abilities to adapt to the
regime's pressing goals—political sustainability of the nondemocratic regime
and thus the curtailing of the anti-Nazarbayev regime opposition. The national
question in Kazakhstan is problematic for the regime if the fragile balance of
compartmentalized ideology is challenged by either nationalist movement—
Russian or Kazakh—or by the growing Islamist religious threat.[3] It is crucial
for the regime to balance all popular views, to diminish nationalist and religious
radicalism as highly dangerous and destabilizing, and as a disastrous outcome
for the country's development.

I define compartmentalized ideology as a separate regime tactic that le-
gitimates discourses about the nation in which different ideologically divided
"audiences" are separated and fed divergent messages about the nation they all
constitute. In Kazakhstan, the audiences are divided on an ethnolingual basis—
those speaking predominantly Kazakh and those speaking mainly Russian. This
shifting of ideological themes constitutes an important asset for the regime's
stability, development, and sustainability by keeping two or more ethnolingual
audiences of the polity within the limits of their own discourse.

These strategies were sustainable in the long term throughout Nazarbayev's
tenure, but the current destabilization—fueled by rumors about the lending of
land as well as the Islamic threat posed by Kazakhstan's ISIS fighters—challenges the mechanisms of compartmentalized ideology. Growing distrust of the
regime's ability to maintain the promised stability is expressed mainly among
ethnic Kazakhs outside the prime centers of power concentration. Until recently, mass protests and terrorist attacks were rare in Astana and Almaty, the two
major central cities of Kazakhstan. In April and May 2016, the marginalized
groups of the ethnic Kazakh electorate, many of them also predominantly
Kazakh-speaking, protested against possible attempts to lend land to Chinese
investors in a movement now colloquially known as "Zher satylmasyn" (The
Land Should Not Be Sold). Major protests that occurred in the towns of Aqtobe
and Aktau in Western Kazakhstan also incited dissenters from major towns in
Eastern and Southern Kazakhstan to protest in Almaty, but this protest was shut
down before it started.[4] The government immediately responded, closing the
"Land Question" by placing a moratorium on the lending of land, but the protest

incentives now expanded into a movement of those dissatisfied with the regime's unpatriotic moves. Land (*Zher* in Kazakh) became the symbol of a deeply rooted and ethnically Kazakhified contemporary national identity project from below, composed of ethnic Kazakhs spontaneously grouped under anti-Land Reform rallies. The leaders of these movements, Max Bokayev and Talgat Ayan, were arrested in 2016 and sentenced to five years in prison. And although these were peaceful protests and demonstrations against the Land Reform, the court termed the actions of Bokayev and Ayan as "social discord," involving the dissemination of false information and a violation of complex legal restrictions on holding rallies, which make such activities almost impossible in Kazakhstan. As some opposition observers noted, the Zher protest movement mobilized only ethnic Kazakhs and supported Kazakh nationalist slogans.[5]

The Zher movement of 2016 was not the first attempt to counter these "rumors" and potential programs for Land Reform. The 1998 attempts to amend Land Reform led to similar speculation and the threat of the "Chinese Question" per se became a field of study in Kazakhstan.[6] However, the harsh economic crisis and double devaluation of the local currency, the tenge, in 2014 and 2015 led to worsening economic conditions, especially on the regional level. Many local observers believe that economic deterioration along with continuous promises of stability and prosperity but with simultaneously diminishing pluralism and political participation for most Kazakhstanis led to the Islamic radicalization of young ethnic Kazakhs who joined ISIS in recent years. The protests incited in Kazakhstan since February 2019 that involved mothers with many children demanding better welfare policies and the write-off of their bank debts are telling examples of how the "stability" discourses promoted by the Nazarbayev regime in Kazakhstan no longer work without actual economic miracles. All these changes and growing distrust toward the regime pose further challenges to the compartmentalized ideology discussed in this chapter.

CONTEXTUALIZING COMPETITION WITHIN THE NATIONALIZING REGIME

Several factors can influence elite competition in a nationalizing regime: elites' position toward the national idea and their personal views, for example, whether they share nationalistic views, their legitimacy and political interests.

Based on my interview data, the power elites in Kazakhstan tend to be more cosmopolitan and pluralistic about ethnic aspects. As noted by one respondent, a former adviser to President Nazarbayev, right after independence "there were not many fervent Kazakh nationalists [among the power elites], it was simply dangerous to allow them into the circle [of high decision making]."[7] During turbulent times in 1994 various organizations guided by ethnic Russian discourses and ideas, for example, Lad, were actively engaged in the political activities and popularization of secessionist or autonomous ideas within the republic based on the ethnodemographic regional representations of the population. The official press was also engaged in framing the discourse of planned (strategic) stability needed in the country:

> Since the beginning [of independence] it was clear that it would be hard to maintain the sovereignty of the republic and not only due to economic reasons. There were great hopes associated with the [following internal and external aspects]: (a) that we would be able to create a state-power [*gosudarstvenno-vlastnii*] mechanism with the President at the top that would be able to regulate the society and to organize it in the new conditions; (b) that Russia, with which Kazakhstan is in very close relations, would be able to become a real democracy and, by overcoming the pro-imperial and pro-chauvinistic tendencies inside it, would lend its hand with helpful and unselfish support and help for the Kazakh republic; (c) that Kazakhstan with its multinational population known before as a republic of "peoples' friendship" would become a country of international stability and Kazakhstani patriotism. Along with that a lot of hope was associated with the role of the Russian nation that constitutes one-third of the population. All these forces that constitute the spine of stateness and the democratic development of Kazakhstan have shown serious cracks [recently].[8]

Despite the need for political elites to legitimate themselves and to do so in the face of the growing majority of titular Kazakhs, the Kazakh elites were far less nationalizing than other elites in the former Soviet Union. This is clearly evident especially in comparison with Latvia. There are several explanations for this phenomenon.

First, elites in Kazakhstan were challenged by the biggest Russian-speaking minority and proximity to their external homeland. Moreover, the Kazakh regime's rather friendly relations with Russia did not allow power elites to choose the *Baltic scenario.* Nor was it technically possible in Kazakhstan because it lacked the initial legitimacy or "national authenticity" available in Latvia by 1990.

Second, legitimation was based on several layers of sometimes conflicting narratives. For example, as noted by many researchers in the field the Kazakh state uses a set of both so-called civic and ethnic narratives in its nation-building.[9] This mere legitimization technique is not unique for Kazakhstan or Uzbekistan, for example.[10] By linking separate narratives to different sociopolitical and socioethnic audiences both on the mass and elite levels, the power elites try to legitimize their ability and right to rule over both the ethnic majority of Kazakhs and the multiethnic society.[11] But they have done so for years of independence without realizing that societal demands for the regime are, in fact, shifting away from the sociolinguistic divide. Finally, the regime was blind to the fact that neither the "multiethnic" non-Kazakh part of the population nor the ethnic Kazakh parts of the population are homogeneous. Another layer of legitimacy lies outside the country: its international legitimacy to the closest kin-state of its largest ethnic minority group (Russia) or wider international community, which accepted the civic rights of minorities.[12]

Third, many current Kazakh elites were politically informed and educated during the Soviet period. Their mindset (*myshlenie*) was formed during that particular regime where some elites were far more ideologically tainted than any mass supporters of the regime. Even though twenty years of independence have changed the initial sociopolitical contexts in the perceptions of the country and elites, the old elites in Kazakhstan still use rhetoric that characterizes forms of Soviet ideological constructions, such as the "friendship of peoples" (*druzhba narodov*) that is based on the assumption of fixed "ethnicity" or universal labor values (a narrative that appeared in Nazarbayev's speech in summer 2012 several months after the Zhanaozen uprisings in December 2011). This way of approaching nation-building from afar (which contributes to its lack of national authenticity) exemplifies the distinctive elite behavior and orientation toward nationalizing on the surface rather than based on core values as in the stable Latvianized national discourse. This fact differentiates Kazakh elites from their Latvian counterparts, although they have a common feature of authoritative protection of defined frameworks of legitimation and national imagination, which are used for the legitimation of both state and elite rule.

Latvian elite development after independence underwent severe structural changes, and this is another reason that differentiates it from Kazakh elites' behavior and attitudes. As was discussed in chapter 2 in the case of Latvia, independence brought a tightening of nationalist ideology and the exclusion of non-Latvian symbolism from ideological content and the exclusion of non-Latvians from the political field. This happened through a series of law enactments (starting with the 1989 Language Law, adaptation of the old Constitution in 1990,

the Citizenship Law of 1994, and, finally, the Education Reform of 2004), which
excluded non-Latvian speakers from the official public sphere and made Latvian
the only official language.[13] Finally, the 1994 Citizenship Law implemented very
restrictive procedures.

Kazakhstan lacked this approach involving aggressive protection of core
national values, in contrast to Latvia's exclusion of vast segments of the non-
Latvian population. Some of the most restrictive discourse movements such as
TB-LNNK required that groups of people who were unable to secure Latvian
citizenship after independence had to leave Latvia and return to their external
(historical) homelands (e.g., Russia, Belarus, or Ukraine). Other groups and parties on the spectrum have supported the idea to allow the most loyal non-Latvian
residents to naturalize through the highly bureaucratic process and restrictive
language tests.

These developments largely contributed to the elite structure and competition immediately after independence, which saw a decline in the number of
Russophone elites in Latvia.[14] Even those Russian-speaking elites and politicians
who supported Latvian independence and were active members of the Popular
Front were excluded from political participation. As one the activist of Latvian-
Russian politics recalled: "The changes were so catastrophic, so sharp and fast, so
traumatic for many people who only yesterday occupied important roles in this
society, who were building this state, this country but today [postindependence]
they found out that they were nobody. Yesterday he was a resident, a citizen and
he voted for the [Latvian] independence and today he turns on the radio and finds
out he is *no one*."[15] Another pro-Russian minority politician recalled:

> In one instance, you are part of the parliament (elections of 1990) and you are in
> the process of making important decisions, voting for independence and in another
> instance you find out this is not your country, you are not a citizen and you cannot
> vote or run for the office. I am fluent in Latvian, Latvia is my country, I have been to
> Russia, it is my historical Motherland (*Rodina*) but my home is here, in Latvia. What
> should I do about that then? Under the new Law that the coalition presented in 1994
> I had to wait to naturalize and if not for the OSCE [Organization for Security and
> Co-operation in Europe] that would've happened only in the 2000s when I wouldn't
> have been able to run for office anymore.[16]

In another discussion with a young bilingual (Russian and Latvian) but ethnically Russian citizen of Latvia and former activist of the ZaRYA movement,

I raised the issue of Russian-speaking representation in the Latvian public administration sector. Mark (name changed) had a successful career working in the Ministry of Integration (in 2001) and had good insight regarding the integration policy of non-Latvian minorities because of his educational background and bilingualism. At the time of his ministerial work he was completing his PhD in Riga. By the time I conducted two subsequent interviews with him in March 2012 and August 2013, he had changed universities twice because of his political activism in what was seen as the "radical pro-Russian bloc ZaRYA."

Mark joined ZaRYA in late 2012 after I interviewed him for the first time. By the time we met again, in 2013, he had already left the party and did not disclose the reasons for his decision. However, I found out from other sources that Mark's successful academic and teaching career at one of the city's universities was terminated, allegedly due to "his radical political views," and that he was able to secure another lectureship in a more liberal but nevertheless good university based on his "tremendous academic achievements."[17] Mark's career was one of the most interesting case studies for me. He identified as an ethnic Russian and was born in Latvia during the Soviet Union. Mark claimed bilingual proficiency in the Latvian language after independence, although he could speak Latvian even while growing up in the Soviet Union. His academic achievements and capabilities paved his way into the influential ministerial structures on integration, where he has worked with famous Latvian politicians in the field of minority relations such as Nils Muzhnieks, who became a professor and Latvian human rights activist before moving to the Council of Europe Commissioner for Human Rights, and Sarmite Ēlerte, who was the former chief editor of *Diena* newspaper and a member of the ruling Vienotiba party.

In our interviews Mark tracked the change in attitudes from a more pragmatic (2012) to a more competitive (2013) approach to the participation of the Russian-speaking minority in Latvian political life. Mark's membership in ZaRYA was a surprise to me. After all, ZaRYA had become increasingly radicalized since its inception, and after 2014 some if its most vocal members even supported the separatist movement in Donetsk and Luhansk. This was evident in the comments of former ZaRYA leaders posted on social media at the height of the Ukrainian civil war in 2014 and throughout 2017. After 2017, the most vocal former leaders of ZaRYA almost disappeared from the news agenda in Latvia and Russia.

In August 2013 Mark seemed disappointed in the direction ZaRYA had taken insofar as he seemed to support the protection and provision of equal rights to both the Latvian and Russian communities rather than justifying radical views.

One hour into the interview we were joined by another Russian-speaking activist from the PCTVL party, which turned our interview into a longer and deeper discussion. I knew that Mark did not openly associate himself with PCTVL, but he actively discussed the referendum on the status of Russian language in Latvia (2012) and the provision for minority schools, which had been the focus of PCTVL political activism since the movement was established in 1998; in 2019 it became known as the Latvian Russian Union.

Because Mark worked in the ministry and was one of the few Russian-speakers involved in Latvian politics after the 1998 abolition of naturalization quotas for non-Latvians, a crucial time for minority rights in Latvia, I asked him why Russian-speakers' participation in political life was so marginal even after the citizenship and naturalization quotas were abandoned:

> The system was already built like that. In the beginning they replaced everyone [including remaining Russians in the political system] based on political views [ideological], they [Latvian elites] needed new cadres who were able to think in new terms [*myslit' po-novomu*]. They started bringing their own people. I haven't seen how everything was "cleaned up" in the Ministries (I came late). But at the beginning of 1990s, I worked at the Riga airport and I saw how they "cleaned it up" there. At first the head of the airport was "parachuted" in and he brought his own team. This team had its own priorities and brought in its own people. Airport and aviation were a completely [ethnically] Russian sphere, but it is a Latvian entity now. . . . How did they do it? The language was key. Yes, you needed to learn Latvian but not in five years but in three months. In three months a commission [the Latvian language inspectorate] would come to check everyone's fluency in the Latvian language. Who can learn the language in three months? Of course, many people had to vacate their positions because of that. . . . I worked there [in the airport] when I was a student. Out of the eighty people (all Russian-speaking) who worked there, only I and one other man remained of the Russian-speakers because we knew Latvian. In the ministries this was done to an even greater extent because they [Latvian elites] had a new hard line and they needed people who were able to think in these new frameworks. Europe "closed its eyes" to these discriminatory developments [against ethnic Russian and Slav minorities] and Russia was also not involved much in these issues, especially during President Yeltsin's times.[18]

A few former ethnic Latvian communists remained in power. Among them was Ivars Godmanis, a key power elite member in the 1990s (twice a prime minister from 1990 to 1993 and from 2007 to 2009) and the architect of Latvian privatization processes. Politicians like Godmanis were part of the communist-turned-nationalists but they were a minority in the Latvian political sphere because political dynamics changed fast and new elites who entered the field were genuinely nationalist and did not have a communist past.

The post-1993 elections were highlighted by the biggest political loss of the Latvian Popular Front as well as the strengthening of Latvian ethnic democracy, its own form of nationalizing regime where the logic of the regime favored ethnic Latvians in official positions but otherwise followed democratic standards and frameworks. The election also saw the development and return of the Western Latvian diaspora—elites and ethnic Latvians who had spent the Soviet occupation in exile and on return to their homeland were perceived as authentic nationalist elites pushing for exclusionist ideologies and Latvianized national identity projects such as the leader of the Samnieks party. Until the mid-2000s the elite field in Latvia was mostly represented by pro-Latvian elites except for the only Russian party PCTVL (*Za Prava Cheloveka v Latvii*—For Human Rights in Latvia), now known as the Latvian Russian Union, which was highly marginalized. The emergence of the Harmony party, which actually claimed to be a centrist party, changed the elitist system in Latvia, thus providing the space for more ethnically heterogeneous party competition.

In Latvia's political life, ideological distinctions existed only on the basis of ethnic division and the elites' orientation toward inclusion or exclusion of a particular ethnic topic, such as minority schools. This framework is most explicitly described by politicians who have been excluded from the postindependent Latvian political system:

The post-Soviet, post-imperial framework led to the search for new identities. The first identity [in Latvia] is based on the family and the second—on language. This is why we have a bilingual and bicommunal society [based on the distinction among Latvian- and Russian-speaking communities] but only a monolingual and monocommunal state! ... For me and for our movement [Russian Union of Latvia] it was important to demonstrate ethnic discrimination and most importantly discrimination against the ethnic opposition. Because with the nonethnic opposition, which exists inside the Latvianized political sphere [nationalizing regime], there the competition is very harsh and it can even lead to short imprisonment [based on corruption allegations, for example], but there is no systematic pressure and forcing out [of the political field] that exists against the pro-Russian parties. This is the focus of our work. Why is this happening? ... Because this was a well-planned and well-executed operation, a system that was created and constructed to feed the interests of pro-Western and Latvian economic interests to exclude vast parts of the non-Latvian population from political and partial economic rights prior to their privatization of the state.[19]

The situation differed in Kazakhstan where elite interest and share in "privatization of the state" did not depend on the primacy of the dominant ethnic group because, although post-Soviet power elites in Kazakhstan were Kazakh, they expressed more cosmopolitan views. In addition, it was more important for the Kazakh elites to construct viable networks of trust based on the abilities and skills of various members of these networks, regardless of their ethnic identity. The compartmentalized ideology of the Nazarbayev regime was a strategy to separate two "audiences" in the state by addressing different messages to them about nation-building in their dominant language—Kazakh or Russian.

CASE STUDY OF THE COMPARTMENTALIZED IDEOLOGY OF NAZARBAYEV'S NATIONALIZING REGIME

The need to address more civic-oriented ethnic minorities with ideas of ethnic harmony and economic prosperity, but simultaneously to address growing ethnic Kazakh communities and their discontent with national policies (e.g., state bilingualism), pushed the nationalizing regime in Kazakhstan to adopt what I term elsewhere "compartmentalized ideology."[20] This ideological practice of reshuffling the content of nationalist and state-building rhetoric is based on pressing contexts (sociopolitical crisis, for example). Under the Nazarbayev regime it was based on the ethnolingual distinction of the audience to whom the message was being addressed. For example, whereas there was an evident trend of ethnohistorical revival of purely Kazakh content in the official rhetoric demonstrated in all five categories of discourses, parallel notions of ethnic harmony, the friendship of peoples (*druzhba narodov*), and the need to avoid ethnic conflicts were also developed.

The difference in language proficiency of Russian-speaking audiences in Kazakh and vice versa had allowed President Nazarbayev to successfully maneuver the coexistence of the discursive domains of ethnic Kazakh revival and the state understanding of multicultural harmony, and thus to equally legitimate the regime in the eyes of these audiences.

Compartmentalized ideology demonstrated its consistency over time to the extent that elites' needs *replaced* some of the regime's main enemies, such as Russian or Kazakh nationalists and their agenda, which the regime framed as narrow-minded and dangerous for the country's stable development. This included the substitution of old referential points and nostalgia for the Soviet Union because elites feared it could spur possible social and ethnic conflicts in the first stage of post-Soviet development. Similarly, all oppositional leaders and other political opponents of the regime and competitive nationalistic movements were branded as threats to the peaceful post-Soviet development. Finally, the division in the population's linguistic abilities, mainly among those who were not fluent in Kazakh, helped Nazarbayev address different messages to various culturally differentiated groups and audiences.

The application of "mild decolonization" or political postcolonial discourses with the delicate and selective use of colonial symbols,[21] the tragic Soviet past (mostly Stalinist purges, and to a lesser extent, the famine of the 1930s), and the glorification of the pre-Russian and pre-Soviet past and heroes, helped create legitimacy in the absence of real resistance or stable interwar independence (as in the Baltic case). The legitimation of the regime was a result of the application of the symbolic triangle of stability–prosperity–president. This allowed the president to maneuver in the political and ideological spheres by building his legitimacy around the idea of his being a guarantor of the interethnic and political stability that led to economic prosperity in the post-transitional period.

The discourse of state-sponsored primordialism and the revival of historic ethnic Kazakh discourse were formed largely dependent on the general legitimation of borders, territory, political community, and the right of indigenous elites to rule in *their own* country. This discourse presented a blend of different historical periods of cultural and ethnic communities, including those of the premodern era, which had occupied present Kazakhstan's territory. These historic communities were united under the narrative of Kazakh *ancestors* from the glorious Kazakh past. Some of the so-called scientific works of progovernmental historians find traces of the Kazakh code not only in Genghis Khan's era but also earlier in history.[22] This pseudo-historical narrative is also expressed in the main symbolism of independent Kazakhstan—the Golden Man, Scythian warrior of the fourth century AD, whose remains were discovered during an archaeological excavation near Alma-Ata in Soviet Kazakhstan in the 1960s.

Historical figures and historical narratives became highlights of state-sponsored primordialism for the following reasons. This helped create at least temporal legitimacy for the Nazarbayev regime by calling for remedial actions regarding the discourses of "Kazakh" and "Kazakhstani" nations envisioned by the regime. The discourse analysis of President Nazarbayev's speeches and addresses from 1989 until the late 2000s (table 6) demonstrates that the most frequent and repetitive discursive narratives were territory, history legitimation, ethnic conflicts, symbols of legacies and traditions, and Kazakh ancestors.

The choice of the ethnonational revival that had helped to legitimize the status of the new nation and the role of the nationalizing regime in Kazakhstan was similar to the processes elsewhere in Central Asia.[23] It also legitimized the policies of the nationalizing regime. After all, the logic presented was that the current nations were descendants of "ancient" civilizations and communities that have occupied this land since time immemorial. This allowed a discourse to form that was similar to the discourse in Latvia—that these were precisely indigenous populations and its elites had full rights to the exclusive choice and construction of ideologies based on the ethnocultural content of Kazakhs.

This ancient right to the territory and the nation can of course be seen from the ethnosymbolic perspective, as Kazakh elites did from early 1991. But more striking is that it is also part of the Soviet legacy. As part of the Soviet Nationalities Policy, the "ancestral" right to territory and pseudohistorical linkage through the primordial narrative was a landmark given to each of the fifteen Soviet republics.[24] Kazakhstan had inherited and applied the same policy as Latvia's, almost unchanged for its own legitimacy.

Certain elites in post-Soviet nationalizing regimes abused the legacy of the Soviet repressive policies and totalitarianism. In their speeches and discourses against the Soviet past, they often cited the center's domination and the periphery's cultural and national suffering. This type of post-Soviet postcolonialism was at the heart of popular sociopolitical discourses such as the Latvian Soviet occupation and Kazakhstan's justification of national revival.

These measures were the sorts of "remedial" actions needed for safeguarding these new post-Soviet national entities. The process of recovering from the negative and positive aspects of the Soviet experience in political developments was accompanied by the vast cultural reconceptualization of this past in Kazakhstan and elsewhere in Central Asia. The language of the oppressed former Asian and African colonies became a ready-made vocabulary of perceived similar experiences.

In 1991 different actors in Kazakhstan's political-cultural field became engaged in processes of readjusting to their new identity and finding a common national identity that would fit the entire population. The legacy of the previous regime was well written in the fixation of finding a common national identity for all divided sociolinguistic or ethnic groups that the regime gradually divided and sustained in separate communities and categories of analysis. It was largely believed that the main role in finding and implementing this project should lie on the abstract framework of the "state" or the "government."

The nationalizing regime's approach to the issue was to provide a rather blurred version of multiple symbolic signifiers within the five dominant categories that the regime perceived as vital for their own nation-building program: (1) territorial integrity and the rights of the titular ethnicity as well as "all people of Kazakhstan" on the country's territory and stable borders; (2) history and legitimation for such claims; (3) the threat of ethnic conflicts that could destabilize the peaceful development of the country; (4) Kazakh symbols and legacies of the traditional (framed) vision of nomadic heritage; and (5) myths of common ancestors. These were the five main discursive categories used in President Nazarbayev's speeches (1989–2013), which are visually represented in table 6.

Other important discourses included the political categorization and objectification of ethnic differences and minorities. The commonly used formula of the "140 ethnic minorities living in Kazakhstan" is a prime example of this dominant discursive categorization, which impedes the development of a more inclusive and political national discourse. For the Nazarbayev regime, it is important to continue separating the electoral and sociolingual audiences and provide different discourses on nation-building and belonging to these different discourses—such as "Kazakhstan our common home" (politically framed multiculturalism), "Prosperous and developed Kazakhstan for all" (modernizing nationalism), "Peace, stability, and a strong president" (politically framed multiculturalism), and "Kazakhstan—the land of our ancestors" (Kazakh national-patriotic).

This discursive representation of the Nazarbayev regime's rhetoric in the first decades of independence (table 6) was only part of the larger discursive network that had allowed the regime to maneuver its ideological messages to different ethnosocial audiences. Table 6 presents only five of the most commonly used textual discourses of the Nazarbayev regime, but it represents the core of the revival discourse in the postindependence era in Kazakhstan. There is also a place for the alternative discourse of the multiethnic nation in this discussion. The multiplicity of discourses and the ability of the regime to reshuffle sometimes

Table 6. Discursive representation in President Nazarbayev's speeches and addresses

	Territory	History legitimation	Ethnic conflicts	Symbols of legacies and traditions	Khazak ancestors
1989	Republic of Kazakhstan and Kazakhs who gave the name to the republic	Colonial expansion	The fear of extremism and calls for harmonic development Examples of Karabakh	Century/History traditions of hospitality	
1990	"Kazakhstani" people and Kazakh people. Republic—common home of all	Before there was a domination from the center (Moscow)	"Poisonous seeds of interethnic conflicts" "Destabilizing explosive processes"	People who were born and grew up in Kazakhstan have the same rights	Ablay khan symbol The land of our ancestors
1991	Borders are very important and delicate but this is ours, in common for all	Abandoning nuclear weapons	The fear of separatism remains and this fear can destroy economic networks	Hospitality and the importance of Kazakhs' culture, the revival of forgotten traditions	Ideas of Olzhas Suleimenov on proto-Turkism and ancestors
1992	Republic of Kazakhstan— national state; territoriality—the ancestral land of Kazakhs	The revival of Kazakhs does not conflict with the rights of other nationalities. Kazakh [ethnic] peoples are like the old and powerful tree whose roots are deep in the earth	The ability of an ethnos to create a state lies in its ability to live in harmony with each other nationalities	Traditions and customs of all people of our multinational country are important to all	Kazakhs—descendants of ancient peoples of Turks, Kypchaks, and so on. Famous names of Kazakh sons Al Farabi, Dulati, Korkyt ata of ancestors and historical epoch
1993	Citizens of the republic, Karakhstani. The independent [territorial] state of Kazakhstan	No significant mention	Political ethnic destabilization as an alarming symbol		Kazakh khans and their achievements for Kazakh statehood
1994	"I am a citizen of Kazakhstan" Kazakhstani people connected to the state.	National spiritual elite of the twentieth century (who were repressed) have focused on the political ideas of nation of that time	The need to live in harmony with other nationalities allowed Kazakhs not to disappear in history	There are no elder and no younger brothers. The importance of Russian culture	Alash Orda of the twentieth century. They developed national culture, they were first to establish Kazakh print capitalism
1995	Kazakh ancestors and the connection of the Kazakh land with the formula "We, people of Kazakhstan"	Kazakh khanate and its origins	Brother-killing wars in the CIS as a reminder of ethnonationalist threats	Internationalism and the friendship of peoples	What is the date of Kazakh state creation? An important point for ideological consideration
1996	Kazakh khanate, our co-citizens who have fought for independence (1986)	Research on events of December 1986 Kazakh independence has ancient traditions	Extremist politicians are a threat	Two hundred years of fighting with the aggressors (colonialism). Long-term resistance of nationalism	Many nations of Eurasia including Kazakhstan are descendants of the Turkic khanate Alash

1997	Kazakhs' special role as state-consolidating people. People of Kazakhstan represent a community of citizens of all ethnic groups	The history of Kazakhstan is a history of all peoples who live in this country	The role of Kazakhs as a state-constructing nationality	Comments on Lenin	Kazakh pre-Soviet intelligentsia plays a very important role in the discourse
1998	Kazakh statehood and territoriality are interrelated	Kazakh intellectuals who contributed to the development of statehood destroyed the previous regime	Our victory is that we killed ethnic nationalist tendencies	Astana and a new place of historical excavations. People who do not remember their history lose their direction	Ancestors' role
1999	Contemporary borders of the republic are closely connected to the ancestral land's borders	Zhanibek and Kerey formed the Kazakh khanate. Other notions of Orda	The threat of ethnic conflicts migrating to Kazakhstan through borders	The friendship of peoples	
2000-2003	Sovereign state and development	Hostile discourse on the previous regime without the notion of "Soviet"	Our path is without blood, tanks, and victims on our way toward development	Former society is destroyed, economic paralysis and legal nihilism	
2004-2008	Astana as a symbol of the new state	The importance of creating historical-cultural heritage analysis	Importance of the discourse of confessional and religious harmony	Freedom and rights to freedom	

completely contrasting ideas became a puzzle for some and a stabilizing effect for various ethnic communities in Kazakhstan.[25]

Compartmentalized ideology did not change much over the two decades of Nazarbayev's rule: the same symbols and narratives remained while the political language started shifting toward his "new" discourses framed around the ideas collaborations between Russia and Kazakhstan regarding the Eurasian Economic Union. However, the civic language of the president's discourse did not affect pro-Kazakh development and its influence in the ideological field: Kazakh culture still predominates in ideological texts and programs along with further strengthening of the role of the Kazakh language, for example, or prevailing "Kazakh" types of monuments that were erected in various regions of Kazakhstan, including Astana, before the celebration of twenty years of independence in 2011.[26]

This type of development is not unique to Kazakhstan; some parallels can be drawn with its close neighbor—Uzbekistan, where Karimov-led ideology developed the same traits of glorification of ancient ancestors, applied narratives

of "pseudo-historiography" and postcoloniality.[27] Interestingly enough, even
the stability–prosperity–president triangle was developed in Uzbekistan in
Karimov's earlier ideological texts.[28] So, further research on substitution for
the absence of ideology should be conducted to consider other Central Asian
political discourses more broadly.

Another vital question posed by the development of substitution for the
absence of ideology in Kazakhstan involves possible ideological developments
in the late and post-Nazarbayev eras. What kind of legacy would remain? Its
development has already presented some crucial challenges to Nazarbayev's
successors. First, decolonization was not complete, which created anxiety in
the growing "Kazakh world" with a "new generation that is hostile to the un-
revealed imperial and colonial past."[29] Second, substitution ideology left other
"hollow spaces," such as growing social and economic inequality in the region
and in larger cities of the country where various groups of indigenous population
such as *oralmans* and members of other ethnic groups have been marginalized.
The ideology of the current regime did not address their problems. Moreover,
it *substituted* pictures of "economic stability and prosperity" for these problems.
But precisely because vast segments of the population do not experience such
developments themselves, this leads to anxiety and unrest. Among the tragic
examples of such problems were the labor disputes and protests in the western
oil-producing town of Zhanaozen, which resulted in seventeen officially reported
casualties in December 2011, during the celebration of the twentieth anniversary
of independence. These challenges, if not resolved by Nazarbayev's regime, will
pose serious problems for the legitimation and rule of his successors.

CASE STUDY ON THE ARTIFICIAL OPPOSITION OF THE HARMONY PARTY IN LATVIA

The Harmony party's victory in the 2011 parliamentary elections was seen in
Latvia as one of the biggest political surprises of the year. By the 2014 elections
the same party was already framed as a party "backing Russian policies" due to
its controversial position on the Ukrainian revolution—many leaders of the party
negatively perceived EuroMaidan and the ousting of President Viktor Yanukov-
ich. Instead they advocated for holding open elections rather than ousting the
elected president. Harmony lost around four seats in the 2014 elections but has
remained the winning party twice in a row since the 2011 parliamentary elections.
After the charismatic domination of the Latvijas Cels (Latvian Way) throughout

the mid-1990s, Harmony became the first successful centrist party in Latvia. It is also the first party to succeed in securing votes from both the Latvian- and Russian-speaking electorates. The party emerged in 2005 when a conglomerate of Tautas Sarkanas Partija formed of the former Latvian Front members, New Centre party, Daugavpils City Party, the Socialist Party of Latvia (chaired by the former communist Alfreds Rubiks), and the Social-Democratic Party of Latvia, and created Harmony Alliance to fill in the centrist gap in the Latvian political spectrum. Since then, the Harmony party has positioned itself as social-democratic, and it advocates for social justice and economic revival through democratic reforms.[30]

Harmony's electoral support increased when it secured seventeen places in the Saeima in 2006, twenty-nine seats in 2010, thirty-one seats in 2011, and twenty-four seats in the most recent 2014 elections (see tables 27–30 in the Appendix). In this section I discuss the rise and fall of the Harmony party in the Latvian Parliament in relation to the "rules of the game" of the Latvian ideocratic nationalizing regime.

Parliamentary elections to the tenth Saeima took place in October 2010. The results included 33 deputy seats won by Unity, 29 seats by Harmony, 22 by the Union of Greens and Farmers, 8 by the Association of Parties "For Good Latvia," and 8 by another Latvian far-right party TB/LNNK.[31] In 2009 Harmony Center secured 43 deputy seats out of 118 in local municipality elections; in the elections for Riga municipality Harmony won 26 out of 60 deputy seats, which gave the party leader Nils Ušakovs his first mandate as mayor of the city of Riga. He became the first ethnic Russian in post-Soviet Latvian history to occupy such a high position. Moreover, according to existing polling in 2011 and 2015, Ušakovs was the most popular mayor of Riga in post-Soviet history, securing 73 percent of votes among the electorate in 2011 and 79.7 percent in January 2015.[32] The popularity of Ušakovs is indisputable; in a separate SKDS survey of possible presidential candidates, he scored 15 percent, which is only 2.5 percent less than the leader of the polls, the mayor of Ventspils, Aivars Lembergs, and 5 percent more than the former Latvian president Vaira Vīķe-Freiberga.[33]

Harmony's electoral success was partially explained by the fact that in 2010 "the voters were already tired of the same nationalistic texts provided by all the leading Latvian parties, [so] Harmony, and Ušakovs looked fresh and had a different agenda."[34] Moreover, in the absence of alternative views on Europeanization and the national question, Harmony represented the strongest voice against austerity, the populist agenda on social justice, and the state's role as the main provider to all its residents. The party's position on interethnic harmony is straightforward but neither evidently pro-Russian nor pro-Latvian. The party program stresses the importance of politically controlled multiculturalism:

> Harmony sees mutual trust among people who belong to different groups as the prerequisite to successful social integration. For the achievement of this goal Harmony engages with the policy of harmonizing [relations]. The goal of this policy is to overcome xenophobia, segregation, and dismissal of interests and needs of all residents of Latvia who belong to different groups....
>
> Harmony sees the strengthening of multicultural education in schools as the key prerequisite for social integration. Multicultural education creates a natural and positive sphere for the development of such relations. It is important to encourage communication among young people who belong to different ethnic groups.[35]

Harmony's victory created a unique situation: the first successful centrist party in post-Soviet Latvia was left with no seat in the government. The party was able to secure a significant percentage of votes both among the ethnic Latvian and Russian-speaking electorate, yet it was marginalized in the Saeima by the pro-Latvian coalition of parties that gained fewer seats but were able to unite against Harmony leaving it in an "artificial opposition." Further developments in political life in Latvia, and more precisely the premature dissolution of the tenth Saeima in July 2011 after less than a year from the previous elections, led to dramatic changes in Latvian politics and influenced the role of Harmony as a new and strong competitor in the elite field.

In May 2011 Valdis Zatlers, the outgoing Latvian president, initiated a referendum on the dissolution of the parliament due to continuing corruption scandals in the highest political echelons. In the referendum on July 23, 2011, a majority of eligible Latvian voters (94.3 percent) supported the dissolution of the parliament,[36] which led to new elections to the eleventh Saeima held in September 2011. In these elections Harmony secured the majority of the votes—28.3 percent and majority of 31 seats in the Saeima, followed by the new party of the former president Zatler's Reform Party (22 seats), Unity, which lost 12.3 percent of the votes or 13 seats in the Saeima (the party got 20 seats in the end), the National Alliance TB/LNNK and "Visu Latvija" got 14 seats and the Union of Greens and Farmers lost 9 seats, securing only 13 deputy seats.

The 2011 elections demonstrated not only a major increase in support for Harmony but also declining support for the leading pro-Latvian parties, such as Unity, and left the major oligarchic groups (especially Ainārs Šlesers) outside the

Saeima. However, Harmony's strong support in both sociolingual communities of the divided electorate did not contribute to its victories in the parliament. They were blocked from forming a government and remained in the opposition. The leading party Unity formed a coalition with the Reform Party (4 ministers), and National Alliance TB/LNNK and "Visu Latvija" (2 ministers), securing 7 ministerial seats for themselves and allowing Prime Minister Valdis Dombrovskis (Unity) to retain his seat.

The political manipulations behind closed doors raised alarm among independent observers in Latvia and contributed to growing distrust even in the Latvian electorate toward the leading Unity party, seen as a key player in this political gaming. "If you look at the evolution of Unity policies over 2011–2014 you can see that Prime Minister Dombrovskis (from the Unity Party) is not as popular as he was when he came to power in 2010," in the opinion of one nationalist leader.[37]

The marginalization of Harmony and other less successful pro-Russian parties and organizations such as ZaRYA (Za Rodnoi Iazik), demonstrate elite competition. But it also shows the attempts of the nationalizing regime in Latvia to marginalize specific parties based on their programs. These are programs that support minorities and might affect ethnic Latvian interests. In other words, competing pro-Latvian parties are willing to go so far as to limit their own opportunities in the political field in parliament in order to circumscribe pro-Russian parties from wider participation in political decision making, for example, they are willing to form a coalition with the far-right National Alliance.

The most important challenge that this "artificial opposition" brought into the structure of Harmony's agenda is that the party had to step away from its centrist position and approve further support for the Latvianized status quo. In other words, the Latvianized nationalizing regime circumscribed the winning party's power in forming a governmental coalition three times in a row (from the 2010 to 2014 parliamentary elections) but it also framed its approach to the national question. To be accepted in the power circle, Harmony needed to shift its ideological program toward a more Latvianized and thus dominant discourse. In the 2014 electoral program, Harmony states, for example, that "the integration policy will be considered successful only in the situation when Latvians are not plagued by doubts over the future development of Latvian culture and when Latvian language is considered as the only state language; and only in a situation when members of all national minorities are confident in the Latvian government's provision for the survival of their [minority] languages and

cultures. These guarantees would contribute to the development of mutual respect among the people living in Latvia and would help to form [a new] national
identity in Latvia."[38] This quote from the new program does not demonstrate any
clear provision or Harmony's plan for the minority language in schools—the
main agenda of pro-Russian parties that do not see Harmony's support for the
Russian-speaking population and their rights. Finally, the party has no clear
demands regarding the status of noncitizens, although its leader Nils Ušakovs
called for the wider inclusion of noncitizens in Latvia's political life. In its policy
on noncitizens, the party "suggests" the same approaches as those called for by
the OSCE HCNM (High Commissioner on National Minorities) since the inception of the 1994 Citizenship Law: provision of automatic citizenship to a child
if both parents are stateless; provision of automatic citizenship for all students
who successfully graduate from high schools and other state educational institutions; and facilitated naturalization for elderly and disabled people.

Russian Language Referendum

The 2012 referendum on the status of Russian language in Latvia was another
good example of how the nationalizing regime has structured and saturated the
nationalistic approach in Latvian politics. The issue of Russian language became
a dividing line in the electoral campaigns, which were structured on support for
one or two state languages. This question also continued to divide the Latvian
political field and competition in the post-2011 parliamentary elections.

The referendum on amendments to the constitution that proposed Russian
language as the second official language in Latvia was held in February 2012.
This was a logical extension after a group of pro-Russian organizations and small
parties (including politicians such as Linderman, Osipov, Gaponenko, and Svat-
kov) initiated a collection of signatures to support such an amendment. This was
done in opposition to the National Association's (TB/LNNK and "Visu Latvija")
collection of signatures to initiate a referendum on changing the educational
system and implementing exclusive Latvian language use in all minority schools.
The referendum on "Amendments to the Constitution of the Republic of Latvia"
posed only one question: "Do you support the adoption of the Draft Law 'Amendments to the Constitution of the Republic of Latvia' that gives the Russian language status as the second official language?" The possible answers included
only "For" or "Against." According to the Central Electoral Commission, 273,347
(24.88 percent) of people cast their votes in favor of adopting the amendments

whereas 821,722 (74.80 percent) voted against. The total vote constituted about a 1.5 million eligible voters—citizens of Latvia excluding noncitizens.[39]

The referendum proved to be one of the toughest challenges for Latvian nation-building. First, it revealed that the nationalities question was still not resolved in Latvia, and thus none of the three attempts to integrate policies and numerous laws in the field of citizenship and language (largely influenced by the European Union) helped improve the situation. It also revealed that the Latvian "Other," the Russian-speaking population, was not ready to integrate fully according to the roadmap suggested by the pro-Latvian politicians who formed a major coalition in the parliament over the years. It also demonstrated the Russian-speaking population's desire to protect its rights and attract political attention to their interests and issues, especially in such an important symbolic domain as language. Second, it created a "political panic" in the context of the dominant Latvian elite field:

> In the past ten years Latvia experienced two very serious and mass demonstrations. First there were demonstrations against school reform [when at least 60 percent of classes in Russian and minority schools were converted to Latvian language use in 2004], and second, the referendum on Russian language. These [events] demonstrated that the Latvian part of the political elite was not ready for this [political competition from nonethnic-Latvian parties]. I mean at the beginning they [Latvian elite] ignored the possibility that referendum could happen [according to the Latvian Constitution there is a need to secure written support of at least 10 percent of the population for a referendum], they didn't think that [the activists for the referendum] would collect the needed amount of signatures [to support the initiative]. Then there was a real scare—what to do? They [Latvian elite] tried to find a "firefighter" [*pozharnika pytalis' naiti*] by presenting the case to the the Constitutional Court. But the Constitutional Court (to its credit) did not support their case. And what we can see now are the results of the scare that this referendum caused—that the requirements for initiation of the referendum were significantly increased, which in the future may affect that same Latvian elite. This is simply leading to restrictions on our democracy.[40]

The feeling of the fright described by Juris Rosenvalds in his interview with me was also expressed in different terms by my other respondents—members of the Unity party and nationalists from TB/LNNK in our subsequent interviews. There were variations in the opinions expressed by different politicians of both parties. Although Unity's politicians were quite cautious about their comments,

their statements about the referendum and disapproval of the amendments on
the state language were parallel to those of the nationalists from the National
Alliance of the TB/LNNK, who openly supported the decision to increase requirements (raising the number of signatures needed) for the initiation of future
referendums.

Third, the referendum exacerbated the existing ethnic divisions in the political
parties' identities in Latvia. Adding to the growing nationalist sentiments of Unity
and the stable demands of TB/LNNK, the pro-Latvian positions of the Union of
Greens and Farmers and the Reform Party, the Harmony party was left in a very
difficult position. On the one hand, it supported the amendments that positioned
it as a "pro-Russian party" and, on the other hand, this could threaten its support
among the Latvian-speaking population. This proved that despite a growing and
positive support of centrist ideas among the population, the ethnic divisions in the
political agenda continued to heavily influence political life in Latvia.

In his analysis of Baltic elites, Anton Steen develops a thesis that Baltic politics
are best understood through the notion of democratic elitism. It is a system
under which "elite orientations are independent of the mass public" and "elites
shape the views of masses. . . . If democratic consolidation is a process where
liberal elites are established, and where the mass public slowly complies with
elites' liberal orientations—as democratic elitists argue—one would expect a
considerable differences of views between elites and the mass public in the early
stages, and a gradual convergence of views over time."[41] In his rather tentative
conclusion, he writes that, after all, democratic elitism provides "a better explanation of *degree of congruence* and the persistent elite-mass gap in confidence in
new core institutions related to regime change, than liberal democratic theory."[42] However, he acknowledges the greater role and influence of new elites on
institutions and the whole political system, its stability, and economic reforms
after the regime change.[43] As this chapter has demonstrated, the new elites do
provide stability of the nationalizing regime insofar as their agenda is in line
with the previously established political consensus on Latvian nation-building.
The ethnic opposition of any non-Latvian segment of the political spectrum
continues to threaten the stability and the whole ideological essence of the Latvianized nationalizing regime and is thus framed as the greatest political threat
and enemy. Steen's argument about Latvian democratic elitism in particular is
correct but incomplete.

Missing in this discussion is the important power of the Latvianized political field to frame the competition within the limits of the nationalized (pro-Latvian) discourses that legitimize the expulsion of democratically elected parties such as Harmony that represent a position that deviates from the nationalizing regime and the dominant discourses it produces. In other words, both the elitist coalition and its ability to continue to safeguard and control the primacy of the dominant national discourse pushes out non-Latvian parties and their agenda from the wider political discussions, despite these parties' continuous electoral victories in open and democratic elections. How is this type of competition different from the Kazakh case? In Kazakhstan the dominant multiple discursive systems (compartmentalized ideology) not only legitimize the regime's power and sustainability in various multiethnic communities and sociolingual groups but also diminish the competition from other political parties and actors. The Nazarbayev regime simply occupies all the available political discourses on nation-building and development, disallowing alternative views in each political field as well as framing the political competition as threatening to the *only* bright path of development promised by President Nazarbayev himself.

Dominant discourses and their appropriation and manipulation in political competition play a significant role in elites' contestations in nationalizing regimes. The alternative parties and views are unable to secure better positions within this system without changing the status quo in Kazakhstan or altering the elite consensus in Latvia. Of course, important differences between the two regimes exist: elites' bonds in the nationalizing regime are either connected to their loyalty to the dominant discourse (Latvia) or to their loyalty to the dominant political leader in power that guarantees elite stability (Kazakhstan). I want to conclude by detailing these different approaches in the structure of the nationalizing regimes.

First of all, the power of the Nazarbayev regime is singular and personalized, the dominant discourses are inevitably connected to the charismatic figure of the president, a typical development in authoritarian regimes, as discussed in chapter 1.[44] The president dominates the discourse and the elites' competition, and the regime remains unstable in the long-term perspective because it cannot provide guarantees for the future smooth transition to the post-Nazarbayev era. A change of this personalized regime will most probably lead to the intensification of the Kazakh national-patriot discourse in the light of new elites' competition for legitimacy via growing Kazakh nationalism and populism. In Latvia, the regime is more stable because elite pluralism is only limited to the competition within the ethnic democracy, for example, by excluding a pro-Russian agenda or participation of Russian-speaking politicians in the government formation. This also creates possible instability in the long run. But as this chapter has demonstrated, any viable non-Latvian opposition has to conform to the rules of the dominant discourse in order to accede to power via the government formation. So far Harmony has had only hypothetical chances to form an alternative ruling coalition in government, but ceded this opportunity to Latvianized party solidarity. The ruling coalition remains the domain of the nationalizing regime.

Second, the nationalizing regime in Latvia is a more stable, successful ideological field than it is in Kazakhstan. The persistence of the Latvianized agenda, amendments to the preamble of the Constitution in June 2014 being the most recent example, and the elites' personal beliefs in the system allow the nationalizing regime to develop further. The elites in Kazakhstan are divided on the question of the nationalizing regime. The majority of the power elite remain cosmopolitan but the new elites who will possibly come to power in the future, such as the ideological team of the leading Nur Otan party, are more patriotic and Kazakh-centered. This trend will guide the development of the nationalizing regime in Kazakhstan in the near future. The growing popularity of the national-patriotic field and the growing demographic position of ethnic Kazakhs will influence the agenda as well.

The level of elite competition in the nationalizing regime rises in Kazakhstan when the competing elite network or group foresees these opportunities and tries to increase its chances of attaining a more powerful position. In either case the nationalizing regime will continue framing the political competition. This happens in part because alternative views, such as political nations or pluralistic approaches to national identity outside the regime's dominant field, do not reach a level capable of challenging these hegemonies. As will be discussed in chapters 4 and 5, the persistent dominance of both nationalizing regimes in Latvia and Kazakhstan have virtually eliminated the possibility of viable non-Latvian and non-Kazakh projects of national identity. Kazakhstani Russian identity or Russophone Latvian identity cannot represent strong alternatives to the existing nationalizing frameworks without being considered and framed (by the political elites) as threatening, secessionist, and potentially as dangerous as the Novorossiya project in Eastern Ukraine.

4

"LOST IN TRANSLATION"

RUSSIAN NATIONALISM, MINORITY RIGHTS, AND SELFHOOD OUTSIDE RUSSIA

Anna, a middle-aged ethnic Russian, was born in Soviet Alma-Ata and moved to Jurmala, a sea resort town outside Riga, in her early twenties. She obtained her medical degree in Moscow and spent most of her adult life in Latvia. She worked as a beautician in one of Jurmala's sanatoriums to which many Soviet citizens used to come for recreational purposes, and where, in her own words, "there was no need to learn Latvian" because everyone spoke Russian. Anna spent most of her life in this small seaside town before moving to Riga in the mid-1990s. As a noncitizen and the ex-wife of a former Soviet soldier (*militia*), she could not legally buy her apartment in Kengaraks before she married another ethnic Russian who was able to naturalize in the early 2000s. I sit in Anna's two-bedroom apartment and she is reluctant to talk about her multiple failures in trying to learn Latvian:

> I failed the language test, you see, three times in a row. Sometimes I feel like nothing, I mean nothing can help me pass it. I did try, you know, I took classes, I bought books to learn Latvian [special language manuals were distributed to noncitizens for free in 1997–2002 and a number of language manuals were sold on the market by the time I came to Latvia in 2012, 2013, and 2014]. I attended special language classes to prepare for the language test because for me Latvian citizenship status

means more than just an opportunity to be a citizen of the EU or to be able to vote in the elections. I don't believe my vote can change much but I just don't want to be a noncitizen, it feels degrading and humiliating because I have lived in this country for so long that it feels as if Latvia is the only home I have.

I ask Anna about her family and their citizenship status insofar as many families are divided along citizenship lines: some have the red Latvian passport of a citizen and others have Russian passports but still live in Latvia. Anna's elderly parents still live in Almaty in Kazakhstan, she says, and explains that she tries to visit them every year. Anna continues, and says that even though old places in Kazakhstan remind her of the past, too much has changed in Almaty since the collapse of the Soviet Union. So, while she discusses the micro district and city *raion* where her parents still live, she slips into memories of her Soviet youth before she moved to Moscow. The central park in Almaty still looks somewhat the same, she says, but old Soviet restaurants have faded away. Every time she returns, she sees they have been replaced, and "every new place is always named in Kazakh," she says. Even small city districts are renamed, and so are major streets, "though people still remember the old, Soviet street names, so it is hard to get lost in my Alma-Ata," she smiles calling it by the old name. Even though the memories and pride of being a *korennaia almatinka*, somewhat elevated status of original urban resident and not a migrant from another city or village, make Anna happy, she concludes that she no longer feels that it is her homeland. After the collapse of the Soviet Union, she did not claim a Kazakh passport and instead remained a noncitizen in Latvia secretly hoping that the citizenship law would be changed to allow her to gain Latvian citizenship automatically.

Anna's ex-husband had to be reallocated to Russia under a special agreement for Soviet militia mobility outside the three Baltic states, and she says he found his way in the new homeland. Anna's older daughter is married and lives in Poland as a Polish citizen, although she was able to naturalize in Latvia after 1998.

She [Anna's daughter] could speak Latvian because she learned it in school, but she did not want to naturalize before 1998 when the age-based quota system was in place. In many ways we were hoping that there would be changes and [that] they [political elites] would allow all noncitizens to gain citizenship without naturalization. There was still a hope in the 1990s, maybe up until the mid-2000s when many people who speak Latvian already went through this process. I also secretly hoped they [political elites and the Latvian regime] would lift the language conditions and allow those older residents to gain citizenship automatically, but I am still a noncitizen as you can see [Anna moved as if embracing an imaginary person in a gesture of desperation]. I can travel to the Schengen zone states and I visit my daughter now and then, I could even invest in this apartment with the help of my husband who is a Latvian citizen, but my status is unchanged, I am a *nepilsoni*, I have a blue Latvian passport [special noncitizen passport] and I also have a Russian passport. I had to get the Russian passport so I'd feel better as a *proper citizen* of at least some state, not having *a normal passport* made me feel depressed.[1]

Hundreds of thousands of people in Latvia share sentiments similar to Anna's feelings of deprivation and humiliation because of being unable to gain Latvian citizenship or acquire Latvian language. Although there are many reasons for not naturalizing, including open protest against the regime's nationalizing policies, many members of the so-called Russian-speaking communities are simply unable to pass the language and history tests. Their monolingualism and status as Russian-speakers leave them in a precarious position: they are unable to secure better jobs and some even escape to the peripheries of the major Latvian cities to eliminate the possibility of failing the language checks done by the Language Inspectorate. One of my respondents of Ukrainian descent mentioned that her multiple failures to learn Latvian in the early 1990s left her in a constantly challenging position and even in fear of losing her job:

I am scared of [the] Language Inspectorate. If they find out my Latvian language level is not enough even for the job I have here [place anonymized], and for my job [as a service provider], they will fine me. What is worse I could even lose my job and then who knows how long until I find another job? We moved to Latvia from Ukraine when I was a teenager, in the 1980s. Back then there was no need to learn and speak Latvian, everyone in Riga spoke Russian, even Latvians! [The] majority of people still speak Russian in Riga; I get by just fine. My younger sister was studying Latvian in school and she was the first member of my family to get proper Latvian citizenship in the early 2000s. She speaks Latvian fluently and I think she speaks more Latvian now than Russian, her native language! At least she has a nice job at the bank, and she is well off. I told both of my children to study well in Latvian. They both went to a Russian, "minority" school but after ninth grade both of them took 60 percent of their classes in Latvian, even chemistry! Sometimes my son asks for my advice with homework, but I cannot help him because it is in Latvian. As soon as he graduates from school, he will be able to study in Latvian

> University, with 100 percent of classes just in Latvian. His sister, my older daughter
> studied at Latvian [State] University and now she moved to Germany and lives
> there. I can visit her; she is also better off outside Latvia.[2]

Latvian language as one of the prime discourses of the loyalty non-Latvians
had to demonstrate to the new nation became a form of economic capital but
also transformed into a battlefield for the cultural rights of minorities and their
representatives. The Minorities School Reform of 2004 and the Referendum
on Russian Language in 2012 were the most visible and significant examples
of these struggles. Ethnic differences and language became the key discursive
frameworks of both nationalizing regimes, which claimed cultural hegemony
over the establishment of dominant discourses and rules of the game (as we
have seen in previous chapters). After independence, Russian-speaking groups
that found themselves in the position of "minorities" naturally followed these
rules of the game, being unable to shift or change the agenda for their benefit.
Because language and ethnicity of the dominant group of each nationalizing
regime (to varying degrees among Latvians and Kazakhs) became sacred,
Russian-speaking groups' advocacy for the inclusion of their linguistic rights and
ethnic determination was seen as a threat to the dominant order and discourse.
This is why any "Russian" parties in both Latvia and Kazakhstan are portrayed
by the respective nationalizing regimes as a threat to sovereignty and viability
of the nation even though the nation itself may not be defined as clearly Kazakhified in Kazakhstan as it is ethnicized in Latvia.

THE RUSSIAN-SPEAKING "OTHER" AFTER INDEPENDENCE

By 1989, based on numbers and categories, ethnic Russians composed almost
40 percent of Kazakhstan's population and 34 percent of the Latvian population
(see figure 4 for a comparison). Twenty years after independence, the titular
population (Kazakhs and Latvians) of the respective countries had established
a firm majority, 63.1 percent in Kazakhstan in 2009 and 62.1 percent in Latvia
in 2011, leaving Russians (specifically defined by ethnicity) as still a substantial
minority—23.7 percent and 26.9 percent, respectively (see figure 4, second part).
These numbers, categories, and labels played an important role in the way the
"state" saw its own citizens and noncitizens. There was an out-migration of
different ethnic groups to Russia, Germany, Israel, and other countries all over
the post-Soviet space, but specifically in Central Asia where many more people

out-migrated due to the heightened economic crisis. However, these statistical data also reflected the ways in which respective post-Soviet states categorized and divided their own populations into titular ethnic groups of Latvians and Kazakhs and other groups of minorities—either into the elusive conglomerate of all Slavs and those ethnic groups for whom Russian was a dominant language in Latvia or into the formula of "140 different ethnic minorities." Both tactics, used in Latvia and Kazakhstan, respectively, diluted the agency of Russian parties or communities to wield their will in political bodies such as parliaments and local administration bodies. The codification of ethnicity disempowered those who were not considered the dominant ethnic group, even in pure statistics calculated and provided by the state agencies.

Different approaches to the most powerful numerical minority have determined the logic by which both nationalizing regimes developed. Kazakhstan guaranteed and applied universal citizenship to all its permanent residents before December 16, 1991, when it became independent. Until 1995 certain republics even had a dual-citizenship policy that allowed many ethnic Russians to obtain both Russian and the respective country's passports. In Kazakhstan, many permanent residents obtained Russian passports for various personal reasons. Some did so to obtain better pensions, others—for property rights, especially in transborder regions, and still others—as an "insurance policy in case things get worse in Kazakhstan."[3]

The worsening economic conditions led to the peak of Russian out-migration from 1994 to 1999, when the share of the Russian population dropped by almost 6 percent. The Latvian Republic chose to rely on the legal historical continuity of its interwar republic and reapplied the constitution, legal body, and parliamentary structure of the interwar republic. For approximately 42.9 percent of its Russian-speaking non-Latvian population it meant a special noncitizen status. Noncitizenship (negrazhdane in Russian) meant that permanent residents of Latvia who were not ethnic Latvians and whose parents or ancestors did not possess citizenship before 1941 when the Soviets first incorporated Latvia were not citizens but permanent residents with no political rights. For many external observers, including the European Union (EU), this move was presented as a "sovereign" and legal decision for dealing with "domestic" politics. Many Russian activists in Latvia still view this as an infringement on their rights.

Latvia's largest cultural and linguistic Other—"neo-migrants who [by the logic of ruling Latvian elites] were sent to post-war Latvia to 'Russify it,'" or "in the favorite words of Latvian far-right politicians, Moscow's *fifth column*,"[4]

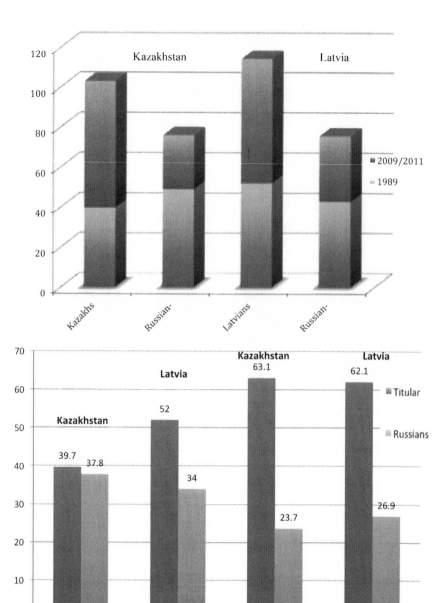

Figure 4a and b. Comparison of titular groups ratio to Russian-speakers group in Kazakhstan and Latvia, based on population censuses in 1989 (all-Soviet census), 2009 (Kazakhstan), and 2011 (first post-Soviet census in Latvia).

created a great obstacle for the nationalizing regime. The way Latvian elites were able to pack the discourse on the legal continuity of the interwar republic and the trauma of the Soviet occupation for the EU and Organization for Security and Co-operation in Europe (OSCE) officials is truly fascinating. Since the first day of the discussions on the new citizenship law in Latvia in 1994, the European observers were constrained by this framework of the legal jus sanguinis. Confidential reports of the Council of Europe experts on the Latvian citizenship law started with the acknowledgment of the historic trauma experienced by the Latvian nation during the Soviet occupation and forced migration. This migration was presented as planned and controlled "by Moscow" of Russian-speaking population Latvian elites had to deal with after independence.[5] The fact that many European officials did not dispute the grounds of quota-based naturalization but contested the *ways* in which this system would be put into place was a complete disappointment to the Russian-speaking, noncitizen population, many of whom regarded it as their political defeat.

In Kazakhstan, the elites masked the sociopolitical tensions of Russians and Kazakhs. According to President Nazarbayev, both groups of "narrow-minded nationalists" threatened to disrupt the balance of interethnic stability—a crucial condition for successful attraction of international investments.[6] By 1993 Kazakhstan had accepted its first constitution, which stated: "We, the people of Kazakhstan, ... based on the inviolability of Kazakh statehood, acknowledging the priority of human rights, ready to create a democratic society and a state based on the rule of law, in the desire to provide civic peace and interethnic harmony and guided by the desire to create good living conditions for ourselves and our offspring, accept this Constitution and declare the following bases of constitutional building: ... the Republic of Kazakhstan is a form of statehood of the self-determined Kazakh nation [and] provides equal rights for all its citizens."[7] The Constitution of January 28, 1993 was changed completely during the August referendum of 1995. The opening preamble was changed to just "Peoples of Kazakhstan," where there was no clear notion of any specific ethnonational entity, for example, the Kazakh nation, but most important, the second constitution virtually fully empowered the president, bypassing the system of checks and balances in all branches of power apart from the executive branch. Now the president had the power to appoint the government, dismiss the parliament, veto any law, create presidential decrees that could have the same legal power as laws in the absence of a legitimate parliament, and appoint regional governors himself, solely by his sovereign power. His power over decision making also determines interethnic relations. His power sustains the dominant paradigm of harmony and stability in these relations.

Did the Kazakh nationalizing regime decide to apply affirmative action policies toward its largest ethnolingual minority for its own legitimacy in the major electoral group and in order to sustain peaceful ethnopolitical conditions within and outside the country given its famous 6,846 kilometer border with Russia? The answer is yes for both. The dual application of state and official languages (Kazakh and Russian, respectively) with no open restrictions on minority, in this case Russian-speaking schools, as in Latvia, the Kazakh regime nevertheless continued supporting its Kazakh-speaking population by rewriting the history, renaming topography, and replacing monuments of Lenin with those of national Kazakh heroes.[8] In parallel to minority cultural empowerment, these are "ethnic Kazakhs" who continue "monopolizing the corridors of power and bearing the name of the new republic," and "justify this through a program of Kazakh cultural revival."[9] Although many Russian elites remained active in the Kazakh political field (e.g., the former prime minister Sergey Tereshenko, in office from October 1991 to October 1994) and many non-Kazakh elites control financial groups (e.g., clans such as the Mashkevitch Eurasian Economic Group and the Shkolnik oil and gas sector), many prominent Russian-positioned activists such as Evgeny Zhovtis and Sergei Duvanov also remain popular and maintain their pressure groups especially during the turbulent early post-Nazarbayev era of early and mid-2019. These voices are specifically heard during court hearings of those who were arrested while protesting. But their proportional representation, even within the growing forms of civic engagement, is still not as significant as that of the ethnic Kazakhs in power—the nationalizing regime—especially proportions of ethnic and Kazakh-speaking Kazakhs in the state structures of the regional administration.

In 1994, however, Kazakhstan and not Latvia saw a significant decline in numbers of the Russian-speaking population, consisting mainly ethnic Russians, Germans, Jews, and Poles returning to their respective ethnic homelands.[10] From 1989 to 1999 Kazakhstan lost more than 1.5 million of its ethnic Russian population and more than half of its ethnic German population, which accounted for almost 600.000 people.[11] In contrast, Latvia lost only 7.1 percent of its ethnic Russian population from 1989 to 2011 (see figure 4 for a comparative perspective).

The share of ethnic Kazakhs in the traditional southern regions, such as Kyzyl-Orda in southern Kazakhstan, has grown, and the linguistic and socioethnic divide has ruralized for Kazakhs and urbanized for Russians and

Russian-speakers of non-Russian or non-Slavic descent. Russian language continues to dominate the social and economic lives of most of Kazakhstan's citizens and constitutes an estimated 95 percent of proficiency among the population, in comparison to 63.1 percent of speakers of Kazakh, the official state language.[12]

The sociolinguistic landscape of both Kazakhstan and Latvia is represented by the regional concentration of specific ethnic groups. The ethnic Kazakh majority traditionally resides in southern and western Kazakhstan whereas, historically, the ethnic Russian population has predominantly occupied the northern and eastern parts of Kazakhstan as well as the industrial centers, for example, in Karaganda but not in western Kazakhstan, which remains predominantly Kazakhophone.

Among Latvia's noncitizen and thus predominantly Russian-speaking population, the lack of Latvian language proficiency and overall apathy toward citizenship are perceived as major reasons that the remaining 14–15 percent of noncitizens are concentrated in cities. For example, this accounts for 22 percent in Riga and 11 percent in the neighboring Pieriga region, and in the eastern regions, in Latgale—10.9 percent, and in Kurzeme in the west—10.4 percent (see table 7).

As table 7 demonstrates, in the most recent data, in 2011 Latvia had about 14 percent noncitizens, or 290,660 people, the majority of whom are residents of the city of Riga—50 percent, and the Riga region—14 percent. The only other post-Soviet country that employed a citizenship policy based on the principle of jus sanguinis was Estonia where rates of noncitizens were around 32 percent in 1992, 12 percent in 2003, and 6.5 percent in 2014.[13] In 1993 Latvia had 730,000 registered noncitizens and an estimated number of 165,000 nonregistered noncitizens, or approximately 30 percent of the total population, excluding around 40,000 vulnerable people—Soviet military personnel who had to leave the country by 1995.[14]

A majority of applicants for naturalization in Latvia are Russian-speaking groups followed by Poles (5,325 applications from 1996 to 2010) and Estonians and Lithuanians (4,759 applications, respectively). With a failure rate of about 15 percent on the Latvian language test, Latvian proficiency is among the major obstacles for noncitizens.[15]

The most active group applying for naturalization in Latvia consists of people ages eighteen to thirty, who account for more than 30 percent of applications. This trend is confirmed by the growing number of school enrollments with Latvian language as the medium of instruction, even before the 2004 education

Table 7. Citizenship composition in regions of Latvia based on the 2011 census

	Latvia	Riga region	Pieriga region	Vidzeme region	Kurzeme region	Zemgale region	Latgale region
Total population	2,067,887	657,424	369,638	211,233	270,168	255,200	304,224
	100%	100%	100%	100%	100%	100%	100 %
Citizens of Latvia	1,732,880	488,760	323,243	199,469	234,916	222,371	264,121
	83.7%	74%	87%	94.4%	86.9%	87 %	86.8 %
Noncitizens of Latvia	290,660	146,964	41,032	10,801	28,146	30,338	33,379
	14%	22%	11%	0.5%	10.4%	11%	10.9 %
Citizens of Russian Federation	31,394	15,032	3,359	497	5,781	1,630	5,095
	0.15%	0.22%	0.09%	0.02%	0.2%	0.06 %	0.16 %
Citizens of Ukraine	2,468	1,301	381	70	297	158	261
	0.11%	0.019%	0.01%	0.003%	0.001%	0.006%	0.085 %
Stateless	188	70	40	13	27	10	28
	0.009%	0.001%	0.001%	0.0006%	0.0009%	0.003%	0.009 %

Source: Latvijas Statistikas—Latvian Statistics.

reform that introduced a 60 percent ratio of Latvian language instruction in secondary schools (figure 5). Latvian school enrollments showed steady growth throughout the first decade of independence with a parallel decrease in Russian schools and classes taught in Russian in mixed-language schools (figure 6). Mixed-school enrollment also declined in the second part of the 2000s after the introduction of the education reform (see figure 7), although the number of classes taught in Russian in mixed schools have increased in recent years (see figure 7).

The 2004 reform introduced a 60/40 ratio of classes taught in Latvian in ninth through twelfth grades in minority schools, where most classes are now taught in Latvian after ninth grade. The Latvian nationalist party TB/LNNK's controversial demands to "nationalize" all schools in Latvia and achieve a ratio of at least 80/20 of Latvian/Russian instruction in minority schools sparked opposition activities among Russian-speakers. However, the new ratio was not adopted, and minority schools in Latvia continue providing classes taught in Russian language in primary schools, and 40 percent in ninth through twelfth grades in minority schools. The reform seemed to have little effect on the steadily growing Latvian school enrollments and somewhat decreasing enrollments in mixed and Russian schools (figures 7–8).

The overall sociolinguistic situation and transformation developed differently in post-Soviet Kazakhstan than in Latvia. With almost similar ratios of

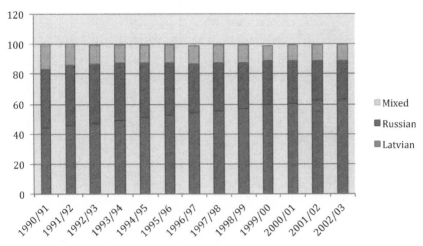

Figure 5. General full-time school enrollment by language of instruction in postindependent Latvia before the 2004 Education Reform. *Source:* Latvijas Statistikas—Latvian Statistics. Central Statistical Bureau of Latvia, Annual Reports on Education Data, csb.gov.lv.

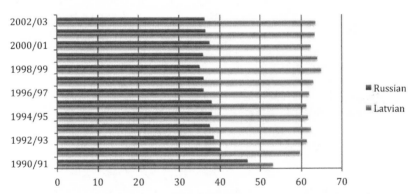

Figure 6. General full-time school enrollment by language of instruction in mixed-language schools in in postindependent Latvia before the 2004 Education Reform. *Source:* Latvijas Statistikas—Latvian Statistics. Central Statistical Bureau of Latvia, Annual Reports on Education Data, csb.gov.lv.

Russian-speaking minority groups, the two countries varied in the ways they accommodated these minorities in the political (citizenship), social, and cultural (education, identity inclusion, provision for minority language development) contexts. For a specific comparison of the Kazakh and Latvian regimes since independence, see table 8.

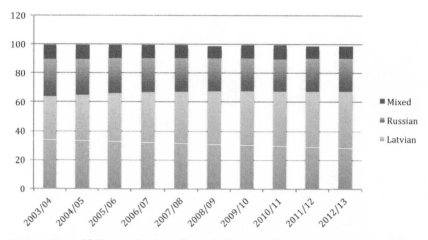

Figure 7. General full-time school enrollment by language of instruction in postindependent Latvia after the 2004 Education Reform. *Source*: Latvijas Statistikas—Latvian Statistics. Central Statistical Bureau of Latvia, Annual Reports on Education Data, csb.gov.lv.

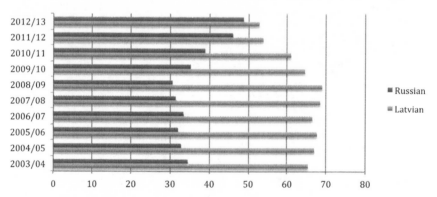

Figure 8. General full-time school enrollment by language of instruction in mixed-language schools in postindependent Latvia after the 2004 Education Reform. *Source*: Latvijas Statistikas—Latvian Statistics. Central Statistical Bureau of Latvia, Annual Reports on Education Data, csb.gov.lv.

However, there was another factor in understanding why and how the Russian minorities and groups "got lost in the translation" and the transition period in the nationalizing regimes framework. So far this framework of decision making and power seeking has been discussed from the domestic perspective and in view of internal elitist struggles, but it was also legitimated and sustained based on external factors, such as the approval of citizenship policies by specific

Table 8. Comparison of post-Soviet Latvian and Kazakhstani nationalizing regimes

	Latvia	Kazakhstan
Regime type	**Democratic**: Ethnic democracy:* interests of indigenous majority are put above the interests of the minority **Parliamentary republic**: Democratic parliamentary elections are held every four years. The Cabinet of Ministers is elected by the majority of votes in the Parliament (usually by coalition). The prime minister is the leader of the winning party. The president is appointed by parliamentary majority every six to seven years. The president has the power to dissolve the Parliament based on an all-country referendum (Parliament was dissolved most recently in 2011 due to corruption scandals). Electoral democracy	**Hybrid regime**: with democratic basis but nondemocratic rule **Presidential republic**: Democratic elections are held every five years for the Lower Chamber of the Parliament (Majilis) and every six years for the Senate of the Parliament. The president appoints seven of forty-seven senators; the Assembly of Peoples of Kazakhstan has a mandate for nine seats for its representatives in the Lower Majilis chamber of the Parliament. The president appoints the prime minister and the cabinet and has the power to dissolve the Parliament
Citizenship structure	Automatic citizenship was granted to descendants of interwar independent Latvia (before 1941) or to ethnic Latvians (including children of at least one Latvian parent permanently residing in Latvia). Type of citizenship: jus sanguinis. All other permanent residents were obliged to naturalize or leave the country. Latvia operated on quota-based naturalization (the quota was defined by the Parliament), which was abandoned in 1998. However, currently about 18 percent of Latvia's nonindigenous population remains in the status of noncitizens—permanent residents with no political rights and restricted economic rights	Universal citizenship was granted to all residents of the Republic of Kazakhstan and the Kazakh SSR who were residents at the time. A special quota for ethnic Kazakh returnees and diaspora abroad (*oralmans*) was introduced in 1997 but was suspended during program modification in 2012. A new program for Kazakh *oralmans* was to be introduced in 2014. Type of citizenship: jus soli.
Language policy	Latvian is the only official language of Latvia. Russian has no official or special status. Proficiency in Latvian is a guarantee of and prerequisite for public office or any representational position	Kazakh is the state language of the Republic of Kazakhstan, and Russian is the official language of interethnic communication. Proficiency in Kazakh is a prerequisite for public office jobs but much of the employment market is sustained by the monolingual role of Russian
Education policy toward minorities	Since the 2004 Education Reform, all secondary schools for minorities in Latvia (after ninth grade) have a 60 percent quota requiring Latvian as the language of instruction in classes (including Latvian for core classes like biology, chemistry, and physics)	The 2004 Education Reform provides for multilingual instruction in minority, private, and public schools. The 2012 reform in education required all schools to teach three languages—Kazakh, Russian, and English beginning in first grade

Note: *Steen, "Ethnic Relations."

watchdogs outside the state organs themselves. In the next section I discuss the historical-legal aspects of the role external actors played in legitimating the nationalizing regime in Latvia and accommodating some of the policies regarding minorities in Kazakhstan. In general, the mechanism aimed at protecting the "minority" from external actors, actually trapped the "minority" in its own limited category as an agentless group requiring symbolic representation in terms of language and cultural determination. This same categorization provided a very narrow perspective for dealing with decision making regarding their destiny or identity within the state structure or the limits of the nationalizing regime, where alternative voices could play out as a balancing force for both Latvia and Kazakhstan.

HOW RUSSIANS AND RUSSIAN-SPEAKING GROUPS BECAME A "MINORITY"

One of the structural weaknesses for the formation of alternative identities and movements of the so-called Russian-speaking minorities against their nationalizing regimes was that they became framed as "minorities." And this, as previous chapters have shown, was a complex process from within the state, based on the nature of the nationalizing regime itself, and also from outside players, namely, international observers, despite the influence of Russian Federation diplomatic discourses about their co-nationals in the *near abroad*, which even today continues to play an important role in the post-Soviet geographical imagination. The most evident example of this claim is Russia's annexing of Crimea from Ukraine in 2014 based on claims that the Russian minority was under threat. However, it is important not to view Crimean annexation as a consequence of very recent developments in Ukrainian politics and internal political struggles on the peninsula. The story of Crimean nationalism is far more complex and longitudinal rather than a snapshot of the 2014 struggles.[16] It is among the key examples of how external forces manipulate and categorize minority status. One way to approach this "minority" framing is through the legitimation of external observations and reports.

The OSCE categorization of post-Soviet state development played an important dual role in European and Western labeling of democratic and non-democratic events as well as the regimes' reevaluation of their own positions regarding minorities (Kazakhstan) and the fragility of the dominant nationalist ideology (Latvia). This response to the negative aspects of integration is usually overlooked in analyses of these push-and-pull relations of external actors and domestic powerful elites of the regime. This is clearly demonstrated in the ways in which the nationalizing regime in Latvia used criticism in its rhetoric. For example, it critiqued OSCE recommendations and evaluations so as to back up its own policies and course of development aimed at deeper and further nationalization of its public sphere through defending its sovereign right to "protect the nation in the name of the nation" that had suffered during the Soviet period. The discourse of national protection allowed Latvian elites to frame their integration under conditions provided by the nationalizing regime—without allowing much leverage for the counter-elites, that is, the Russian-speaking political potential, while also promoting the idea of an alternative "European" future in the EU. This goal emphasizes the power struggles since independence and has helped legitimate the nationalizing regime and its Latinized elites. However, the visual changes to the legislation that I discuss in the sections on Latvian Europeanization and the role of the OSCE High Commissioner on National Minorities (HCNM) in Latvia are acknowledged as great improvements in this nation-building policy.

In addition, these processes were contradictory in themselves. The protection of minorities and values such as human rights, democratization, and open dialogue became more politicized than real dialogues for implementing change in the political system. Minorities, too, became objectified and "trapped" in a specific ethnolingual framework in which many of them simply did not fit anymore. Moreover, supranational frameworks of political identities, European and Eurasian, did not prevail over the existing structures of the nationalizing regimes. European values played an important role in Latvian society but did not influence change in regard to the Latvian–Russian Other identity dichotomy, either within or even outside Latvian borders in migrant circles in the EU. The facts that the naturalization quota existed for at least four years before Latvian elites realized the catastrophically small numbers of naturalization rates per year; and that the noncitizen problem is still a pressing issue for the Russian-speaking community clearly demonstrate that European values did not influence the change in attitude of the Latvian nationalizing regime, but on the contrary, heightened the level of minority distrust of the regime.

For many leaders of Russian-speaking political movements, ZaRYA, PCT-VL, the Latvian nationalizing regime was only democratic and European at the outset, whereas the actual circumscribing of political and even human rights continues against these minorities.[17] Similarly, Eurasian identity is still a work-in-progress at the overall regional level and is very vaguely recognized by the Nazarbayev regime in Kazakhstan. To further understand the nature and development of the triadic nexus and beyond, it is crucial to include these interconnections with other actors in the analysis. In the next section I discuss European values and European organizations such as the OSCE and the Council of Europe in the Baltic States, focusing on Latvia in particular, and focusing on Kazakhstan as well.

OSCE, HCNM, Council of Europe, and European Union in Latvia

In November 1993 the OSCE Missions to Latvia and Estonia were established. The head of the Mission in Latvia, Hugh G. Hamilton, indicated that the main issues in post-Soviet Latvian state-building were democratization, the withdrawal of the remaining Russian (Soviet) troops from Latvian territory, ethnic relations and divisions in society, security and political tensions in the political field, including parties and political movements. The Mission was established to observe, monitor, and advise the Latvian government and the OSCE headquarters based on these observations. All the monitoring materials were sent back to Vienna and open for any OSCE member states to read and comment on. The well-known war of statements of the Russian delegation opposing the "exclusivist" citizenship laws of Latvia and Estonia against the Russian-speaking minorities from 1994 up to 2004, for example, was one result of the Mission's external response to Latvian internal politics, but it did not bring substantive changes domestically.

In addition, in July 1992 the Commission on Security and Cooperation in Europe (currently the OSCE) established the High Commissioner on National Minorities mandate under the Helsinki Summit Document. The Mandate of the HCNM was envisioned as "an instrument of conflict prevention" and its main focus up to the present day is "early warning" and "early action" toward rising tensions "involving national minority issues which have not yet developed beyond an early warning stage, but, in the judgment of the High Commissioner, have the potential to develop into a conflict within the OSCE area."[18] In the words of the first High Commissioner, known in OSCE circles as the legendary master of "quiet diplomacy," a Dutch former foreign minister, Max van der Stoel, the main mission of the HCNM was: "First, to contribute to solutions of particular inter-ethnic problems and, in this way, to contain and de-escalate tensions involving national minority issues. Secondly, to regularly inform and, if necessary, alert OSCE participating States about developments relating to national minority issues in the OSCE area. And thirdly, to work with OSCE participating States to develop long-term frameworks for the protection and promotion of national minorities."[19] The "early warning" approach included the collection and analysis of information regarding minority issues and the assessment of the earliest stages of potential conflict threats in the OSCE area.[20] It is important to note that the HCNM role in OSCE preventive diplomacy was mainly as a tool for conflict prevention whereas the OSCE Missions established in Estonia and Latvia in 1993, and the Liaison office in Tashkent in 1995, were monitoring tools for democratic and human rights in the respective states and regions of the Baltics and Central Asia. However, all three instruments were used to sustain stability, first in Europe and only then in the wider OSCE region.

One of the first instances of cooperation and recommendations made by the Council of Europe and the OSCE in Latvia involved issues and several drafts of the Citizenship Law of 1994. At that time, almost three years after independence, there were 730,000 registered noncitizens and an estimated 165,000 nonregistered noncitizens.[21] The citizenship law had been a matter of deep consideration and discussions focusing on naturalization processes. The prepolitical consensus established in the political discourse in Latvia argued for (1) each country's own choice in dealing with the immigrant population's naturalization process; (2) Soviet-era immigrants (all those who entered the country after 1940) to be automatically considered as the only candidates for citizenship (excluding zero-option citizenship as was adopted in thirteen other post-Soviet states, including Lithuania);[22] and (3) a specific quota system to be in place for these immigrants to naturalize over the next few years and not all at once. National identity and Latvianness were at the core of the decisions establish a quota system as the vast majority of newly elected Saeima members feared that a zero-sum option would not motivate many Russian-speakers to learn Latvian and acquire Latvian values, thus again (repeating the Soviet occupation experience) endangering Latvian culture and the Latvian nation.

The HCNM commissioner, Max van der Stoel, sent his comments on the citizenship law to the minister of foreign affairs of Latvia, Georgs Andrejevs on December 10, 1993. In the letter he called for expanded consideration of citizenship that would allow more groups to be prioritized for naturalization. At the time, the Saeima was discussing the level of naturalization rates—each year only a certain number of people who qualified for citizenship (permanent residents of Latvia before independence) had to pass the Latvian language test and history exams to acquire Latvian citizenship. Several narratives laid down by the international community (CSCE, the Council of Europe, and even the Russian Federation) were later present in van der Stoel's letter. The postulate of international law, namely, of the country's own right to decide on its internal affairs, was transformed in Latvia into the idea that ethnic Latvian political elites had a sole right to determine the country's internal policies by virtue of their having won the 1993 elections, in which noncitizens could not participate either as candidates or voters.

The OSCE became a field of contestation of foreign policies and a place for hostile comments made by the foreign ministers, but it provided little in terms of interstate participation on the ground. For example, in 1994 discussions on the Latvian Citizenship Law, the Russia's foreign minister said:

> We consider our relations with Lithuania as stable and fairly good and we don't have any claims to Lithuania in the field of human rights. . . . The question of army pensioners—there are around 10.000 of them in Estonia and 30–40.000 of them in Latvia. The requirement of their migration [from Estonia and Latvia to the Russian Federation] with their families and in a very short time became a humanitarian problem. We want to call for a deeper and more attentive consideration of this issue from the governments of Estonia, Latvia and international community. . . . Latvia is about to adopt the same approach as Estonia did in May last year [1993] when in a very short time a set of laws were adopted that either deteriorated or legally discriminated against the Russian-speaking population. A new Law on local elections was adopted [in Latvia that excluded non-citizens from any political rights even on regional level]. In respect to that [the Russian foreign minister] A. Kozyrev sent a special request to ministers of foreign affairs of CSCE participating States and to the heads of international organizations attracting their attention to the fact that this Law completely does not conform either to Latvian realities or to the standards of international law.[23]

The set of narratives on international law protecting Latvian domestic affairs included an acknowledgment of Latvia's historical tragedies because of being occupied; it also recognized the consequences of what European discourse on Latvia framed as "forced Soviet migration," which was used by Latvian politicians as a tool for legitimation domestically and abroad. Thus, a space for Latvia's justification of its nationalizing policies was created throughout the OSCE. Foreign policy was formed in such a way that it used the same OSCE narratives against aggressive oppositional rhetoric, even from abroad and mainly from Russia, to back up Latvia's sovereign right to deal with its own population. For example, the growing debate over citizenship rights of noncitizens in Latvia spurred discussions among Russian and Latvian representatives at OSCE headquarters. This happened almost immediately after the first OSCE Mission reports from Latvia became available to OSCE member states. The Latvian defense against the Russian Federation's rhetoric was as follows:

> One of the arguments used by the distinguished Russian Representative was that while drafting the citizenship law the Latvian authorities neglected the realities that have emerged in the country. We can assure the participating states that the Government of Latvia is aware of the realities and considers them more carefully than anybody else. At the same time the fact that during more than fifty years of occupation the Baltic nations were not able to control the immigration and the borders of these nations were redrawn without their consent must not be forgotten.
>
> Even if no state finds enough political will to assume the responsibilities for the crimes committed by the communist regime, the Baltic states should not be left alone facing the consequences of these crimes.[24]

The Russian Federation's involvement in these debates was, however, limited to foreign policy. The embassies of the Russian Federation in both Estonia and Latvia offered fast-track acquisition of Russian citizenship and passports, provided pensions for elderly ethnic Russian noncitizens, and established a special educational-cultural system for Russian language and Russian education. However, even today a majority of the Russian-speaking activists in Latvia are critical of the Yeltsin regime, stating "he did not do anything to support us [Russians in Latvia]."[25] In 2013 in Daugavpils, the city with the second greatest number of Russian-speakers in Latvia, people expressed little hope for Russian state involvement. "We are sending our students there for summer programs, student exchanges, and so on," said one of the leaders of the Russian-speaking movement in Daugavpils and Latgale,[26] "but we must be realistic—no one came to 'protect us' in the 1990s and no one would do it today," he concluded in our interview in late August of 2013. The situation has dramatically changed and evolved with the Peoples' Republics discourse and war in Eastern Ukraine in 2014. Only ZaRYA was actively involved in supporting separatist movements in Ukraine and sought support from Russia. Eventually one of its leaders, Illarion Girs, applied for political refugee status in Russia after he burned his Latvian passport in 2016. Girs was a Latvian citizen and even after burning his passport, he was issued a new Latvian passport, which he said he did not request or need and asked for the Latvian state to issue him a blue, noncitizen passport. His fervor, however, did not last long and soon after his official migration to Moscow, he moved to the United Kingdom. ZaRYA also disappeared from active discussions in Latvia, Russia, and Ukraine by 2018.

Prolonged discussions about the citizenship law, the expert assessment of the legal basis for the citizenship law by the Council of Europe, several visits of the HCNM to Riga, and four drafts of the citizenship law caused a crisis of the government in Latvia and led to the final acceptance of the law on July 22, 1994.[27] The law still included differentiation based on the legal status of post-1941 migrants and quota-based naturalization. The legal continuation of the 1938 citizenship law of Latvia was never clearly opposed by any of the external forces involved in the process of recommendations and evaluations.

The Saeima accepted most of the recommendations made by the Council of Europe regarding the citizenship law, including, for example, a clear definition of the body of citizens, abolition of dual citizenship, a delineation of the number of categories for quotas on naturalization for noncitizens based on the priority given according to age for those who were born in Latvia. The HCNM at first proposed abandoning the quota system but then suggested grouping by categories,,prioritizing those who spent more time in Latvia. Max van der Stoel's initial recommendations to abandon the quota system, grant automatic citizenship to stateless children born in Latvia, and simplify the process of language and history tests during naturalization were only accepted in 1998, after long discussions and meetings with high-ranking officials in Latvia and Vienna. The decision to follow van der Stoel's initial recommendations was also the result of very low naturalization rates under the quota system.[28]

Some scholars did not think Van der Stoel's efforts had influenced the Latvian and Estonian governments.[29] I agree that he had only a limited effect. Today, more than 14 percent of noncitizens remain in Latvia, which clearly demonstrates the OSCE's limited effect there. The changes that the Latvian parliament had to adopt were minimal but in light of the political struggle were considered far from marginal by the OSCE Mission. These included recommendations on abolishing the quota system introduced in 1998 and simplifying the language and history tests required for naturalization, granting automatic citizenship to children of stateless parents who would otherwise become stateless as well, and exempting some vulnerable groups from the language and history tests for naturalization, for example, pensioners and the disabled. The main group of those disappointed in these outcomes were the Russian-speaking activists themselves. In a confidential report, the Mission stated that in 1999, the HCNM met with Tatjiana Zhdanok and Boris Tsilevich to discuss the limitations of the education reform that was to be implemented in 2004, limiting the use of Russian language in Russian minority schools. The Russian-speaking activists were not happy about the outcome of the meeting—their concerns were taken into consideration, but no promises were made. The 2004 Education Reform was adopted by the Latvian government with the same ratio of 60 percent Latvian language instruction from ninth to eleventh grades in minority schools.

The vagueness of defining minority rights was noted by Britain, France, Turkey, and also supported by United States in 1992 when the Helsinki Document established the mandate for the HCNM and insisted on restricting the title to commissioner "on" instead of "for" national minorities. This has created a space in which Estonian and Latvian citizenship legislations could legitimize the quota system. This was achieved by the active legitimation of the Soviet occupation discourse, where many far-right politicians in Latvia accused Europe of "leaving" Latvia to deal with its own problems when it was occupied by the Soviets in 1941. The occupational discourse was also strong in foreign policy, specifically because the three Baltic states used it first, as a coalition to destroy the remaining Soviet military bases and remove Soviet army officers from Latvian soil, and then to join NATO and the EU.

The vagueness and absence of a united and uniform agreement on citizenship and minority rights in Europe also posed legal constraints on pressuring the governments of Estonia and Latvia. The exchange of letters between the HCNM and Estonian and Latvian foreign ministers throughout the 1990s included, for example, a strong rebuttal based on European conventions of human rights as well as considerations and comparisons of different citizenship laws in EU member states. The sharp criticisms Russia tried to put through the OSCE forum not only failed to help change the situation but even made it worse. Since then, Russo-Latvian foreign policy has been in a stable but hostile situation regarding the remaining border disputes on which post-Soviet border agreements were reached in 2007.[30]

So even though these discussions did not lead to a positive outcome for the minorities, they provided a space for contesting and shaping the most aggressive policies of exclusive nationalizing regimes. In this way, the OSCE, EU, NATO, Council of Europe, and other international organizations involved in the evaluation of national policy in the Baltic states played the role of a fourth element of the aforementioned triadic nexus as well as in the discursive field itself. I contend that every major decision made, especially the passing of minority-sensitive laws, such as the citizenship law, law on aliens, law on local elections, language law, committee on (Russian) army pensioners in the Baltic states, and so on, provided unique discursive fields in their own right, where contestations of different perceptions of rights, law, and international standards of legislation took place.

The multiplicity of actors and opinions in the OSCE largely contradicted the ideals it attempted to project regarding Latvian minority issues. In this way, the OSCE was never a solid actor representing a consistent opinion and insisting on the same line of argument. Different parties and different states in the OSCE expressed various opinions that influenced the final outcome. Despite criticisms for being unable to make significant changes, the only figure who did remain consistent in demanding changes in national legislation in Latvia was Max van der Stoel, the first HCNM. For example, he insisted on the abolition of quota systems for four years. The same line of pressure came from van der Stoel on the matter of language law and the choice of language use in the private sphere without the strict imposition of Latvian. However, one person could not change or even substantially influence a whole system that was driven by the interests of the ruling political elites.

The OSCE exerted multiple layers of pressure on Latvian politics before its accession to the EU and specifically before the Mission closure in Latvia, which was extended by six months more than it was in Estonia precisely because van der Stoel's recommendations (e.g., on the language requirements for non-Latvians running for office and on education reform), were accepted very reluctantly by the Latvian officials. Multiple OSCE pressures,[31] achieved by using various institutional units (ODIHR [Office for Democratic Institutions and Human Rights], HCNM, the Mission) to monitor and recommend actions in different fields, made the quadratic nexus more complex than just the contestation of three or four actors. With the role of OSCE institutions, any nexus expands to include multiple actors because the OSCE is made up of separate countries (e.g.,Russia, the United States, Great Britain) or a coalition of countries (the European bloc, in the early 2000s GUUAM [Georgia, Ukraine, Uzbekistan, Azerbaijan and Moldova]) pursuing different interests.

The goal and mandate of the HCNM was undoubtedly to guarantee security within the European borders and to control dangerous situations such as secessions, ethnic clashes, and wars.[32] It is hard to tell whether the actual rights of minorities were the essence of the debates because none of the parties involved pushed for the full consideration of Latvia's remaining noncitizen population. In December 2000, the OSCE Mission to Latvia reported that the numbers of noncitizens declined from 735,000 registered noncitizens in 1995, when the citizenship law took effect to 555,000 in 2000, or 25 percent of Latvia's population.[33] Also, by 1999 about 22 percent of noncitizens still did not possess a noncitizen passport.[34]

The problem with OSCE regulation of citizenship and minority rights was the political resistance coming not only from Latvia's ruling elites and parties throughout the 1990s but also from within the OSCE and participating states. The idea of Fortress Europe and the acceptance of the "Soviet-era migrants" label for Russian-speaking minorities that appeared in much of the OSCE internal correspondence suggested that the internal ideological and value system did not allow many of these international agencies to argue for full inclusiveness of the Russian-speaking minorities. This allowed the Latvian ruling political elites to maneuver their limited citizenship policy into Parliament without overtly challenging the core European values of political (but also exclusivist) democracy and multiculturalism. These processes ultimately also shaped the ways in which the rights of Russian-speaking minorities were negotiated and the ways different types of "minorities" were established within this group.For example, the group could include more favorable long-term residents or less-favorable ex-militia, ex-KGB, or ex-communists, whose rights were significantly limited and not protected. The external evaluation of Latvia's relation to its largest minority also set a precedent in which democratization favored nationalization of the public sphere and domestic politics. It allowed one dominant ethnic group to claim historical injustices against the other and to assert more leverage in defining the rights and procedures for less favorable minorities to gain these rights. These were predominantly ethnic Russians and Slavs who migrated to Latvia after 1943.

Case Study of the OSCE and Kazakhstan, a Different Type of Europeanization?

Although the OSCE engaged with Central Asia more than any other European organization, its influence did not lead to any significant and positive changes even after Kazakhstan's chairmanship of the OSCE in 2010 and the first OSCE Summit (OSCE summits began in 1999) that was held in Astana in December 2010.

The OSCE established the Central Asia Liaison Office in Tashkent in April 1995. It was supposed to "facilitate contacts and promote information exchange with the Chairman-in-Office as well as with other OSCE institutions and the OSCE participating States in Central Asia; establish and maintain contacts with local universities, research institutions and NGOs; promote OSCE principles and commitments as well as co-operation between countries of the region within the OSCE framework; assist in arranging OSCE regional events, *inter alia*, regional seminars and visits to the area by OSCE delegations; perform other tasks deemed appropriate by the Chairman-in-Office or other OSCE institutions."[35] The promotion of human rights, and rule of law are the key components of the human dimension of the OSCE. Although these are also key components of a democratic regime, the values are associated with the "West" in post-Soviet countries. In countries like Latvia the adoption of these values was seen as a return to normalization and thus a return to Europe.[36] However, because of the OSCE's influential role in both cases in terms of the promotion of values of equality, human rights, and rule of law and the respect for national minorities, which was not always successful, I would argue that much of the rhetoric was part of the fuzzy field of Europeanization.

Europeanization is usually perceived as policies and values of the European Union; however, Latvia and Kazakhstan represent a peculiar interplay of Europeanization beyond the EU. In Latvia, Europeanization was operationalized on multiple levels of various organizations, including the OSCE, Council of Europe, NATO, and the EU. Kazakhstan largely experienced Europeanization via the OSCE and to a lesser extent the EU or Council of Europe because, unlike Latvia, Kazakhstan was never a member of either the EU or the Council of Europe.

In Kazakhstan the situation was completely different situation: pressure was placed on normalization via the democratization of the political system. The political elites in Kazakhstan always viewed the OSCE as their way into Europe and considered the ODIHR and election monitoring important prerequisites for the regime's legitimation abroad. However, to the disappointment of Kazakhstan's political elites, none of the country's post-Soviet elections were proclaimed open and fair by the OSCE. In his autobiographical analysis of Kazakhstan's politics, Kassym-Jomart Tokayev, then the former prime minister and frequent occupier of the Ministry of Foreign Affairs office, and currently the second president of Kazakhstan, wrote the following bitter comment about the report of the presidential elections of 2005 by the ODIHR and other international observers:

Some international journalists hurried to declare the elections not trustworthy and the results incredible, [stating] that it is impossible to score so many votes in a democratic system [according to the official results, President Nazarbayev had more than 90 percent of the votes]. Foreign politicians did not hurry with conclusions as they were waiting for the international observers' verdict. They came to Kazakhstan in vast numbers—more than 1,500 people. What was the final verdict of the international observers beforehand, for us it was not a secret. In fact, there was division among them according to specific interests: some want to see the good and others are focused on the negative. It is not hard to guess why such a dichotomy was formed because big politics dominated the final evaluations and reports.

Two months before the elections I half-joked but half-seriously told my colleagues in the government: "I already can tell you know what the ODIHR of the OSCE is going to say about the elections. First, they will say that there were some slight improvements from the previous elections but then claim that there would be serious violations that do not conform to international standards. And don't expect more from the European observers—everything is predetermined." I remember how somebody said this was defeatism and there was no point in going to the elections with such attitudes. But I insisted on my opinion because I was completely sure of my rightness.

In the end everything turned out the way I had predicted it. And I say this without any satisfaction and with great disappointment. When one can predict the reaction of one of the biggest international organizations down to every single detail, it is a good reason to start seriously evaluating what is going on in that type of organizations, its bias, and how one can change this dangerous tendency.[37]

The ODIHR reports stated, for example, that "the 3 April [2011] early presidential election in Kazakhstan revealed shortcomings similar to those in previous elections" and that "the election was technically well-administered, the absence of opposition candidates and of vibrant political discourse resulted in a non-competitive environment."[38] In the 2012 early parliamentary elections, again the ODIHR focused on the limitations of the parties' competition. For example, parties were suspended from registration or "a significant amount of time has been allocated to coverage, especially on state-owned television stations of Kazakhstan's achievements in the 20 years since independence ... [which] *de facto* provided the ruling *Nur Otan* party with an informational advantage."[39] The permanent Mission of Kazakhstan to the OSCE (office in Vienna), nevertheless, viewed these reports and evaluations as a very important technique of legitimation abroad. Kazakhstan's statements to the OSCE highlighted only positive sides of the reports, for example, the Kazakh ambassador (to the OSCE) Doulat Kuanyshev commented on the ODIHR Election Observation Committee on presidential elections that "according to the [ODIHR] report voting was conducted in a generally calm atmosphere. Observers assessed voting positively in 92 per cent of polling stations visited."[40]

After Kazakhstan's first president, Nursultan A. Nazarbayev, resigned on March 19, 2019, and the Senate Speaker, Kassym-Jomart Tokayev, whose discontent with the OSCE ODIHR mission I quoted above, was appointed as interim president, he promised that the next presidential elections would be fair and open. This was not the first time political elites in Kazakhstan promised fair and open elections. But some in the movement called "You Cannot Run from the Truth" that grew after the April 2019 protest, who had seen the activists Asya Tulesova and Beibarys Tolymbekov imprisoned for fifteen days, saw this as the first opportunity for possible political competition. These were the sixth consecutive presidential elections and first elections since independence in which Nazarbayev was not participating except for endorsing the interim president as the candidate for "stability" of the country. When it was officially announced that voting day would be June 9, 2019, the Central Elections Commission started registering the candidates. The procedure is legally complex: candidates cannot be self-nominated, must be citizens of Kazakhstan by birth, and be officially residents of the country for the past fifteen years, which technically prohibits any exiled politicians or recent migrants (e.g., Kazakh returnees, *oralmans*) to run for president. Most important, candidates for the presidency have to pass the Kazakh language test,[41] to be nominated by a political party or a political movement, to have no criminal record, have a higher education, and be older than forty.

The registration period for presidential candidates lasted for only a week between April 28 and May 3, and many observers voiced fears that not all candidates could satisfy all the requirements in such a short time frame. The question remained whether the Central Election Committee and the nationalizing regime itself would allow an "alternative" candidate to be placed on the ballot. In the list of candidates backed by pro-regime parties—whose names were appearing in the wider public space for the first time and were largely unknown to voters, despite their seats in the parliament—only three names were familiar. Key on the ballot was Kassym-Jomart Tokayev, who was known as a leading figure in the country's foreign policy, former secretary-general of the United Nation's office in Geneva, and interim president after Nazarbayev. The other two known politicians were one of the leaders of the pro-Nazarbayev Communist Party, Zhambyl Akhmetbekov, and the "oppositional" candidate nominated by the Ult Tagdyry national patriotic movement public association, Amirzhan Kosanov.

In this trio, the figure of Kosanov, the former press secretary of the exiled ex-prime minister and oppositional leader Akezhan Kazhegeldin (prime minister in 1994–97), stood out as the only "opposition" candidate to Nazarbayev's regime. Kosanov was actively involved in the Kazakh opposition after Kazhegeldin's exile. He actively participated in the attempts to be elected of the unified oppositional forces in the mid-2000s alongside the businessman and politician Bulat Abilov, the publicist and national-patriot Ryspbek Sarsembai, the former prosecutor general Zharmakhan Tuyakbai, and others. Kosanov also actively participated in opposition rallies in Almaty, and in December 2011, after the tragic Zhanaozen events when seventeen officially reported people died in rallies. However, at the time, the political opposition claimed that there were more victims who were not reported. Kosanov was arrested twice for unsanctioned rallies in support of the Zhanaozen victims and those who were imprisoned after the events in Zhanaozen. These arrests led many oppositional politicians to resign from public political engagement due to fears of further persecution. Before the 2019 presidential elections there were no viable political opposition structures (parties or movements) that could support any united candidate from the opposition.

Kosanov's reappearance in the political arena was unexpected to some long-term political commentators and he was practically unknown among the younger strata of voters. Yet to many observers in Kazakhstan the fact that any alternative candidate seen at opposition rallies in the early 2010s was a sign of change. As a result of growing changes in civic engagement before the elections two specific and intertwined transformations of Kazakhstan's context are important—the rise of citizen electoral observers and the creation of the Oyan Qazaqstan (Wake up, Kazakhstan) movement. Before the elections several prominent and young journalists, bloggers, activists, social media influencers (e.g., Madina Musina and Aliya Isenova who have a combined 306,000 followers on Instagram, one of the most popular social media platforms for young people in Kazakhstan) announced that they would become independent electoral observers in their respective cities.[42] Most of these independent observers are the first post-Soviet generation born either at the end of the Soviet Union in the late 1980s or during the independence period in the early 1990s. Their political consciousness and engagement rose through the wide use of social media platforms and alternative political rallies organized by the Oyan Qazaqstan movement in different major cities of Kazakhstan before the elections, called *seruen*, meaning "walk" in Kazakh.[43] On June 5, 2019, the movement published its manifesto on the major independent online media resources, Vlast.kz and the-village.kz.

The Oyan Qazaqstan movement's manifesto called for strict adherence to the constitution, which allows peaceful protests without the sanctions and arrests that took place before the elections. Arrests followed when the protest movement ignited across the country and solitary protestors appeared on the streets holding posters or banners supporting the free elections activists "You Cannot Run from the Truth." Many people were arrested even for solitary protests and carrying an empty poster or "imagined" and nonexistent poster and for an actual poster citing the Constitution of the Republic of Kazakhstan.[44]

Oyan Qazaqstan was initiated by urban, middle-class, educated young people, journalists, bloggers, artists, photographers, writers, poets, academics, and activists claiming that "the state is every citizen of Kazakhstan" and that movement aims "to build democratic institutions." They stated, "We believe in institutions that guarantee respect for the rights and freedoms of all Kazakhstanis. Everyone deserves respect, opportunities to achieve their potential and to participate in managing affairs of the state through fair and open elections. We are all equal among equals in our common home."[45] The initiation of the Oyan Qazaqstan movement just days before the presidential elections and active role independent observers played in the elections shifted the perception of "staged" elections in Kazakhstan even beyond the ODIHR's presence or reporting.

Although Oyan Qazaqstan is not yet a viable political party or serious opposition player in the eyes of the ongoing nationalizing regime that continues in the shadow of the former president Nazarbayev and his legacy, this movement is the first attempt to create alternative voices from the younger generation. Giving the movement more legitimacy is the fact that most of Oyan Qazaqstan's activities are carried out in a de-Sovietized form away from nomenklatura institutions of the ruling Nur Otan party or its Young Nur Otan subparty Zhas-Otan, in which young people are mocked for sycophancy when they propose to erect another monument to the Leader of the Nation.[46] Their manifestos and activities, including reports and live updates from polling stations on the day of the last presidential elections in June 2019 and then from police stations and squares during the postelection protests that were broadcast live on their social media platforms, have created an unexpected response from the coercive state apparatus. Online activism and creative activism including unsanctioned banners citing the constitution, the occupation of public monuments, and even graffiti on the pavements in Astana, are seen as unconventional forms of protest by the regime, but as perfectly understandable to the younger generation who just started voting.

To this new generation of voters, the old slogans of the Nazarbayev nationalizing regime might still sound authoritative—slogans of stability and interethnic harmony in contrast to what is seen as the devastating "Ukrainian scenario." Contrasting discourses of the 1990s, such as the "Baltic syndrome" regarding the treatment of "minority groups" within their own borders, are now shifting toward the horrors of the post-Crimean political imagination of annexed transborder territories. The "Ukrainian scenario" remained the most popular anti-activist slogan throughout June–July 2019, even after Kassym-Jomart Tokayev became the country's second elected president, amid condemnations from the ODIHR and other international organizations of the elections and mass detainment of protestors after the elections. However, as President Tokayev wrote in his 2008 political memoir, in his capacities as a former prime minister and diplomat, Kazakhstan rarely expected a more favorable reaction from the ODIHR and the OSCE regarding their evaluation of its political situation.[47]

In Kazakhstan, where the ethnic composition was similar to that in Latvia, but where universal citizenship was applied to all residents of the former Kazakh SSR, the OSCE took an approach that was very different from the one it had taken in Latvia. The self-determination argument that existed in European relations with Latvia was almost totally absent in Kazakhstan as minorities' rights, their citizenship, language, and education rights were not questioned for full nationalization in Kazakhstan, as was the case in Latvia. Besides, Kazakhstan had no high expectations or goals to join the EU, the Council of Europe, or NATO as Latvia had. However, Kazakh elites' desire for international recognition pushed them toward wider consideration of minorities' rights and building a democratic facade, with its picture of harmonious interethnic relations that prevailed in the country throughout the Soviet rule.[48] Whether or not this was a real democracy and harmony is a different issue. The fact that the discourse of harmonious interethnic relations had become one of the pillars of President Nazarbayev's self-legitimation separates the Kazakh case from that in the other post-Soviet states because the Kazakh regime's top elite genuinely believed in this partially civic model, which ascribes to both politically framed multiculturalism and Kazakh ethnonationalism.[49]

Very few of the old elites knew the way out of this controlled model of nation-building, which was actually a case of national division and categorization that made many people minorities, including ethnic Kazakhs themselves. Many discontented Kazakhophone groups believed and continue to believe that they are minorities for linguistic reasons, where Kazakh language is not dominant, and based on more pressing economic issues, where many people in the regions live in insecure and impoverished conditions. This is when the idea of sacred stability propagated by President Nazarbayev tends to fail. The late June 2019 crisis that occurred when an army weapons depot exploded in the small town of Arys in Southern Kazakhstan and the subsequent crisis of refugees entering the city of Shymkent, demonstrated how one event away from the center can affect the whole regime. When more than 40,000 people were hastily evacuated in this emergency situation, the newly elected president Tokayev had to fly to Shymkent immediately. The refugees spoke to the president in Kazakh, demanding better living conditions away from the nearby military base and its weapons depot, write-offs of bank debts, and better welfare for families with many children and socially vulnerable groups. Who the "minority" is in Kazakhstan's context remains an open question.

Democratization and the transition from a totalitarian system to a more open democratic society with viable institutions and market economy was the focus of the OSCE Human Dimension prerogative in Kazakhstan. The scope of the mandate of the HCNM who visited Kazakhstan on many occasions in the 1990s was thus directed toward democratization. The first letter sent to the Kazakh government in April 1994 clearly spelled out that a full consideration of minority rights cannot be conducted in a nondemocratic system or a closed judiciary.[50] The framework of democratization spelled out in various OSCE documents (e.g., 1990 Copenhagen Document on on the Human Dimension) was the dominant narrative in OSCE communications and recommendations to Kazakhstan's government.

The discourse of democratization from the European and OSCE perspective included the following elements: first of all, free elections as an essential prerequisite for the normal and effective functioning of democracy; and second, openness of democratic institutions and their liberation from the legacy of the Soviet totalitarian past as it was referred to in HCNM communications.

Two other issues that were touched on in the letter were language use and the Kazakhification of the state apparatus. These issues were also problematic for the Russian-speaking community in Latvia, but they were never raised as strong concerns by either the OSCE or any other European organizations in Kazakhstan and Latvia.

The first issue was state language dominance over the Russian language. The HCNM concluded that Russian was the native language of 36 percent of Kazakhstan's population. And therefore, according to the HCNM, Russian language in Kazakhstan should not have been endangered or discriminated against. However, recommendations concerning the use of Russian language in Latvia were an ongoing issue of OSCE-Latvia relations until the Mission's closure in 2002. But no European organizations ever made it clear that Russian language or its use was somehow discriminated against in Latvia.[51] In Kazakhstan, on the contrary, the Constitution of 1993 and the new Constitution of 1995 provided the initial background for linguistic dualism on the political level. The HCNM and OSCE were pressuring the government in internal politics to give Russian a legal basis almost equal to that of the state Kazakh language. The OSCE saw potential tension in preferring Kazakh over any other language. This possible tension was specifically true for Russian, which was portrayed as a minority language but actually represented a dominant one. This peculiar deviation from the OSCE's course of relations in various post-Soviet states may partially explain the government's ambiguity regarding language policy in Kazakhstan in the 1990s.[52]

The second issue concerned the Kazakhification of the state apparatus and lower representation of ethnic minorities in public offices. The HCNM raised an alarm about the representation of different ethnic groups in state organs. This is another deviation from the case in Latvia, where the Latvianization of the state apparatus benefited the indigenous ethnic group at the expense of the minorities, many of whom were prohibited from occupying official positions due to their noncitizenship status or lack of knowledge of the state language.[53] However, in the Kazakh case, the OSCE proposed monitoring the ethnic composition of employees in public offices to ensure more inclusion of the minorities in the state apparatus.

All the points specifically raised by the HCNM in the Kazakh case—including ensuring overall interethnic stability and considering minorities' rights in nation-building—are of course considerations of a democratic state in which the rule of law prevails in social and ethnic concerns for specific positions or rights, and all minorities are treated with sensitivity. Developments in Kazakhstan represent several puzzling situations. There was great development in the spheres of language, citizenship, and education requirements. A democratic state offers its minorities rights in these domains, and these were fully incorporated in the Kazakh case. Some may even argue that this was done at the expense of local culture, for example, by marginalizing Kazakh language to specific groups and regions. However, Kazakhstan democratized in the political sphere less than was expected by external organizations: the OSCE, ODIHR, and Freedom House Index evaluations indicate Kazakhstan as "nondemocratic." None of the elections were acknowledged as fully free and open by the OSCE, the internal political field is still dominated by inter-clan competition among elites and elective bodies such as the parliament; and local governing bodies (*maslikhat*) are marginalized in favor of the power and figure of president.

The liberalization of institutions and the fight against corruption, nepotism, and so on continue to be great challenges for Kazakhstan. Despite wider minority rights considerations in Kazakhstan, which were fully prioritized according to the OSCE framework, these rights have never been acknowledged as successful or up to standard. The pervasiveness of the personalized nationalizing regime circumvented any possibility for a viable opposition to develop through political institutions such as political parties, free elections, or seats in the parliament. This prevented all the previous opposition attempts from surviving. Moreover, all previous opposition leaders, parties, and actors came from within the regime itself. Few attempts of civic actors who were vocal about human rights, free elections, and free journalism were not directly associated with the regime, its institutions, or previous experience of involvement in the regime. This was another factor that influenced the growing popular distrust of opposition politicians and a shift toward supporting nonpolitical actors, including activists, artists, and traditional Kazakh *aitys* singers as well as bloggers, social media influencers, and young writers and poets.

The question remains whether the OSCE, among other external monitoring organizations, allowed bias in various aspects of categorizing post-Soviet states. In the case of Latvia, a restricted approach toward ethnic minority groups was considered appropriate for EU accession. However, better treatment of the same minority group in Kazakhstan was nevertheless criticized in regard to overall democratization. Certainly, Kazakhstan's slow democratization pace and even farther fall into a personalistic regime must not be underestimated. But if any categorization of democratic progress exists regarding the treatment of minorities, the Latvia-Kazakhstan dichotomy clearly represents a biased evaluation of a country's efforts and domestic policies toward their minorities.

The dual position of Russian-speaking groups as ethnic and linguistic minorities creates internal and external problems of identification for this group. In Latvia these people and groups were officially framed as a linguistic group of Russian-speaking minorities, but in Kazakhstan the situation was blurred by the presence of many Russian-speaking Kazakhs. However, in both cases the identity and position of Slavs and those identifying with Russian ethnicity or groupness are jeopardized by the fact that their linguistic preference frames them as a "minority" by default. The pro-Russian movements were not particularly successful in forming a solid political or social movement in these two states. Apart from two parties, Harmony and PCTVL, in Latvia and a number of secessionists attempts in Kazakhstan in the 1990s these large social and linguistic groups of people remain depoliticized. Tensions occur only when issues of language and potential threat to citizenship status are raised by dominant nationalist groups in Latvia and growing nationalist movements in Kazakhstan.

The position of the so-called Russian-speaking minorities in Latvia is further aggravated by the fact that a significant number of Russian-speakers have still been unable to naturalize. Their position as *nepilsons*, noncitizens, leads to further marginalization and depolitization of this group. In an age of national states and citizenship regimes these are some of the most vulnerable groups in Latvia. Their linguistic deprivation and the strong correlation of their status with the language they speak frames them as a group "lost in transition" and "lost in translation." The Latvian Russian-speaking minority is an extreme example of the extent to which a nationalizing regime can expand its powers in defining personal and group identities, marginalizing these group identities, and externalizing their status as a "minority." The international community also adds to these discourses as Russian foreign policy and European democratization discourses further "cage" Russian-speaking groups as a linguistic and cultural minority, impeding the group's further integration and their resistance to political projects of the nationalizing regime. Below I briefly problematize the concept of "Russian-speaking minority" drawing on the data from my ethnography.

There is a distinct difference between Kazakhstan and Latvia in separating ethnolingual minorities and blurring the lines of the ethnopolitical identification. The category of Russian-speakers continues to slowly melt into a social rather than ethnic category in Latvia. In Kazakhstan this category is double-faceted: it is applied *culturally* to monolingual Russian-speaking Kazakhs and *ethnically* to Russians and other Slavs.

Throughout my fieldwork and my experience of growing up as a bilingual

Kazakh- and Russian-speaker in post-Soviet Kazakhstan, I found it difficult to differentiate between or apply concepts like "ethnic Russians" or "Russian-speakers," which are ubiquitous in predominantly Russian–speaking Riga, Almaty, and even Astana where I conducted my fieldwork. However, in the words of my respondents and in their daily experiences terms such as "Russkii" (Russian), "russkoiazychnyi" (Russian-speaking), "orys tili" or simply "orys" (Russian language in Kazakh), "Krievu valoda" (Russian language in Latvian), and "Russian-speaking population" or "Shala Kazakhs" (Russian-speaking Kazakhs) were almost never confused or misused. They signified specific and interchangeable categories of identification dependent on the contexts.

The use of the terms "Russian–speaking" or "Russian–speaker" in Kazakhstan is contextual. To identify a Russophone Kazakh one would typically evaluate his or her education and place of origin. The geographical region in Kazakhstan where one comes from may easily identify linguistic capabilities; for example, people from Western Kazakhstan and the city of Aktau might be more Kazakhified than Kazakhs coming from Eastern Ust-Kamenogorsk. However, the urban-rural divide can also influence the speaker's hypothetical ability to communicate in the Kazakh language. For example, rural areas in most parts of Kazakhstan apart from Northern Kazakhstan would be considered more Kazakhified. The proximity of *oralman* (Kazakh diaspora returnees) neighborhoods or *oralman* identity would also signify better proficiency in the Kazakh language.

Because Kazakh-speaking Russians and other non-Kazakh non-Central Asians are very rare, no special connotation is needed for Slavs for whom Russian *should naturally* be a native language. In other words, it is a socioethnic imposition of a language on Slavs but a contextual characterization for Central Asians, that is, Uzbeks and Uyghurs "ought to speak Kazakh because these languages are so similar." But an urban ethnic Kazakh from the north of Kazakhstan or from a predominantly Russified Almaty would *most probably* be less fluent in Kazakh but "ought to have at least colloquial understanding of the native language." Other factors like physical appearance (*metis*, for example, in the Kazakh context refers to a mixed ethnic background even if it is a combination of Tatar and Uzbek) or general appearance influence the sociolinguistic identification of the speaker. Ripped jeans or any other very fashionable outfit can place one (even an ethnic Kazakh) in the Russophone category or even in a foreign category (e.g., Japanese or Asian American). Additionally, the language of Slavs does not distinguish their ethnic background particularly; for example, a Kazakh-speaking Russian named Sanya (short for Alexander) from Shymkent might Kazakhify his name to Sabyr or Sake, and be highly respected in his community for knowledge of the Kazakh language but might remain psychologically "Russian" (*orys*) in the eyes of the same community. A Russian-speaking Ukrainian would still be regarded affably as "khokhol" (Ukrainian) in the neighborhood and would automatically relate to Russian-speaking Koreans and Germans.[54]

In this context, the term "Russian-speaking population" does not represent a specific category in the mindset of Kazakhstan's multiethnic citizens. This is also true in Latvia. It was envisioned as a tool for homogenization of Latvia's ethnic and lingual Other (unlike Kazakhs, a very small percentage of Latvians is not fluent in their native language). Before further discussion, the classical use of the term needs brief clarification. Work conducted by David Laitin in Estonia, Latvia, Kazakhstan, and Ukraine concluded that "a new category of identity, the 'Russian-speaking population' has emerged in all four republics. . . . This conglomerate identity includes Russians, Belarusians, Ukrainians, Poles, and Jews, all of whom speak Russian as their first language in republics outside their putative national homelands. The Russian-speaking population is not a 'nationality,' but there is a reason to believe it will take on the feel of nationality, just as the Palestinians in the Middle East and the Hispanics in the United States."[55] These identities were still forming and took a very interesting turn both in Latvia and Kazakhstan where titular ethnic group members could either be bilingual in Latvian or Kazakh and the Russian language or fluent in only one (precisely the case of urban Kazakhs). While evaluating the sociological data on ethnic composition of these populations it is important to pay attention to both ethnic identity and sociolinguistic background as the two do not always go together.[56]

The spread of the Russian language was determined by a significant migration of ethnic Russians to Kazakhstan and Latvia from the time of the colonial conquest of these countries by Russia in the late eighteenth (Kazakhstan) and nineteenth (Latvia) centuries. The size of the Russian-speaking population in Soviet Kazakhstan and Latvia kept growing. This was occurred as a consequence of vast modernization projects for which qualified workers and laborers were in great demand. One of the biggest projects attracting mass Soviet migration was the 1950s Virgin Lands campaign in Northern and Eastern Kazakhstan, an area that even today remains vastly Russian-speaking. Population growth before the war and during the Stalinist era in general was also influenced by deportations of Germans, Koreans, Uyghurs, Dungan, Chechens, Meskhetian Turks, and other nationalities primarily to Kazakhstan but also to other parts of Central

Asia. The regional spread of the Kazakh population in Kazakhstan is broad; however, ethnic Kazakhs are predominantly rural compared to the urban share of Russian-speakers (excluding urban Kazakhs). This divide constituted not only a socioethnic divide but also sociolinguistic and ideological divisions in post-Soviet Kazakhstan. This was one of the main reasons for the regime's division in its nationalizing policy, which applied strategic ambiguity in addressing the national question.[57] Another factor was division among the elites themselves on the question of which policy to apply.

The nationalizing regimes in both Latvia and Kazakhstan demonstrated remarkable resistance to the challenges of integration—changes and the harmonization of the legal system toward inclusion of minorities or interrelations with the minority kin-state, Russia. International organizations such as the OSCE and even the European Union became battlefields for debates between nationalizing regimes and kin-states in cases of Russo-Latvian relations. Despite numerous efforts and an effective value system transmitted by these international organizations, the role of minorities and their rights still remains highly objectified in a very narrow way and does not enhance their positions in the respective nationalizing regime. The fact that almost a quarter of Latvian residents are still noncitizens and most of them belong to minority groups clearly demonstrates these outcomes of a highly bureaucratized but inefficient system of categorization and unequal treatment of member states in the OSCE and the EU political structures. The Eurasian Economic Union (EEU) does not yet influence the main goals of the nationalizing regime in Kazakhstan. Sociological data from the latest Eurasian and integration barometers demonstrate that Kazakhstan's population expresses an affinity to neighboring Russia, but mostly in economic and security cooperation, not political relationships. Eurasian identity, which could have been shared across the region of participating states of the EEU currently led by Russia's Vladimir Putin, is not clearly defined and cannot compete with projects of the regime in Kazakhstan. National belonging to the Kazakh state is still strong among the citizens of Kazakhstan. The borders and rights of titular ethnicity and identity (Latvian or Kazakh) also remain intact, despite the turbulent challenges of integration in both states.

The Kazakh government's new projects demonstrate this argument. These include the Kazakhified national idea of *Mangilik El*, the Eternal Nation and further talks about the empowerment of Kazakh language and enforced migration of ethnic Kazakh returnees (*oralmans*)[58] and ethnic Kazakh citizens to the northern capital Astana and northern regions that are predominantly populated by ethnic Russians. Further European integration does not affect deviation or effective change in the Latvian nationalizing regime's policies, as demonstrated by the Latvian regime's further nationalization of the public sphere in minority schools with the minority education reform accepted in 2004, and further disempowerment of Russian minority's political will with amendments to the referendum law after the 2012 Russian language referendum.

5

HOMOGENIZING THE NATION

COMPETING DISCOURSES AND POPULAR SUPPORT

I t is not surprising that the national question and national rhetoric became a dividing line for political and cultural elites in post-Soviet states since it is such a dominant discourse of the ruling regimes. It has also become a defining feature in segmenting the electorate and political party agendas during the elections. Both regimes tried to use popular reception as forms of their legitimation. This is also an essential aspect of nationalizing regimes—with their many fixations on rediscovering, reviving, or restoring justice in nation-building. This focus on the national character of internal and ideological politics inevitably affects the entire political field. Because legitimation became a key factor of both the democratic and nondemocratic regimes, Latvian and Kazakh elites were equally trying to build their legitimacy on popular support. This, however, led to divergent results when the Nazarbayev regime was more popular in Kazakhstan due to its ambiguity in nation-building and its accommodating approach to all ethnic groups, and it was less successful in Latvia due to the regime's fixation on non-Latvian competition in the public sphere.

A few questions remain open in this discussion. How do the *practices* and *policies* of nationalizing regimes affect the populations of the respective countries in which these regimes operate? In contrast, how do the masses influence elites and their decision making in regard to practices and policies of nation-building, especially in ethnically divided societies such as those in Kazakhstan and Latvia?

In this chapter I analyze sociological data from Kazakhstan and Latvia to focus on the interdependency of nationalizing regimes and popular responses to their nationalizing policies and practices. What constitutes popular support of the Nazarbayev regime and why is the post-Nazarbayev regime transition considered locally as a cause of significant sociopolitical anxiety?[1] How can we understand some of the most important social processes and developments in relation to the evolution of nationalism? Here I refer to the increase of out-migration in Latvia, which was widely associated with the failure of the regime to deliver on its promises to citizens and noncitizens alike. With EU accession in 2004, and even before that, the Latvian demographical situation was in decline. Migration reports of the Organization for Economic Cooperation and Development (OECD) show that "between the 2000 and the 2011 Census, Latvia's population had fallen by almost 13 percent, to 2.07 million" and in 2012 it fell to 2.04 million.[2] Many of these people do not reside in Latvia permanently and work abroad but keep their legal status at home. In 2019 this number fell further to account for only 1.9 million of Latvia's population.

These developments in Latvia account for negative net migration of –14,262 in 2013, and led to "suitcase voting," a silent protest and mass distrust and de-politicization of the population. The latest voter turnout, for example, did not exceed 58 percent which is considered low for formerly politically active Latvia.[3]

I contend that the fixation of the elitist paradigm and elitist regimes on ex-clusive nation-building policies in Latvia has narrowed the political agenda and political competition outside the nationalist rhetoric. Although nationalizing is the prime field of operation for the political elites, far from addresses societal demands and the need for economic interests on the ground. This has already led to growing concerns over the vast migration of both non-Latvians and ethnic Latvians from the country.

In Kazakhstan, the growing ambiguity of the nationalizing regime and its division into different dual polar groups of interests has resulted in the radi-calization of the Kazakh-speaking electorate. There were also various waves of protest against nationalization to apolitical radicalization from cosmopolitan Kazakhstanis. But this process of ambiguity has also resulted in a general depo-liticization of the population.

My argument in this regard is twofold. First, I contend that the essence of the groupings (minority and titular) in the analysis of popular and unpopular response to the nationalizing regime is incorrect—groups of support and discontent on the ground are formed regardless of the ethnic identity. Social masses react to the nationalizing regime based on other factors, among which economic and political development is the most important. Second, I argue that discontent as a reaction to the nationalizing regime and its policies is transmitted through multiple social groups and their identification within the nationalizing regime. The class and expectations of the specific electoral group would define the response to the nationalizing regime.

In this chapter I distinguish two types of such reactions: *skeptical citizenry* (Latvia), which represents discontent and disenchantment with the nationalizing regime agenda and the reaction via active emigration and the "suitcase vote"; and *stable citizenry* (Kazakhstan), which consists of those who accept one or two ideological narratives of the regime based on economic development factors. The latter scenario is characterized by the stability of the vote and social and ideological alienation and active separation from the nationalist agenda of the majority of electorate. Support for the regime is primarily expressed through support of its promises to modernize and provide welfare. But when these promises are unfulfilled, the protest mood peaks, as happened in Kazakhstan beginning in early 2019 with the mass protests after the death of five children from the same family in one of Astana's most impoverished neighborhoods of migrants.

TOWARD A POPULAR RESPONSE

Do popular responses to the projects of the nationalizing regime matter? In other words, on the level of mass support, are nationalizing regimes shaped not only by competition within the elite field but also by challenges to its legitimacy outside the regime? By evaluating secondary sociological data, I follow the logic of each nationalizing regime's creation of discourse and practices under the specific challenges of skeptical and stable but disinterested citizen responses. Two hypotheses are formed. First, the nationalizing regime in Latvia has not been influenced by the popular vote of the Latvian population (with a persistent 15 percent vote for the far-right movement since independence), and it is exclusively embedded in the political field, which leaves little room for societal consideration. Based on this hypothesis I analyze and compare the dominant discourse of nation-building and national framing in Latvia since independence and the results of opinion polls on these major discourses—citizenship, patriotism, and popular beliefs about democracy.

The second hypothesis compares popular responses to the seemingly authoritarian but stable regime in Kazakhstan. I hypothesize that despite, and precisely due to, the regime's ambiguous ideological framework to the national question, it allowed the divided society to stabilize around a more or less civic ideal of economic growth and stability. This ambiguity, however, has also caused a further fragmentation of opinions in the political and societal field and will continue to create more anxiety for those who stop investing in the regime as the economic crisis grows.[4]

The Skeptical Citizenry in Latvia

The goal at the heart of the Latvian nationalizing regime was to establish a dominant nationalizing discourse—the legal continuity of the Latvian interwar independent state despite fifty years of Soviet occupation (1941–91): "[In post-Soviet Latvia] a 'legitimizing identity' [following Castells] very well describes the way in which the state-related identity of Latvians was constructed, as was the synergy which that identity ensures between the Latvian community and the country in which, on the one hand, the civic constructs national identity in an active and responsive way while, on the other hand, also rationalizing and strengthening the state power."[5]

The main challenge to the construction of this identity and legitimacy in Latvia is the vast Russian-speaking minority of the bulk of Soviet-era migrants who, in contrast to Latvians, "base their identity on collective memories which confront collective memories about Latvia's 'regained' history—the interwar period."[6] The "regained" Latvian nationalist discourse has been developing since late perestroika with the inception of the Latvian National Front (Latvijas Tautas Fronte) and was finalized by 1993 with the debates on citizenship law in the first post-Soviet democratically elected parliament (out of one hundred elected members only six were Russians). The Latvian nationalizing regime has solidified the discourse of nation-building pursued to the present—an exclusivist ethnic democracy with the domination of indigenous elites, culture, language, and national symbols. This was achieved by strictly defining the citizenry discourse legally, historically, and nationally as exclusively Latvian, and by restricting naturalization quotas until 1998 (when under the pressure of the Organization for Security and Co-operation in Europe [OSCE] and European Union [EU] the quotas were finally abandoned).

The context of societal involvement is very important in the further analysis

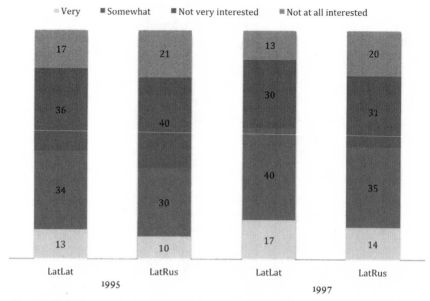

Figure 9. *Baltic Barometer*, 1995–1997. Data on political interest and involvement in the divided society (the ethnic groups are listed as Latvian Latvians and Latvian Russians). Question: "How interested are you in politics?" *Sources*: Ross, *Baltic Barometer III; Baltic Barometer V*

of Latvian social and political involvement. For example, the *Baltic Barometer* survey tracks the political awareness of the people in both socioethnic groups and demonstrates the level of political interest among Latvians and Russian-speakers. Both groups were relatively equal with regard to a negative version of political involvement in the Russian community in 1995 due to the limited discussions on the citizenship law. The data from my Russian ethnographical interviews with noncitizens and with Russian activists indicate that at the time "Russian-speakers, who represented the majority of the noncitizenry were already disappointed and alienated from the regime."[7] That situation can be described in the words of one of the so-called Russian-speaking noncitizens, Valery Kravtsov:

> Then the Citizenship Law was adopted. At the beginning, the difference didn't
> look so much but I started to feel it pretty fast. Because of where I lived, I was not
> allowed to register even as a permanent resident and obtain an ID code. It was part
> of a campaign to squeeze out of Latvia assigned young specialists like me. Without
> the ID code I had no rights to a municipal apartment, and this is lost forever. I must
> say it's really *unbelievable*: I had to spend half a year trying to prove my right to be a

... non-citizen! Well, I overcame that, obtained my *non-citizenship status* and started a private business. The free border regime with Russia has helped a lot, the business was successful and allowed me to forget political problems for the next ten years.

The situation changed with the introduction of the "school reform" that directly affected my children. I understood that I was still sitting in a cage—a golden one but a cage nevertheless; I couldn't protect my children.

I can afford a private school for my children. My elder daughter now studies in Birmingham University, another had the misfortune to get under the reforms' steamroller but now she's in Birmingham too, in a good private school. . . . But private schools aren't available for everyone. I know that regular schools are not prepared for these reforms, the quality of education will suffer. But *nobody cares*— and I'm not the only one who understands this.[8]

The political disbelief was, however, widespread in both sociolinguistic communities in the 1990s. As has already been mentioned, the period of the 1990s under scrutiny was highlighted by sociopolitical and economic transformations and redress from the previous regime. These were also highlighted by "the remedial actions used by Latvian politicians against the Russian-speakers, not only in terms of political re-establishment when there [was] no more space for the Russians but also in terms of private property (restitution),"[9] as well as military personnel settlement when many minority groups felt vulnerable and powerless. The same feeling of powerlessness among citizens who unable to change the position of the local or republican governments is also visible in the responses of both Latvian and Russian residents with evidence of elite-mass division (see figure 10).

The data from sociological opinion polls also demonstrate that Latvian citizens and residents did not entirely share the nationalizing regime's zealous guardianship of the boundaries of citizenship, national identity, and membership in the country's political community. According to the *Baltic Barometer* survey data, in 1997, 50 percent of ethnic Latvians in Latvia agreed that anyone born in Latvia or anyone who has lived in Latvia for more than ten years must have a right to vote in the parliamentary elections (the provision of basic political rights were not available for noncitizens). However, another 42 percent ascribed this right only to those who were citizens before the 1941 Soviet occupation. This would have left around 10 percent of ethnic Russians in the electorate (roughly judging by the 1935 Latvian census). In 2000 the *Baltic Barometer* found a decline in a similar question but on wider citizenship rights. The opinion that only citizens

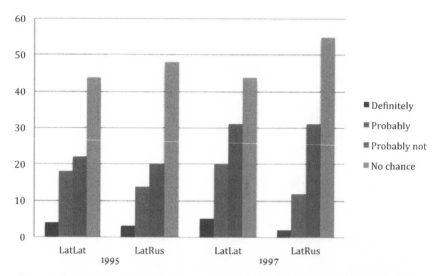

Figure 10. *Baltic Barometer*, 1995. Data on question "If the local authorities made a decision which went against people's interests, do you think you could do something about it or not?"

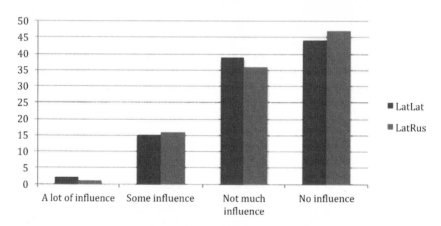

Figure 11. *Baltic Barometer*, 2005. Data on "Under our present system of government how much influence do you think people like yourself can have on government?"

before 1941 *should be granted Latvian citizenship* was held by 24 percent of ethnic Latvians, whereas 63 percent of ethnic Latvians supported the view that citizenship should be granted to those (1) who were born in Latvia (39 percent), (2) had lived there for more than ten years (17 percent) or lived there at independence (7 percent)[10] (see figure 11).

Table 9. Latvian opinions about citizenship rights, 1997–2005 (pre-EU and post-EU; %)

	1997		2000		2005	
	LatLat	LatRus	LatLat	LatRus	LatLat	LatRus
Only those whose families were citizens before 1940	42	4	27	3	27	2
Everyone born in the country	33	24	39	36	41	40
Everyone who has lived here for more than ten years	17	24	17	22	11	23
Everyone living here at independence	5	17	7	18	10	14
Any former Soviet citizen living in this country	3	30	4	20	5	19

Source: Baltic Barometer.

Table 10. "The views of Latvia's citizens on who should not be allowed to become a citizen of the country by nationality and citizenship"

Nationality citizenship	Those who wish to preserve their traditions and culture	Non-Latvians	People from other countries	Members of former repressive organizations (KGB, Soviet militarists)	Those to whom Latvia's interests are unimportant	Those who ignore Latvian law (paying taxes, etc.)
All	13.6	15.6	27.1	55.3	63.4	63.9
Latvians	18.5	21.9	35.9	70.7	76.3	71.4
Russians	7.0	8.1	14.5	32.0	44.1	54.7
Others	6.5	3.7	15.9	40.7	50.6	50.1

Source: Zepa and Kļave, "National Identity."

Note: Latvian Human Development Reports had been published since 1995 in cooperation with the United Nations Development Programme to "report on the development of the global population in the context of most important global processes." In Latvia these reports "typically are focused on a specific subject, and the development of the nation is reviewed under a conceptual framework related to same. This makes it possible to ensure that the reports offer evidence of the nation's development as part of a research project" (from Zepa and Kļave, Human Development Report 2010/2011). This report was specifically focused on national identity and mobility and prepared by a special group of researchers in a project on "National Identity in Latvia" under the auspices of Latvia's most renowned sociologist, Brigita Zepa.

Although to an outsider this division in opinions might be perceived as a strict prerequisite of citizenship, it must be noted that opinions shared by the Latvian electorate were more "liberal" and open than those propagated by the Latvian nationalizing regime. According to the 1993 Citizenship Law, all those permanent residents of the newly independent Republic of Latvia who were not citizens of Latvia or descendants of citizens of Latvia before 1941 were required to undergo a process of naturalization, including passing tests in Latvian language and history.

After the quota system was abandoned in 1998, the naturalization rates went up. However, today, about 15 percent of noncitizens in Latvia, for various reasons, are either not able or not eager to naturalize. During the whole time, and despite international pressure from the OSCE and Council of Europe, the OSCE High Commissioner on National Minorities, the Latvian elites were reluctant to make changes in the citizenship and naturalization laws.

Despite these policies and practices of intentional subjugation of the noncitizen population, a majority of whom are Russians or Russian-speaking, the Russian component of the Latvian population is almost as loyal to the Latvian state as the Latvians themselves. In a 2011 survey on national identity (Latvia Human Development Report), more than 82 percent of ethnic Latvians expressed their sense of territorial belonging to Latvia along with 72 percent of Russians (33 percent of whom also expressed their territorial belonging to Russia). In the same year, 84.7 percent of the total population of Latvia, or 93.1 percent of Latvians and 72.2 percent of Russians, agreed with the statement that "all people in Latvia must speak Latvian language."[11] However, only 46 percent of Russians and 89 percent of Latvians agreed with the statement that the "foundation for unity in Latvia should be Latvian language and culture." This echoed divisions into two discursive ideas of the nation—the ethnopolity dominated by Latvian content and the political nation dominated by multiculturalism and cosmopolitanism, as frequently heard in my interviews with many centrist and pro-Russian politicians.

In the same 2011 poll, 21.9 percent of Latvians agreed with the statement that "non-Latvians should not be allowed to become a citizen of the country," which demonstrates little shift in radical attitudes.[12] About 8 percent of Russians agreed with the same statement. Latvians, in general, are more patriotic than other groups in the study; thus, more than 76 percent of Latvians agree with the statement that "those to whom Latvia's interests are unimportant" should not be granted citizenship (table 10). The same statement is supported by 44 percent of Russians. However, Latvians also expressed relatively high doubts about being able to do much if the political majority decided on some measure the Latvian citizen did not agree with. The *Baltic Barometer* data from 1997 to 2005 show gradually increasing skepticism of the Latvian electorate, although they still believed in and valued democracy.

Two questions are crucial to the discussion based on popular responses and identity perceptions on the ground. These are questions about the political nation and about consistent competition between the Russian content of the political nation, persistent Latvianized nationalizing regimes, and growing distrust among the Latvian population toward the government and state institutions in general. As was evident in my interviewees' responses to discussions about the political nation in Latvia, its presence and the myth of a civic–ethnic national divide continues to haunt the Latvian political elite, but this is completely separate from interests and opinions on the social level.

With more than 20 percent unemployment among Latvians and Russian-speakers in Latvia in 2010 and with a monthly unemployment benefit of only €57, Latvia has experienced enormous official and unofficial outflow migration since independence in 1991. Those leaving Latvia are mostly young and educated—68 percent of leavers in 2000–2010 were between eighteen and thirty-four years old, with the highest proportion in the university-educated group.[13] The majority of migrants were women (57.2 percent) and the study showed that women were less eager to return. Employability of Latvian migrants abroad was also higher than that of those who stayed—87 percent in the migrant group and 54 percent in the broad group (ages eighteen to seventy-four) of those who stayed in Latvia. Those leaving Latvia are Latvian citizens because noncitizens have restricted working visas in the EU. The same data also show the deteriorating demographic situation in Latvia—half of its "adult population [is] living abroad with a spouse/partner," 56.4 percent and 58.8 percent in the Zemgale and Latgale regions, respectively, and around 40 percent of the registered population in Riga.[14]

This tendency was known as the second wave of the "suitcase vote" (the first was initiated by some far-right politicians during the Citizenship Law—"Soviet migrants had to go" was a very popular discourse among the radical nationalists). "People leave because of the frustration that their state and their nation is unable to deliver on all those promises of independence," commented an anonymous interviewee in Riga.[15] The main challenge to the nationalizing regime in Latvia is thus its concentration in the political field and its inability to address growing anxiety about state institutions (worsening attitudes toward democracy), a decreasing sense of belonging to the nation, which results (along with economic pressures) in vast out-migration of the adult citizenship.

The Stable Citizenry in Kazakhstan

The sociopolitical context in Kazakhstan differed from that in Latvia. The regime's practice of nationalization was strategically ambiguous and tried to provide enough room for maneuvering two different messages to two sociolinguistic audiences.

The regime provided universal citizenship to all its preindependence residents, however, a vast majority of Russians (up to 13 percent) left the country in the first two decades of independence from 1991to 2009. This factor along with the growing demographic conditions of ethnic Kazakhs (see table 10) by 2009 firmly established Kazakhs as a majority (63 percent) of the population. In the same year there were also developments toward resolving ambiguity in the nationalizing process and calling for the so-called civic identity of Kazakhstani citizens under the Doctrine of National Unity.

The vast out-migration in Kazakhstan was partially explained by worsening economic conditions. Only official levels of unemployment in pre-2008 crisis data show around 8–9 percent of unemployment (see table 23 in the Appendix of Tables).

By 2009 a majority of ethnic Kazakhs was firmly established in eleven regions of Kazakhstan apart from the traditionally Russian dominated industrial regions of Karaganda, Kostanay, and North Kazakhstan (also in Pavlodar). The regional representation of different ethnic groups in Kazakhstan in 2009 is shown in table 12. Ethnic Kazakhs are also more politically aware of and concerned about the situation in the country. The Doctrine of National Unity, which spurred Kazakh nationalist opposition, is discussed below.

The doctrine was elaborated and written by the Assembly of Peoples of Kazakhstan and the presidential administration. It stated that "interethnic and interreligious consolidation and civil unity is the most important condition for the *development* of Kazakhstan, realization of the socioeconomic and political modernization strategic goals."[16] The development and modernization in the context of nationalism and national politics is one of the most important principles (along with the discourses on the president's role and ideology) of the nationalizing regime in Kazakhstan. Unfulfilled Soviet promises of stability,

Table 11. Natality (birthrate) among major ethnic groups in Kazakhstan, 1999–2008

	1999	2007	2008
Kazakhs	90,026	165,363	193,005
Russians	−22,915	−15,484	−9,452
Uzbeks	7,130	10,838	12,219
Ukrainians	−6,270	−6,203	−5,239

Source: Agency for statistics of Kazakhstan and Kazakhstan Institute for Strategic Studies (KISI) report on sociodemographic parameters in Kazakhstan 2009.

Table 12. On regional representation of different ethnic groups in Kazakhstan, 2009

Regions	Kazakhs	Russians	Uzbeks	Ukrainians	Uygurs	Tatars	Germans
Kazakhstan	9,540,806	3,869,661	463,381	422,680	241,946	226,803	220,975
Akmola region	330,885	265,473	850	46,846	274	14,799	30,155
Aktobe region	555,212	90,897	678	34,447	114	9,743	6,672
Almaty region	1,070,326	295,196	3,266	9,282	153,442	14,957	12,763
Atyrau region	458,100	32,639	375	1,251	56	2,528	544
East-Kazakhstan region	764,327	581,820	1,150	10,806	1,436	21,967	20,079
Zhambyl region	711,449	143,220	24,620	4,218	2,751	10,693	6,694
West Kazakhstan	438,937	141,327	263	15,213	79	9,059	1,503
Karaganda region	594,251	532,649	2,605	62,615	732	34,423	39,455
Kostanay region	316,663	363,290	863	103,482	162	16,857	33,365
Kyzylorda region	614,514	12,266	926	508	110	1,758	155
Mangystau region	366,245	38,187	509	3,305	111	2,173	431
Pavlodar region	342,359	288,723	764	48,788	273	15,512	23,988
North Kazakhstan	218,552	313,441	1,073	36,521	139	14,529	23,839
South Kazakhstan	1,669,606	145,779	414,932	8,218	3,727	21,565	3,726
Astana	403,385	160,952	4,080	19,522	574	11,279	9,868
Almaty	683,995	463,802	6,427	17,658	77,966	25,321	7,738

Source: National Statistical Agency of Kazakhstan and Kazakhstan Institute for Strategic Studies (KISI) report on sociodemographic parameters in Kazakhstan 2009.

economic growthm and modernization are fully incorporated by the Nazarbayev regime.

The doctrine's program proposed a blurry but *frameworked* project—meaning that it tried to provide a framework for itself, but in trying to achieve the frame it remains empty of meaning—of full civic citizenship based on the equal

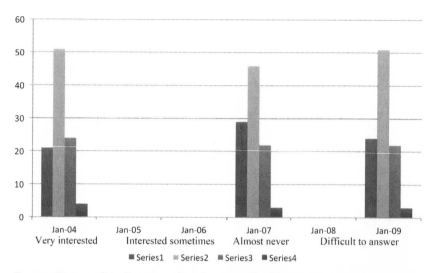

Figure 12. Data on political interest and involvement in Kazakhstan, 2004–2009. *Source:* Strate-giya sociological survey, Kazakhstan: Report on "Peculiarities of the identity and consolidation [processes] of Kazakhstani population, March 2009."

rights of all citizens regardless of race, ethnicity, religion, language, or any other discriminatory basis. It also called for state provision of mutual development of the state Kazakh language, the Russian official language, and languages of all ethnic groups. Minority languages of ethnic groups were estimated to encompass around 140 groups, which were represented in the doctrine. Support of the state language monopoly (Kazakh nationalism discourse) divides the political sphere in Kazakhstan, where nationalists are viewed more negatively than, for example, the far-right movement was in Latvia. The linguistic dualism of Russian and Kazakh is a more dominant and powerful discourse.[17] So, when discussions arise on the matter of the partial disempowerment of the Russian language in Kazakhstan, for example, by excluding it from official status, it creates a deeper sense of ideological conflict than in Latvia. Put differently, demands to decrease the status of Russian language and increase the use of Kazakh are perceived as negatively as Russo-Latvian language parity in Latvia's policyh.

The doctrine's goal was to "establish priorities and mechanisms of national unity provision in Kazakhstan on the basis of civic identity [*grazhdanskoi iden-tichnosti*], patriotism, spiritual-cultural unity, provision of stability, interethnic and interreligious *concord* in society."[18] The proposed values were:

- Our common history as a unifying basis since the beginning of independence;
- Free choice of one's own destiny, complicity with the destiny of the country and future generations of its citizens;
- High level of tolerance toward lifestyles, traditions, feelings, opinions, ideas, and religions of all members of all ethnic groups, confessions, and social class;
- A multiplicity of dialogues between different ethnic groups in the country to remain as a source of constant development and prosperity of all Kazakhstanis; and
- Traditional moral values as deeply established in Kazakhstani society: respect for the elderly, respect for the institutuion of family and traditions of hospitality.[19]

Some of the recommendations included further antidiscriminatory measures for all ethnic group members to freely participate in public, political, and other activities. It also made recommendations for the development and enhancement of Kazakh language in the public sphere. "Kazakh language acquisition must become a natural condition for each citizen," stated the doctrine in the paragraph on languages. [20] This subsection (the text of the initial doctrine is not presented in clear sections but rather as a long text) on languages made recommendations not only for the development of services for the acquisition and use of the Kazakh language but also for learning programs related to the ethnic languages of minorities and the wider use of the Russian language.

The doctrine's justification for these recommendations is curious. It stated that "the basis of the stability and concord in society demonstrated the initial choice of [the society and the state] toward the formation of a civic and not an ethnic community."

> Time has shown that the wisest approach to the coordination of interests of all citizens of the country regardless of their ethnic identity is highly valued in the world. Contemporary Kazakhstan has formed its own model of interethnic concord [harmony]. . . . The Constitution of the Republic of Kazakhstan guarantees protection of the interests of all citizens regardless of their ethnic, racial, religious, or any other identity. The norms of the main law [constitution] have laid [down] principles for mutual trust and respect among all ethnic groups. Priorities of interethnic and interreligious concord were also reflected in strategic programs and projects of President Nazarbayev. . . . This theme is also reflected from all sides in Head of the State, president Nazarbayev's books, e.g., "A history stream," "Critical Decade," in his reports and speeches to the Assembly of Peoples of Kazakhstan.[21]

The results of the Strategiia sociological agency in Kazakhstan survey, conducted in March 2009 with 1,601 respondents in all fourteen regions (oblasts), Almaty, and Astana with Kazakhstani citizens above the age of eighteen, and fifty-one experts,[22] confirm the hypothesis about the authoritarian legitimacy of the regime. The vast majority of the respondents were aware of the pro-presidential party Nur Otan (92 percent of the sample had full awareness) and the presidential ideological discourse of prosperity–stability–strong presidential rule.

The report's results on self-identification look a bit too optimistic in the context of the heated debates on the Doctrine of National Unity that followed in the late fall of 2009. However, the results of this study demonstrated high civic attitudes: more than 75 percent of respondents self-identified with citizenship (primary civic identity) and only 12 percent—with ethnic identity.

The focus groups revealed two dichotomous tendencies that are still present in Kazakhstan despite growing awareness of the civic identity: "The Kazakh-speaking community will always value the importance of the ethnic identification," the report concludes,[23] drawing attention to the existence of a consistent group of people for whom ethnic identity is not important and who express doubt about ethnonationalism.

Debates arose in various political fields but were widely heard among Kazakh national-patriots, or simply nationalists. For them, the doctrine circumscribed the rights of the Kazakh nation and nationality, who "have suffered enough," as they still blamed the past, reflecting on the postcolonial approach to the most recent Kazakh history.[24] They announced a mass hunger strike and several demonstrations in resistance to the doctrine.[25] The political party Ak Zhol and its main ideologue Burikhan Nurmukhambetov were among the most constructive critics of the doctrine's approaches. Nurmukhambetov attacked the doctrine for "not answering the main question of how to define the *nation*—Kazakh or Kazakhstani."[26]

Resistance to the "hastily written" doctrine seemed to unite various political groups under the same agenda aimed at providing a better and clearer version of the nation-building framework. For example, nationalists were always dispersed and represented by various groups and individuals. This differs from the traditional leaders of the movement—the writer Mukhtar Shakhanov, activists around the *Ana tili* (Mother tongue) newspaper, and former December 1986 participants like Zhasaral Kuanyshalin, who has also been directly linked to the radical opposition since 1995, and Dos Kushim, a former leader of the Azat movement in the 1990s.

The more recent tier of Kazakh nationalists is represented by figures like Mukhtar Taizhan, Aidos Sarym, and Rasul Zhumaly who can be characterized or identified as independent public figures with previous experience in the official institutions of the regime—both Taizhan and Sarym worked in the administration of the president at different times in the early 2000s, and Zhumaly had a career as a foreign officer in the Middle East.

There is also a younger generation of very dispersed and competitive Kazakh nationalists. One noteworthy figure is a young politician and journalist Zhanbolat Mamay, who became famous after his articles in *Zhas Alash*, a Kazakh newspaper, criticizing inequality and corruption. After the December 2011 riots in Zhanaozen (the result of a six-month mass strike by workers of oil-producing companies), Mamay traveled to Western Kazakhstan (an oblast where Zhanaozen is a small industrial town) along with the leader of the opposition party Alga, Vladimir Kozlov, and the prominent theater director Bolat Atabayev. All three were arrested and held in prison for several weeks. Only Kozlov was sentenced to seven years in prison in August 2012 for "inciting social hatred" (Article 164, point 3 of the Criminal Code of the Republic of Kazakhstan), "calling for the overthrow of the constitutional order of the state" (Article 170, point 2), and "creating and managing an organized criminal group with a view to committing one or more crimes, as well as participation in such a group" (Article 232, point 1).[27] Mamay's imprisonment led to several protest actions by his supporters in Almaty, Astana, and Western Kazakhstan. On his return to Almaty he established a new opposition newspaper Ashyq alan/Tribuna (Open Tribune) with a group of young activists, among whom Inga Imanbay is the most well-known. The newspaper, which was supported by the Foundation of Altynbek Sarsenbayev—a deceased opposition leader (assassinated in 2006). This bilingual independent weekly newspaper (currently published only in Russian) became very popular and is hard to find after Friday when it is published. However, Mamay was not engaged in the doctrine debates in 2009 in which the opposition party OSDP Azat's Amirzhan Kosanov, Zharmakhan Tuyakbay, a parliamentary fraction of the new (post-Baimenov and post-opposition) Ak Zhol party, and dispersed groups of Kazakh nationalists were involved.

This discussion, especially about the connotation of the Kazakh and Kazakhstani nation, did not result in a constructive debate, and an amended version of the doctrine was ultimately accepted, which specified and prioritized a strong role of the Kazakh language. National identity, the theme of the most heated debates, also remained ambiguous—it is now a voluntary decision for a citizen to state or not to state nationality. The decision to allow citizens their own choice in official and unofficial self-identification along with state identification (citizen of Kazakhstan) was concluded as the most acceptable situation at the time: "The attempt to introduce the concept of the 'Kazakhstani nation' instead of the Kazakh nation is a serious blunder. Along with other gossip about selling the territories of Kazakhstan to China and about the background with the Customs Union, this whole muddled situation leads to the activation of the Kazakh nationalist wing [of the political field]. . . . There is a need for further pluralism of ideas, for further discussions, and there is also a need for further openness of the system to resolve these disputes and problems [about national identity and nationalism]."[28] These same debates occupy the minds and work of younger representatives of cultural and public activist groups, that is, the new circle of contemporary artists, writers on both sides—urban Russian-speaking cosmopolitans and youth groups of Kazakh nationalists—because democratization is an important value in the Kazakhstani society.[29]

It is important to demonstrate how the doctrine project completely failed to address these issues to the society at large. The sociological survey after the introduction of the doctrine, conducted in January 2010,[30] demonstrated very limited acknowledgment and awareness of the doctrine (see figure 12). Only 5.5 percent of respondents have read the doctrine, although it was available online. The ANK (Assembly) also had a program for promoting the doctrine, but most of the information came from the debates and speculations on the ground, which were discussed in the media.

Studying popular support and/or distrust of the nationalizing regime and nationalizing policies is valuable in revealing the dynamics of and pressures on a given nationalizing regime. The results demonstrated in this chapter show that the nationalizing regime in Latvia is least affected by popular support of its nationalizing rhetoric on the ground. The country's vast out-migration became a greater socioeconomic problem. It demonstrates the hidden discontent seen in the "suitcase vote" of the Latvian population. Growing depoliticization and lack of trust in the state institutions including the Saeima and the government continue to demonstrate this trend. The political agenda of the nationalizing regime in Latvia is far from the mass perceptions and moods. The transformation of sociolingual and, most important, socioeconomic identities in the post-Soviet space define electoral and regime support in both Latvia and Kazakhstan. Social class and living expectations became more dominant influences in peoples' choice to support or distrust a particular party or government. The development of modernizing nationalism in Kazakhstan, for example, has demonstrated two trends. First, it depoliticized minority ethnicities from political participation and equally promoted neoliberal ideas in both socioethnic communities advocating for the stability of the Nazarbayev (nationalizing) regime and its policies of economic development. And second, it was done instead of political participation and nationalization demands.

Based on the surveys, I have distinguished two types of mass reactions to the nationalizing regime—skeptical, which is characterized by weak political participation and high levels distrust of the state and regime; and stable, which is characterized by the steady and gradual depoliticization of citizens in matters of nation-building. This categorization of citizens and their response to the nationalizing regime's rhetoric and policies is not constructed by the specific regime itself. Rather the policies and competition in the Latvian nationalizing regime led to discontent regarding the political institutions. In contrast, the regime in Kazakhstan aimed at outcomes of success in modernizing nationalism and substitution ideology, which produced mass support for President Nazarbayev and his rhetoric of stability and gradual economic development.

Surprisingly, the nondemocratic regime (Kazakhstan) aims at focusing on major societal demands for economic prosperity and stability. In this way, the regime in Kazakhstan is more accommodating toward its multiple domestic "audiences." The persistence of substitution ideology also supports this point. The ubiquitous thesis on "geography, and most important, demography" as the most important structures for the nationalizing regime in Kazakhstan continue to influence the situation on the ground.

The more democratic political regime but closed nationalizing regime in Latvia, on the other hand, proved to be more inward looking and concentrated on ethnopolitical competition in the political field. The problems of wider social concerns were vaguely acknowledged, and electoral campaigns and overall political competition are still tainted by the persistence of ethnic democracy and the Russo-Latvian divide. The nationalizing regime's logic continues to reproduce this dichotomy and competition.

These findings are important for the further explanation of structures external to the regime that influence its further development to one degree or another. In the concluding chapter, I further detail specific trends in the foreign policies of nationalizing regimes and argue that the distinctions made by external international observers can affect the regime's policy outcomes and legitimacy abroad.

CONCLUSION

S o which nation do you want to talk about?" was the question that was often directed at me during my fieldwork, elite interviews and ethnographies, in conversations and in debates, and in confusion when people could not decide what their nation was and give straight-forward answers and citations of the constitution. In fact, the concept of "nations" is complex and diverse in all these contexts regarding whether or not nations are to be understood as deriving from Russian *natsia*, an individualized bottom-up perception of the hybrid ethnolinguistic, ethnosocial, and political-patriotic perception of the self. But nations are also understood through the ambiguous all-welcoming idea of Kazakhstan or Latvia, where despite manipulation of and confusion about these concepts, it is an idea of citizenship and self-expression through political will (including open and free elections) and protection of one's rights and dignity.

Is a nation still about belonging or a sort of collective consciousness as described by Ernest Gellner? Is it possible under the conditions of ever-growing globalization and out-migration? Surprisingly, for both Latvian and Kazakhstan's citizens the bitter joke of London as the second capital of their respective nation-states is no longer funny. The two countries represent very distinct nationalizing regimes whose policies and these regimes' influences are nevertheless pervasive and not always accommodating or fair for all, despite the promises of the ruling elites. Growing economic problems and frustration about "the few changes independence brought," to paraphrase my friend Laima, mentioned in the introduction to this book. Migration pushes too many citizens as well as those who are no longer citizens of the nation away from their sacred borders.

In this book I have argued that the nationalizing-regime framework is better suited for analyzing and understanding post-Soviet state- and nation-building and power relations. Where political competition is fixated on control over the discourses dominant in the nation-building field, it creates a situation of constant domination over decision making that moves away from the interests and desires of the broader public.

The problem with nationalizing regimes is that they produce a set of guiding and structural frameworks for political elites but not for the wider citizenry and their perceptions and imagination of the nation and state. As one former presidential candidates put it in an interview with me, "For every public politician the idea of the national revival and the development of national consciousness is something sacred, nobody can doubt this idea or question the necessity of development [of national consciousness], neither in Kazakhstan nor elsewhere. If anything, there should be a discussion about discourses worth exploring [in nation-building] and the pace of its development."[1] What is clear from this interview excerpt, as from many other discussions with party leaders, former advisers, fathers of state-building, and ideologues of independence, none of the post-Soviet political elites in Latvia and Kazakhstan questioned the necessity and form of nation-building. Consensus was reached at the highest level that new "states" will have old nations and old ways of dividing, categorizing, and ruling the state with all its complex institutions and bureaucracy guided by the telos of the chosen nationalizing regime. Whether in the name of the sacred nation or in the name of the sacred leader and the economic stability he never fully achieved, the nature of post-Soviet nationalizing regimes, elitist fields, and mechanisms of decision making, was strictly controlled and shaped by the power elites.

The closeness of the nationalizing regimes and the consensus of its elites to circumvent any alternative discourses prevailed as hegemonic structures above and beyond the democratic and nondemocratic development of these states. These regimes emerged under very distinct geopolitical, economic, and political conditions because the framework of historical and contemporary elite development caused these structures to influence elite decision making.

The study of this framework and its future implementation in other cases makes its greatest contribution to the fields of nationalism studies, the sociology of elites, Eurasian and Baltic studies, and the history of communist and post-communist states. By focusing on the role of the producers of the nation and by bringing in rich empirical findings this study has been able to shed light on and offer in-depth discussion of the most significant outcome of the Soviet Union's collapse—the rise of nations and their incumbent elites.

The discussion here has focused on this influx of ever-changing contexts and elites as well as on the mundane shuffling of projects of national identities and ideological texts (compartmentalized ideology) in some states' nation-building and the ingrained worsening categories of national divisions in other states.

So how can one use the nationalizing-regime framework to further study post-Soviet states? This framework encompasses the following important components of analysis: elite composition and elite network formation; national discourses and narratives; the nationalizing regime working as a mechanism to regulate the operation of these narratives and the actions and behaviors of participating and ruling power elites; external structures, that is, popular or unpopular responses from the society within a state that has a nationalizing regime; and finally, external factors, such as unionist nationalism. Latvia and Kazakhstan are telling examples of the way this framework can work, and in this regard, further studies can be done.

ELITE COMPOSITION AND NETWORKS

The nationalizing regimes are composed of elites, those men and women who are able to gain the political power to define political and ideological development in a state. Their election and selection into power differs in the Kazakh and Latvian political systems in the contemporary period. I have argued throughout the book that the two regimes are hybrid: Latvia must be specified as an ethnic electoral democracy and Kazakhstan as a hybrid nondemocratic regime with a presumably open electoral system, but in reality a closed one. This distinction is crucial because it leads to the differentiation of elite composition in both regimes.

Latvian ethnic electoral democracy provides political rights only to citizens. To become a citizen one either needs to be born into citizenship (jus sanguinis) or naturalize into it by passing a Latvian language and history test after at least ten years of permanent residency. Most noncitizens who did not gain citizenship after the implementation of the 1994 Citizenship Law were also restricted from applying for naturalization for at least four years from 1994 to 1998, based on the quota-based system that was in place initially. Moreover, many active former politicians were banned for life from applying for naturalization and citizenship. This created a restricted ethicized field of political participation for the Russian-speaking minorities in Latvia and opened up more space for ethnic Latvian political demands and activities. Kazakhstan identifies itself as a democracy (in the official discourse of its constitution), but none of the external electoral evaluations, which are now considered as legitimating and categorizing apparatuses for non-Western democracies, have identified any elections in Kazakhstan as open and fair. There are two main types of elections in Kazakhstan—presidential and parliamentary. Local administrative positions are appointed by the president rather than by election.

These electoral and selection frameworks are very important in defining the logic of the nationalizing regime's development. Elite formation is dependent on elite election and selection. In both countries these systems engage this process through formal institutions such as political parties. These formal institutions channel different agendas and formally guide the competition. The party system reflects a combination of the political and nationalizing regimes. Party formation in Latvia is restricted to citizens and thus shadow organizations such as the Non-Citizen Congress have no real political power. In Kazakhstan, the party system is controlled by the personalized regime of President Nazarbayev, which promotes the regime and interelite stability and channels political participation.

Elite mobility upward to become the power elite is also differentiated based on the distinctions of the two regimes. In Latvia the power elite is usually formed from the ruling coalition in the parliament. The vitality of the ruling coalition is usually defined by elite consensus and the wider sociopolitical context. Corruption scandals and overall political distrust in the late 2000s toppled the currently powerful coalition of so-called Latvian tycoons—Ainārs Šlesers and Aivars Lembergs (via his connection to the Union of Greens and Farmers) in the Saeima. This led to the further rise of the Unity party and its prime minister, Valdis Dombrovskis. The party dominated the Latvian political field beginning in the late 2000s and it continues to hold leading positions in the ruling coalition today, despite the Zolitude tragedy (see chapter 1) in Riga, which ended Dombrovskis's political career. The ruling coalition in Latvia is more than just a simple political coalition. It has extensive powers to set the tone of political competition for parliament's highest-ranking positions and thus can exclude even those parties that technically win the elections, as in the case of the Harmony party (discussed in chapter 3). However, the ruling coalition is not limited to formal institutions only. Latvia's political field is inevitably connected to interests that stretch beyond political power via extended elite links and sponsorships outside formal politics.

A similar situation is observed in Kazakhstan where formal institutions are heavily intertwined with informal ones. Some scholars believe that "there is no set hierarchy in the relationship between the two forms of politics and that informal politics does not always dominate the formal and neither do formal institutions always shape informal political relations and behavior."[2] Political will depends on context and often reacts to events that happen unexpectedly like tragedies in Arys in Kazakhstan in June 2019 (see chapter 1).

This nuanced approach to the study of power elites in Kazakhstan is the most effective way to understand the complexities of this hybrid regime. Similarly, in chapters 2 and 3, I have argued that power elite selection in Kazakhstan is connected to loyalty to President Nazarbayev. This web of relations and "connections" forms the structure of Kazakhstan's nationalizing regime, in which multiple discursive frames of compartmentalized ideology, a system of providing messages to Russian-speaking audiences that differ from messages to Kazakh-speaking audiences so as to legitimate Nazarbayev's rule, is not openly challenged by the members of the nationalizing regime. This happens largely due to their dependency on the president's dominant role. However, some dissident voices express more nationalistic views within the Nazarbayev nationalizing regime, but these positions are negated by the overall necessity to conform to the regime's rules and goals of stability.

Kazakhstan's temporality is distinct. The information space is limited due to the restrictions of nondemocratic state coercion, which diminished all existing and short-lived open and independent media initiatives, but left behind the grappling "new media" either due to the inability of the coercive apparatus to understand it or by sheer accident. In this limited space of information sharing, often described by local nonelite players as Facebookstan, where everything seems to happen at once, and the news cycle is so rapid that an event as drastic as someone's death or the social protests it spurs gets lost in the mediascape as fast as it appears. This is to say that the rapid change of significant, earthshaking events forms a sense of insecurity and lasting division in the community of those who participate in these events. A partial reason for this is that in social media, people can either be exposed to content and discussions or close their eyes to an event; they can be banned from discussions on a popular blogger's

site or in popular social media groups. It might be too early to grasp these rapid
changes of the decisive year of 2019 in the contemporary history of Kazakhstan. And it might soon be too late to analyze them in a coherent manner. This
is because of the storm they managed to create in the changing fabric of the
complex web of Kazakhstan's wider society, political community, and its many
nations. These matters should be considered beyond the limitations of Kazakh-
or Russian-speaking, such as the Nazarbayev regime's attempt to divide them
over decades of postindependence nation-building.

THE POWER OF THE DISCOURSE

Elite settlement before regime formation and even before formal independence
are key to the stability of a political regime in general and the consolidation
of a nationalizing regime in particular. Consensus must be achieved at some
point to create at least ideational unity within the elitist field to provide the
telos for future development. This happens through consensus on dominant
nationalist discourses. Three aspects are of great importance for the study of
a nationalizing regime, in this case connected to the above-mentioned idea of
post-Soviet temporality.

First, elite settlement does not always depend on or take place based on the
temporal and political ruptures of the old (Soviet) and the creation of a new
(independent) reality. The Latvian-Soviet Awakening wave (Atmoda) of nationalist movement started as far back as the famous publication and discussions
about the Daugava river hydroelectric power plant in 1986.[3] This event created
a temporal link to the first inception of the movement and was framed as the
initial point of late Soviet resistance. Historically, however, the real political and
intellectual struggle in Latvia actually began openly only in 1989. The interview
data that I collected in Latvia suggested that the agenda became Latvianized
only after formal independence. The majority of the Russian-speaking activists
I interviewed conveyed this message in their evaluations of the unfair citizenship
legislation discussions that commenced in the political sphere in 1991. However,
it is important to focus on more detailed historical comparisons and distinguish
the Atmoda from the pro-independence movement. Atmoda was a highly Latvianized intellectual movement and only later a political one, whereas the pro-
independence movement was a spontaneous multifaceted, multiethnic struggle
for further economic, political, and social liberalization, in which many saw their
own interests in breaking away from the union. Similar to many other examples

of social movements and revolutions the Latvian scenario encompassed a variety of voices, all representing very different views. However, consensus on the Latvianized national discourse was formed separately in Atmoda and only then transformed into an all-Latvian movement for independence by 1989–90. By May 1990, the makers of the post-Soviet Latvian nation were symbolically connecting its new independent discourse to the historical period of interwar independence and its symbols.

This crucial historical understanding of ruptures and connections throughout the late 1980s and to the present is a key component for unraveling these complex processes of making nations. As I have argued throughout the book, nationalizing processes must be understood from the perspective of elites and the structures that guide their decisions—interests, competition, personal beliefs and values, and mindset (*myshlenie*).

Second, temporality does not enhance the power of the dominant national discourse. In other words, a Latvianized regime is far more consolidated than Kazakhstan's ambiguous regime for reasons other than its earlier inception and empowerment. As I have demonstrated in chapters 2 and 3, Kazakhstan's regime was able to consolidate only after the implementation of the second constitution of 1995, which granted more powers to the executive branch and to President Nazarbayev directly, leading to further consolidation of his autocratic personalized rule. Until 1995 the elites and counter-elites in Kazakhstan were not only in antagonistic ideological competition but also in a state of great disunity. Interviews with former high-ranking politicians at the time suggested: (1) complex manipulations of elections to power positions (e.g., in the parliament and government), and (2) a pressing need to consolidate a discourse that would keep the country and society in balance. This meant that many nationalistically concerned Kazakh politicians had to moderate their nationalizing agenda or were moderated by the political apparatus. Post-1995 developments in Kazakhstan demonstrated a hybrid authoritarian regime that further encompassed and tightened the grip on both Russian and Kazakh nationalist groups, their agendas, and the framing of political opposition to President Nazarbayev.[4]

Finally, the power of the discourse depends on the level of input from the elites. In other words, the nationalizing regime's dominant discourse is only as powerful as the degree to which it is backed by its own members. Here the double interplay of the power of a nationalizing regime is in place—the discourse empowers its actors but it also depends on the actors to choose to empower themselves through a particular discourse. The Latvianized nationalistic agenda is believed to empower ethnic Latvian politicians and negate the agenda of ethnic minorities or centrist parties like Harmony, but the persistence of this dominant agenda/discourse lies within the power of its representatives to enact it and control its further development. In this study I have identified two distinct development scenarios—a consolidated Latvian regime based on occupation discourse and the legal continuity of previously independent Latvia of 1918–41, and the scenario of the unstable and personalized (Nazarbayev) regime in Kazakhstan. These overarching discourses of the regimes also develop into a series of smaller discourses—guiding principles of legislation in citizenship, language, education, and other spheres.

THE RULES OF THE GAME

In chapter 3 I indicated the ways in which possible competition to the dominant discourses of the nationalizing regime is negated and excluded. I argued that a nationalizing regime is potentially a very powerful framework for elite exclusion. This same argument was demonstrated in the case study of the centrist party, Harmony, in Latvia whose political deviation from the dominant discourse of the Latvianized regime cost it the chance to win even one seat in the cabinet. This was done through the power of the ruling coalition (formal and informal institutions) to block Harmony from forming a feasible counter-coalition as well as by framing Harmony's future agenda closer to the dominant discourse. The powerful Latvianized field, the nationalizing regime in Latvia, was able to frame the political competition not only on the level of excluding the Other electorate from political participation but also on the level of parliament by excluding non-Latvian parties and non-Latvianized agendas from participating in open competition. Harmony, which is not even the strongest proponent of the rights of all minorities but rather a pro-business party with centrist views, is categorized within this frame. The power of being able to frame a discourse in Latvia resides with the nationalizing regime composed of political elites who sympathize with its values and goals and is a collective action of the ruling coalition. This is why the political competition/opposition against the dominant regime in Latvia is highly marginalized and unsuccessful.

The rules of the game in Kazakhstan are defined by the powers of compartmentalized ideology—a quasi-ideological tool created by the regime to manipulate multiple sets of discourses addressed to varying ethnolingual audiences. The ability of the regime to position President Nazarbayev as the sole guarantor of the country's development and stability allows the regime to legitimate itself to the vast majority of the population. Other legitimating techniques the regime uses include the creation of an extended network of loyal party men via the Nur Otan pro-presidential, majority party; the contextual use of nationalistic slogans and economic gain at various levels of elite standings; and so-called clans, or as I term them here, political-financial groups. President Nazarbayev's role forms a dominant discourse and framework in its own right. It serves as a balancing function for intra-elite competition at the highest-rank level and also serves interchangeably to represent the regime itself, even though various processes of power elites change. They can be fired, framed negatively in the public discourse, or imprisoned. The nationalizing regime in Kazakhstan, thus, is a very narrow representation of powerful actors, most of whom are tightly connected to the president's closest circle of power elites.

POPULAR RESPONSE

The questions of popular response and popular support, or the ways in which a majority of the population in a specific country narrates and perceives nation-making processes and projects represent the missing piece of the larger picture. I addressed this issue in chapter 5, focusing on the wider societal implications of the policies and processes initiated by the nationalizing regimes in their respective countries. The *new national question* became a focus in Latvian and wider Baltic social sciences area studies and thus provided an array of secondary sociological data and barometers, but Central Asia still lacks a coherent set of barometers and archives of available data for further analysis. This is one of the limitations of academic study in the region. However, the combination of state-provided data, available opinion polls on some of the regime's rhetorical projects of nation-building, and existing opinion allows us to sociologically evaluate the contemporary situation. I further contend, however, that Nazarbayev's regime approach to delineating the population according to static and Sovietized notions of ethnicity and sociolinguistic divides is both outdated and erroneous. Support for the regime or for specific policies is less homogeneous in either Kazakh- or Russian-speaking groups. These points of analysis require further methodological and analytical rethinking and in-depth study. The complexity of the "Kazakhstani" identity is equally overlooked by the regime as the tremendous failure of the Doctrine of National Unity has demonstrated. The making of citizens in both Kazakhstan and Latvia is an ongoing and complex process of overlapping and contextual identities—an issue that is often overlooked by the nationalizing regime.

The results of these numerous studies reveal that the nationalizing regime in Latvia is the least integrated with the views and interests of its population. After the first postindependence election, political participation in Latvia dropped to almost 30 percent and popular response to the reforms demonstrated almost equal distrust in political institutions across the two ethnolingual audiences. Even the mid-2000s *Baltic Barometer* data showed that a vast majority of respondents believed they did not really have any influence on political decision making. The dominant Latvian discourse of the regime is also slowly losing popularity among the Latvian and Russian groups. More Latvians support extending citizenship rights to people who live in Latvia regardless of their ethnic identity. Welfare and unemployment are considered more important social issues than the nationality question on the ground, but heated debates about the nation at the elite level continue to exacerbate these divisions. In the summer 2014, the ruling coalition bulldozed amendments to the preamble of the Latvian Constitution, for example, giving ethnic Latvians the sole role as the nation's creators. The biggest challenge for Latvia today is the out-migration of the country's most capable citizens.

Vast out-migration of nontitulars was also one of the Kazakhstan's greatest problems in the 1990s. In the first decade of independence, almost a quarter of the country's large Russian and Slav minorities migrated to Russia and elsewhere in the Commonwealth of Independent States. By 2009, ethnic Kazakhs had firmly established themselves as the majority at more than 60 percent. In reality this could have produced a shift in the nationalizing regime's agenda as well.[5]

Kazakh-language media became more prominent and a new generation of Kazakh national-patriots formed. However, it could not compete with the regime's agenda and powerful channels of communication. As a result, a Kazakhified agenda remained separate from wider public discussions due to the lack of Kazakh language knowledge among vast parts of the urban population. The popular response to the regime and its multidimensional substitution ideology has been positive overall. Nazarbayev continues to secure the popular vote largely due to the regime's course of modernizing nationalism and promises of development and welfare for all. The multifaceted approach to presenting legitimation to various ethnolingual audiences is a temporal yet successful strategy.

The interplay and interrelations of the elites already in the nationalizing regime depend on their ability either to change the dominant discourse completely (an example of the failed attempt of pro-Russian parties in the 1990s in Latvia or the contemporary situation of the Harmony party) or to engage with the discourse, appropriate some of its strongest features, and use them for their personal political capital gain. Another scenario can be demonstrated on the example of the charismatic former mayor of Almaty and Astana, Imangali Tasmagambetov, who was seen as one of the favorable "nationalists" in the Nazarbayev nationalizing regime. Tasmagambetov, an ethnic Kazakh from Western Kazakhstan and a former Komsomol activist, joined the nationalizing regime right after independence and paved his own path toward gaining legitimacy. Tasmagambetov is known as a builder—a former mayor of both capital cities, Almaty and Astana, he initiated the construction of major buildings and supported the development of ethnic Kazakh museums and cultural programs. He is known as someone who takes great interest in the development and proliferation of the Kazakh cultural heritage. For example, he contributed heavily to the "Kazakh Hall" of heritage and the collection in the Museum of the First President of Kazakhstan in Astana and sponsored many heritage and Kazakh cultural events. In the future, in the post-Nazarbayev era, this scenario of legitimacy building in Kazakhstan's ambiguous nationalizing regime might be a way out of the growing pressures of Kazakh nationalism and increasing insecurities among the non-Kazakh part of the population. In other words, even restricted nationalizing regimes might provide a space for alternative players if the regime risks its own relegitimation and needs to rely on the charismatic leadership of single actors like Tasmagambetov in Kazakhstan or centrist bilingual politicians of the type of Nils Ušakovs in Latvia.

The nationalizing regime as a novel framework for study of the "new" nationalisms provides a more nuanced approach to examining nation-building processes from the perspectives of those who construct and guard them—the power elites. Kazakhstan and Latvia offered a useful terrain for this research and discussion because they have differentiated conditions but similar sociodemographic compositions. There are many more scenarios of nationalizing-regime development and some of the most interesting features of such divided regimes can be studied in future work focusing on Ukraine, Azerbaijan, and Kyrgyzstan. The significance of this framework is in its ability to grasp processes on the ground, to trace and evaluate the mechanisms of elite-led mechanisms and the development of these nationalist ideologies. It sheds more light on the process of making new nations and incorporating an agency-based approach to such studies.

Table 13. Social knowledge and acknowledgment of the Doctrine of National Unity, January 2010

		Percentage
24. "Do you know/Have you heard about the Doctrine of National Unity of Kazakhstan?"	Yes, I read the doctrine itself	5.5
	Yes, I am aware of some of its points	9.1
	Yes, I heard something but cannot say anything concrete [about it]	28.8
	No, I didn't hear anything/don't know	56.6
25. "What is your opinion about the Doctrine of National Unity of Kazakhstan?"	Approve	47
	Approve some things but not all	37
	Do not approve	6
	I have an indifferent attitude toward it	6
	Difficult to answer	4

Source: Strategiya sociological agency, Kazakhstan.

Table 14. Latvian parliamentary elections, June 5–6, 1993, Fifth Saeima: breakdown by party

	Party	Votes, no.	Votes, %	Seats, no.
1	Latvia's Way	362,473	32.41	36
2	LNNK National Independence Movement	149,347	13.35	15
3	Harmony for Latvia – Revival for the Economy	134,289	12.01	13
4	Latvian Farmers' Union	119,116	10.65	12
5	Equal Rights Movement	64,444	5.76	7
6	TB—For Homeland and Freedom	59,855	5.35	6
7	Latvian Christian Democratic Union	56,057	5.01	6
8	Democratic Centre Party	53,303	4.77	5
9	Latvian Popular Front	29,396	2.63	0
10	Green List	13,362	1.19	0
11	Party of Russian Citizens in Latvia	13,006	1.16	0
12	Latvian Democratic People's Party	10,509	0.94	0
13	Electoral Union "Happiness of Latvia"	9,814	0.88	0
14	Citizens' Union "Our Land"	8,687	0.78	0
15	Saimnieciskas Rosibas Liga	8,333	0.75	0
16	Latvian Social Democratic Workers' Party	7,416	0.66	0
17	Anticommunist Union	5,954	0.53	0
18	Republican Reform	5,075	0.45	0
19	Conservatives and Peasants	2,797	0.25	0
20	Independents' Union	1,968	0.18	0
21	Latvian Liberal Party	1,520	0.14	0
22	Latvian Unity Party	1,070	0.10	0
23	Liberal Alliance	525	0.05	0
	Total	1,118,316	100.0	100

Table 15. Latvian parliamentary elections, September 30, and October 1, 1995. Sixth Saeima, breakdown by party

	Party	Votes, no.	Votes, %	Seats, no.
1	Democratic Party "Saimnieks"	144,758	15.22	18
2	People's Movement Party (Siegerist)	142,324	14.97	16
3	Alliance "Latvia's Way"	139,929	14.71	17
4	Union "For Fatherland and Freedom"	114,050	11.99	14
5	Latvia's Unity Party	68,305	7.18	8
6	United List of Latvia's Farmers' Union, Latvian Christian Democratic Union, Latgale Democratic Party	60,498	6.36	8
7	Latvian National Conservative Party and Latvian Green Party	60,352	6.35	8
8	Latvian Socialist Party	53,325	5.61	5
9	National Harmony Party	53,041	5.58	6
10	Coalition "Labour and Justice"	43,599	4.58	0
11	Political Union of Economists	14,209	1.49	0
12	Union of Latvian Farmers	13,009	1.37	0
13	Party of Russian Citizens of Latvia	11,924	1.25	0
14	Latvia's Popular Front	11,090	1.17	0
15	Political Association of the Underprivileged and Latvian Independence Party	9,468	1.00	0
16	Party "Our Land" and Anticommunist Union	5,050	0.53	0
17	Democratic Party	2,546	0.27	0
18	Latvian Liberal Party	2,163	0.23	0
19	Latvian National Democratic Party	1,367	0.14	0
	Total	951,007	100.00	100

Table 16. Latvian parliamentary elections, October 3, 1998, Seventh Saeima, breakdown by party

	Party	Votes, no.	Votes,%	Seats, no.
1	TP-Popular Party	203,585	21.30	24
2	LC-Alliance "Latvia's Way"	173,420	18.15	21
3	TB/LNNK	140,773	14.73	17
4	National Harmony Party	135,700	14.20	16
5	Latvian Social-Democratic Alliance	123,056	12.88	14
6	New Party	70,214	7.35	8
7	Latvian Farmers' Union	23,732	2.48	0
8	Alliance: DP (Labour Party); LKDS (Latvian Christian Democratic Union);LZP (Latvian Green Party)	22,018	2.30	0
9	Popular Movement for Latvia	16,647	1.74	0
10	Democratic Party "Master"	15,410	1.61	0
11	Latvian Revival Party	5,000	0.52	0
12	National Progress Party	4,522	0.47	0
13	Latvian Unity Party	4,445	0.47	0
14	Social Democratic Public Organisation	3,133	0.33	0
15	Popular Movement "Freedom"	3,099	0.32	0
16	Latvian National Democratic Party	2,927	0.31	0
17	Conservative Party	2,318	0.24	0
18	Maras zeme	2,238	0.23	0
19	Helsinki-86	2,088	0.22	0
20	Democratic Party	792	0.08	0
21	Latvian National Reform Party	464	0.05	0
	Total	955,581	100.0	100

Sources: http://www2.essex.ac.uk/elect/electer/latvia_er_nl.htm and http://cvk.lv/pub /public/28361.html (Latvian Central Electoral Committee).

Table 17. Latvian parliamentary elections, October 5, 2002. Eighth Saeima, breakdown by party

	Party	Votes, no.	Votes, %	Seats, no.
1	The New Era	237,452	23.9	26
2	Union of Political Organizations "For Human Rights in a United Latvia" (PCTVL)	189,088	19.0	25
3	Peoples Party	165,246	16.6	20
4	Latvia's First Party	94,752	9.5	10
5	Union of Green and Farmers	93,759	9.4	12
6	TB/LNNK	53,396	5.4	7
7	Union "Latvia's Way"	48,430	4.9	0
8	Latvian Socialdemocratic Worker Party	39,837	4.0	0
9	Light of Latgale	15,948	1.6	0
10	Union of Social Democrats	15,162	1.5	0
11	Social Democratic Welfare Party	13,234	1.3	0
12	Political Alliance "The Center"	5,819	0.6	0
13	Russian Party	4,724	0.5	0
14	Latvian Party	3,919	0.4	0
15	Latvia's Revival Party	2,558	0.3	0
16	Freedom Party	2,075	0.2	0
17	Mara's Land	1,446	0.2	0
18	Party "Our Land"	1,349	0.1	0
19	Progressive Center Party	1,229	0.1	0
20	United Republican Party of Latvia	826	0.1	0
	Total	997,754	100.0	100

Table 18. Latvian parliamentary elections, October 7, 2006, Ninth Saiema, breakdown by party

	Party	Votes, no.	Votes, %	Seats, No.
1	**The People's Party**	177,481	19.56	23
2	**Union of the Green and Farmers**	151,595	16.71	18
3	**The New Era**	148,602	16.38	18
4	**Concord [Harmony] Centre (Sarkanas Centrs)**	130,887	14.42	17
5	**Latvia First Party and Party Latvian Way Electoral Union**	77,869	8.58	10
6	**Latvian National Conservative Union TB/ LNNK**	62,989	6.94	8
7	**Union of Political Organizations "For Human Rights in United Latvia" (PCTVL)**	54,684	6.03	6
8	Latvian Social Democratic Workers' Party	31,728	3.5	0
9	Political Patriotic Union "Motherland"	18,860	2.08	0
10	Party "All for Latvia"	13,469	1.48	0
11	New Democrats	11,505	1.27	0
12	Political Organization "Party of Pensioners and Seniors"	7,175	0.79	0
13	Mara's Land (Maras Zeme)	4,400	0.48	0
14	Political organization "Eurosceptics"	3,365	0.37	0
15	Party "Our Land"	2,065	0.23	0
16	The Party of Social Justice	1,575	0.17	0
17	National Power Unity	1,172	0.13	0
18	Nationally Political Latvian defense organization Latvian Latvia	1,130	0.12	0
19	Party "Union of Fatherland"	1,114	0.12	0
	Total	908,979	100.0	100

Table 19. Latvian Parliamentary Elections, October 2, 2010, Tenth Saeima, breakdown by party

	Party	Votes, no.	Votes, %	Seats, no.
1	Unity	301,429	31.2	33
2	Association of political parties "Harmony Centre"	251,400	26.0	29
3	Union of Greens and Farmers	190,025	19.6	22
4	National Association TB/LNNK	74,029	7.6	8
5	Association of Parties "For Good Latvia"	73,881	7.6	8
6	Union of Political Organizations "For Human Rights in United Latvia" (PCTVL)	13,847	1.4	0
7	"Made in Latvia"	9,380	0.9	0
8	"The Last Party"	8,458	0.8	0
9	"For Presidential Republic"	7,102	0.7	0
10	"RESPONSIBILITY—Social Democratic Association of Political Parties"	6,139	0.6	0
11	"People's Control"	4,002	0.4	0
12	Christian Democratic Union	3,488	0.3	0
13	Party "Daugava—For Latvia"	1,661	0.1	0
	Total	994,841	100.0	100

Table 20. Latvian parliamentary elections, September 17, 2011. Eleventh Saeima, breakdown by party

	Party	Votes, no.	Votes, %	Seats, no.
1	Harmony Centre	259,930	28.36	31
2	Zatler's Reform Party	190,856	20.83	22
3	Unity	172,563	18.83	20
4	National Association TB/LNNK and "All for Latvia!"	127,208	13.88	14
5	Union of Greens and Farmers	111,957	12.22	13
6			2.41	0
7	Union of Political Organizations "For Human Rights in United Latvia" (PCTVL)	7,109	0.78	0
8	"Last Party"	4,471	0.49	0
9	"For a Presidential Republic"	2,881	0.31	0
10	"People's Control"	2,573	0.28	0
11	Latvian Social Democratic Worker's Party	2,531	0.28	0
12	Party "Freedom. Free from fear, hate and anger"	2,011	0.22	0
13	Christian Democratic Union	1,993	0.22	0
	Total	916,469	100.0	100

Table 21. Latvian parliamentary elections, October 4, 2014. Twelfth Saeima, breakdown by party

	Party	Votes, no.	Votes, %	Seats, no.
1	"Harmony" Social Democratic Party	209,887	23	24
2	Unity	199,535	21.8	23
3	The Union of Greens and Farmers	178,210	19.5	21
4	National Alliance TB/LNNK and "All for Latvia"	151,567	16.6	17
5	Latvian Association of Regions	60,812	6.66	8
6	"From the Heart of Latvia"	62,521	6.8	7
7	Latvia's Russian Union	14,390	1.58	0
8	"United Latvia" Party	10,788	1.18	0
9	"Latvian Development"	8,156	0.89	0
10	Party "Freedom. Free from fear, hate and anger"	1,735	0.19	0
11	"Political Party Development"	1,515	0.17	0
12	"Sovereignty"	1,033	0.11	0
13	The new Conservatives	6,389	0.7	0
	Total	912,553	100.0	100

Source: http://cvk.lv/pub/public/28361.html (Latvian Central Electoral Committee) and website of the Latvian Parliament, saeima.lv.

Table 22. Movement of Kazakhstan's residents abroad and to the Commonwealth of Independent States (CIS) from 2005 to 2009

	2005	2006	2007	2008	2009
Total number of visitors–residents of the Republic of Kazakhstan who have moved abroad (excluding those who left for permanent emigration)	2,974,869	3,687,849	4,544,440	5,242,643	6,413,943
To the CIS	2,577,026 85.2%	3,179,915 86.2%	3,749,996 82.5%	4,557,146 87%	5,797,478 90.3%
To outside the CIS	397,843 13%	507,934 13.7%	794,444 17.4%	685,497 13%	616,465 9.6%

Source: National Statistical Agency of Kazakhstan Report "Kazakhstan in Numbers, 2010."

Table 23. The economic context of Kazakhstan's development 2005–2009 (pre- and postcrisis years)

	2005	2006	2007	2008	2009
Level of population's economic activity	69.4	69.7	70.4	71.1	70.7
Level of unemployment	8.1	7.8	7.3	6.6	6.6
Level of population's economic passivity	30.6	30.3	29.6	28.9	29.3

Source: National Statistical Agency of Kazakhstan Report "Kazakhstan in Numbers, 2010."

NOTES

INTRODUCTION

1. Name changed. Here and elsewhere in the text, names of the respondents are either anonymized per their request, changed for their own privacy, or left open and official if requested during the interview. Laima discussions, February 2013, Riga, fieldwork notes.

2. The third Atmoda is a distinct Latvian National Awakening wave that took place between 1986 and 1991 and is associated with nationalist activism initially among the Latvian intelligentsia (writers, artists) and then among wider Latvian population. What Laima referred to in our discussions was her own participation in mass mobilizations on the central squares where people sang traditional Latvian songs in protest against Soviet hegemony. On the third Atmoda, see Karklins and Zepa, "Political Participation in Latvia"; and Eglitis and Ardava, "Politics of Memory."

3. Mills, *Power Elite*, 3.

4. Przeworski and Teune, *Logic of Comparative Social Inquiry*.

5. Kandil, *Power Triangle*, 2.

6. Higley and Pakulski, "Elite Theory versus Marxism," 229.

7. See Bauman. "Love in Adversity"; Karabel, "Towards a Theory of Intellectuals"; Motyl, "Inventing Invention"; Suny and Kennedy, *Intellectuals*; Verdery, "Civil Society or Nation?"; Zake, "Inventing Culture and Nation"; and Zaslavsky, "Nationalism and Democratic Transition." I also discuss this process in detail in Kudaibergenova, *Rewriting the Nation*, on the example of Kazakhstan's cultural elites who produce the dominant narratives for the national imagination but lose the political battle for pragmatic nomenclature before and after independence.

8. Badie, Berg-Schlosser, and Morlino, *International Encyclopedia of Political Science*.

9. Brubaker, "Nationalizing States Revisited," 1786.

10. Rivers, "Attitudes towards Incipient Mankurtism," 159; and Kudaibergenova, "Mankurts, Kazakh 'Russians' and 'Shala' Kazakhs."

11. Brubaker, "Nationalizing States Revisited," 1786.

12. On Russia, see Clowes, *Russia on the Edge*; on Uzbekistan, see Adams, *Spectacular State*; on Tajikistan, see Ibañez-Tirado, "'How Can I Be Post-Soviet?'"; and Tlostanova, *What Does It Mean?*

13. Baltic scholars, in particular, have succeeded in developing a field of Soviet postcolonial studies: see Annus, "Ghost of Essentialism"; Annus, "Layers of Colonial Rule"; Annus, "Problem of Soviet Colonialism"; and Kelertas, *Baltic Postcolonialism*.

14. This is still an initial discussion that is intertwined in different debates about defining, structuring, and analyzing the nature of "decolonial," "postcolonial" in the post-Soviet realm, but it is also an outgrowth of local knowledge. Current bottom-up developments in the art field dealing with decolonial and postcolonial debates across the entire former Soviet space clearly signify the importance of critically investigating this issue further.

15. Brubaker, "Nationhood and the National Question."

16. Ivans, *Voin ponevole*; and Kudaibergenova and Shin, "Authors and Authoritarianism."

17. Tilly, *Democracy*; see also Tilly, *Stories, Identities, and Political Change*.

18. Linz and Stepan, *Problems of Democratic Transition*, 3.

19. Wedeen, *Peripheral Visions*, 74.

20. See also Jones Luong, *Institutional Change*; Jones Luong, *Transformation of Central Asia*; Marat, "Nation Branding in Central Asia"; and Schatz, "Access by Accident."

21. Tilly, *Democracy*, 13–14.

22. See Bissenova, "Post-Socialist Dreamworlds; Fauve, "Tale of Two Statues"; Junisbai and Junisbai, "Democratic Choice of Kazakhstan"; Schatz, "Soft Authoritarian Tool Kit"; and Tilly, *Democracy*.

23. Adams and Rustemova, "Mass Spectacle," 1249; see also Bissenova, "Post-Socialist Dreamworlds"; Carlson, "Failure of Liberal Democratisation; Cummings, *Kazakhstan: Power and the Elite*; Dave, *Kazakhstan*; Matveeva, "Legitimising Central Asian Authoritarianism"; McGlinchey, *Chaos, Violence, Dynasty*; McGlinchey, "Paying for Patronage"; and Schatz, "Soft Authoritarian Tool Kit."

24. Isaacs, *Party System Formation*; Jones Luong, *Institutional Change*; Kudaibergenova, "Use and Abuse"; and McGlinchey, "Paying for Patronage."

25. Kudaibergenova, "Ideology of development."; Kudaibergenova, "Compartmentalized Ideology"; and Kudaibergenova, "Compartmentalized Ideology and Nation-Building."

26. Kudaibergenova, "Modernizing the Past"; Kudaibergenova, "Use and Abuse of Postcolonial Discourses"; Laruelle, "Which Future for National-Patriots?" 155; Junisbai, "Market Reform Regimes"; and Isaacs, "'Papa'–Nursultan Nazarbayev."

27. Kazakhstan's political elite became allergic to the word "ideology" after 1995, but the form and content of state programs such as *Ideinaia konsolidatsia*, Kazakhstan-2030, and most important, *Mangilik El*, the Eternal Nation, clearly bear ideological roots and directions. Though these programs are separate, they form a singular message—cementing the Nazarbayev Way for Kazakhstan's development—and they present the first president not only as the Father of the Nation, *Elbasy*, but also as the main guarantor of peace and stability in the country. I discuss the use of ideology in Nazarbayev's regime in chapter 1, citing his own definitions of what he understood by ideology: something that gives direction to the country's development.

28. Rasanayagam, Beyer, and Reeves, "Introduction," 11.

29. Mosley, "Just Talk to People?" 21.

30. Lynch, "Aligning Sampling Strategies," 37.

31. For an analysis of the cultural elite's construction of state ideology in Uzbekistan, see Adams *Spectacular State*, chapters 2 and 4.

32. Kudaibergenova, "Where Is Central Asia?"

33. See Adams, *Spectacular State* and Adams and Rustemova, "Mass Spectacle."

CHAPTER 1. NATIONALIZING REGIMES

1. Kudaibergenova, "'My Silk Road to You'"; and Kudaibergenova, "Where Is Central Asia?"

2. Anderson, *Imagine Communities*.

3. Similar, but less significant, numbers were also observed in Estonia where ethnic Russians constituted 30 percent in the 1989 census and 25 percent in 2010; and in Ukraine with the official 22.1 percent of Russians in the 1989 census and 17.3 percent in the 2001 census. However, in 1989 the majority of ethnic Estonians constituted 61 percent of the population in Estonia and the majority of ethnic Ukrainians in Ukraine constituted 72 percent in 1989. In contrast, ethnic Kazakhs as well as ethnic Latvians showed the biggest proportional growth of the titular ethnic group to minority groups at the time of independence—by 10 percent on average from 1989 to 2011.

4. See Annus, "Ghost of Essentialism"; Kelertas, *Baltic Postcolonialism*; and Kudaibergenova, "Modernizing the Past."

5. Angrick and Klein, *"Final Solution" in Riga*; Annus, "Layers of Colonial Rule"; Annus, "Problem of Soviet Colonialism"; Drifelds, *Latvia in Transition*; Kasekamp, *History of the Baltic States*; Kasekamp, "Radical Right-Wing Movements"; Plakans, *Concise History of the Baltic States*; Plakans, "Regional Identity in Latvia"; Plakans, *Latvians*; and Skultans, "Remembering to Forget."

6. Cheskin, "Exploring Russian-Speaking Identity"; King and Melvin, *Nations Abroad*; Kolstø, *Nation-Building*; Laitin, *Identity in Formation*.

7. I discuss non-Latvian speakers' strategies for escaping the Inspectorate in chapter 4. Many of my respondents who attempted but failed the language test for naturalization shared their fears about Language Inspectorate checks, and relate them directly to the real possibility of job loss. See also Dawson, "Latvia's Russian Minority"; Kolstø, *Nation-Building*; Kruma, "EU Citizenship"; Morris, "President, Party and Nationality Policy; Solska, "Citizenship"; and Tsilevich, "Development of the Language Legislation."

8. Morris, "President, Party and Nationality Policy"; and Solska "Citizenship."

9. Tribes known as Kazakhs were not unified politically. As Svat Soucek writes, "By 1730 the Kazakhs . . . had asserted themselves as a distinct group of nomadic tribes living in the eastern part of the Dasht-i Kipchak, speaking a distinctive Kipchak Turkic idiom, but lacking overall political unity" (Soucek and Soucek, *History of Inner Asia*, 195).

10. Amanzholova, *Na izlome*; Kendirbaeva, "'We Are Children of Alash'"; Kendirbay, "National Liberation Movement"; Kudaibergenova, *Rewriting the Nation*; Sarsembayev, "Imagined Communities"; Surucu, "Modernity, Nationalism, Resistance"; Uyama, "Geography of Civilizations"; and Zardykhan, "Russians in Kazakhstan."

11. In 1989 ethnic Kazakhs were a minority in their own country and constituted only 38 percent of the total population. Moreover, due to the Russification and mass migration of Russian speakers, many ethnic Kazakhs were educated in Russian rather than Kazakh and that led to a shrinking percentage of actual Kazakh-language speakers among urbanized ethnic Kazakhs (Kudaibergenova, "Use and Abuse"; and Yessenova, "'Routes and Roots'").

12. National Statistical Agency of Kazakhstan, "Results," 19.

13. Notwithstanding regular scandals about mistranslations and numerous mistakes in key ministerial reports that are circulating in the media. One of the most recent waves of criticism concerned a report from the Ministry of Culture that contained numerous grammatical mistakes in the Kazakh language.

14. Especially in rural areas such as the Kyzylorda region where more than 98 percent of village schools are taught only in the Kazakh language.

15. See, for example, Yessenova, ""Routes and Roots.'"

16. Wedeen, *Peripheral Visions*, 11.

17. Gellner, *Nations and Nationalism*, 6.

18. Suny, "Constructing Primordialism." See also Edgar, "Marriage."

19. Northrop, *Veiled Empire*, 345.

20. Kivelson and Suny, *Russia's Empires*, 10–11.

21. Gellner, *State and Society*, 40; see also Engels, *Origin of the Family*, and Lenin, *State and Revolution*.

22. So far, the local historical consensus established that the mid-fifteenth century marks the inception of the Kazakhs as a self-aware nationality and political community. In the context of nomadic society is the most easily applied definition of nation and state, despite the very fluid and mobile borders that practically defined the whole mindset of nomads, and was so different from the classical European conceptions of nation and state. For a discussion of the Kazakh medieval nation, see most notably Abuseitova, Masanov, and Khazanov, *Istoriia Kazakhstana*; Abylkhozhin, *Istoriia*

Kazakhstana; and Klyashtornyi, *Istoriia Tsentral'noi Azii*; and on Kazakh nomadism, see Masanov, *Kochevaia tsivilizatsiia Kazakhov* and Tolybekov, *Obshchestvenno-ekonomicheskii stroi kazakhov.*

23. Gellner, *State and Society*, 94.

24. I further discuss this historical development at the beginning of *Rewriting the Nation*, a monograph that explains the ways nomadic lifestyle and traditions were at first discredited by Soviet Kazakh writers in the late 1920s and up to the 1950s when Mukhtar Auezov's seminal historical novel *Abai Zholy* [The Path of Abai] began to restore the image of nomadism among the Soviet cultural elites, nomenklatura, and citizens alike.

25. Gellner, *State and Society*, 94.

26. Mukhtar Auezov describes this nomadic way of living in his seminal work *Abai Zholy*, which documents nomadic life and traditions in distinct detail to partially represent and capture a fading tradition as well as to demonstrate the important role of the Kazakh thinker Abai who condemned rich tribesmen who did not help their kinsmen and were not fair to their people.

27. Gellner, "Nomadism Debate," 96.

28. See Igmen, *Speaking Soviet*; Kamp, *New Woman*; and Northrop, *Veiled Empire.*

29. Hirsch, *Empire of Nations.*

30. See Cameron, *Hungry Steppe*; Kindler, *Stalin's Nomads*; Pianciola, "Décoloniser l'Asie centrale?"; and Pianciola, "Famine in the Steppe."

31. Borrowing James Scott's "agrarian reformers dream" (*Seeing Like a State*, 41).

32. See Akiner, *Formation of Kazakh Identity*; Cameron, *Hungry Steppe*; Kindler, *Stalin's Nomads*; Pianciola, "Décoloniser l'Asie centrale?"; and Pianciola, "Famine in the Steppe."

33. Ro'i, "Soviet and Russian Context" and Amanzholova, *Na izlome* for further analysis of Kazakh nationalist intelligentsia purges and the standardization of Kazakh Soviet culture. See also Boram Shin's forthcoming study of Soviet cultural formation in Stalinist Uzbekistan and Ali Igmen's study of the same topic in Kyrgyzstan, *Speaking Soviet with an Accent.*

34. Brubaker, *Nationalism Reframed*, 17.

35. See Kudaibergenova, *Rewriting the Nation.*

36. Suny, "Constructing Primordialism," 870.

37. Masanov, Abylkozhin, and Erofeeva, *Nauchnoe znanie.*

38. Riga fieldnotes, March 2013.

39. In Russian, *iazik* means both language and tongue.

40. Ibañez-Tirado, "How Can I Be Post-Soviet?"

41. Ibañez-Tirado, "How Can I Be Post-Soviet?" 191.

42. Author's interview with one of the main ideologues of Kazakhstan's post-Soviet regime and the former head of the presidential administration, anonymous, August 22, 2012, Kazakhstan.

43. Author's interview with political elite member, anonymous, July 15, 2018, Kazakhstan.

44. Author's interview with one of the main ideologues of Kazakhstan's post-Soviet regime and the former head of the presidential administration, anonymous, August 22, 2012, Kazakhstan.

45. The temporality of Nazarbayev's own rule is still contested in Kazakhstan's popular discourse, but here I sum up Nazarbayev's initial entry to power as the first secretary of Soviet Kazakhstan in 1989, and not his first presidential election in independent Kazakhstan, up to his official resignation in March 2019, which totals almost thirty years in power in Kazakhstan with its major political changes from a Soviet republic to an independent state.

46. See the website of the Nur Otan party, http://nurotan.kz/structure. For more on the Nur Otan party and party system in Kazakhstan, see Isaacs, "Bringing the 'Formal' back In" and Isaacs, *Party System Formation.*

47. See the report at https://www.nur.kz/1781061-mnogodetnye-kreslo-prezidenta-i-dzaksybe kov-kak-prosel-sezd-nur-otana-foto.html.

48. On the Astana Opera and the opera about Nursultan Nazarbayev, see https://ru.sput niknews.kz/culture/20190626/10692233/astana-opera-oprovergli-informatsiyu-o-premere-spek taklya-v-chest-nazarbaeva.html.

49. Author's interview with Latvian politician, April 2013, Riga,.

50. Author's interview with Latvian politician, April 2013, Riga.

51. Author's interview with Latvian politician, April 2013, Riga.

52. Cummings, *Kazakhstan: Power and the Elite*, 1; emphasis added.

53. Eglitis, *Imagining the Nation*.

54. Eglitis *Imagining the Nation*, 7–8.

55. Grzymala-Busse and Jones Luong, "Reconceptualizing the State," 531.

56. Bogushevitch and Dimitrovs, "Elections in Latvia"; Demurin, *Sovremennaia evropeiskaia et-nokratiia*; King, Vanags, Vilka, and McNabb, "Local Government Reforms; Kruma, "Access to Electoral Rights"; Mole, *Baltic States*; and Vilka, Pukis, and Vanags, "Indicators of Local Democracy."

57. The OSCE Office for Democratic Institutions and Human Rights (ODIHR) preliminary findings and conclusions of the presidential elections on June 9, 2019, reported a number of problems with ballot stuffing and lack of transparency. The preliminary report noted that "counting was evaluated negatively by IEOM [International Election Observation Mission] observers in more than half of polling stations observed, raising serious questions about whether ballots were counted and reported honestly, as required by paragraph 7.4 of the 1990 OSCE Copenhagen Document." See https://www.osce.org/odihr/elections/kazakhstan/422510?download=true for more preliminary conclusions on the latest presidential elections (2019) in Kazakhstan.

58. Bunce, "Subversive Institutions," 331.

59. Latvian Constitution Preamble, accessed June 10, 2016, http://www.saeima.lv/en/legislative -process/constitution.

60. Satpayev, "Analysis of the Internal Structure," 283.

61. OSCE ODIHR Mission has never acknowledged any of the elections in post-Soviet Kazakhstan as free and open or legitimate. Although some politicians and groups in Kazakhstan have called into question "predictable outcomes of OSCE's evaluation" (Tokayev 2008), in the postcommunist space. the OSCE electoral observations have been considered a legitimate and independent evaluation.

62. The Freedom House index graded Kazakhstan's media situation as high as 5—"Not Free."

63. Linz, *Totalitarian and Authoritarian Regimes*, 54.

64. Anacker, "Geographies of Power"; Bissenova, "Master Plan of Astana; Buchli, "Astana"; Koch, "Bordering on the Modern"; Koch, "Monumental and the Miniature; Laszczkowski, "State Building(s)"; Schatz, "What Capital Cities Say."

65. Kudaibergenova, "Compartmentalized Ideology"; Kudaibergenova, "Ideology of Development; Ostrowski, *Politics and Oil*; Weinthal and Jones Luong, "Energy Wealth."

66. Linz, *Totalitarian and Authoritarian Regimes*, 21.

67. Mills, *Power Elite*, 287.

68. President N. A. Nazarbayev's opening speech, Transcript of the meeting of the national committee for state policy under the president of the Republic of Kazakhstan, who was present (at the meeting) about developing the concept of state policies from June 15, 1993 [*Stenogramma zase-daniia natsional'nogo soveta po gosudarstvennoi politike pri Prezidente RK s uchastiem Prezidenta RK Nursultana Abishevicha Nazarbaeva po voprosu razrabotki kontseptsii gosudarstvennoi politiki ot 15*

iiunia 1993 goda], F5H, Op. 1, D. 1753, National Presidential Archive of the Republic of Kazakhstan, p. 2.

69. Nazarbayev, *Ideinaia konsolidatsiia obshchestva.*

70. President N. A. Nazarbayev's opening speech, June 15, 1993, 2.

71. In 1994 the famous dissident writer Alexander Solzhenitsyn published his essay "Kak nam obustroit' Rossiiu" [How do we reconstruct Russia], in which he proposed that vast territories of northern Kazakhstan "have always belonged to Russia." This along with the activation of Cossack movements in Eastern, Western, and Northern Kazakhstan posed another threat to the unity of Kazakhstan. Following these discussions, in 1997–1998 Kazakh elites relocated the capital from Almaty in the south to Astana in the north, a move that expanded the migration of ethnic Kazakhs to the north and east. See Koch, "Monumental and the Miniature"; Laruelle and Peyrouse, *Les russes du Kazakhstan*; Peyrouse, "Nationhood"; Schatz, "Reconceptualizing Clans"; and Wolfel 2002.

72. Writers eagerly accepted these invitations as they also believed in being part of democratic and wide decision-making processes. Many Kazakh writers later became prominent in the political field. Until his death in 1993, Anuar Alimzhanov was actively involved in transition politics and, like many writers and artists of the late 1980s, served as a people's representative (*narodnyi deputat*); Olzhas Suleimenov was actively involved in party politics and even almost ran in the presidential elections of 1995 but was effectively exiled when he was assigned as an ambassador first to Rome and then to UNESCO in Paris; Abish Kekilbayev occupied important roles as chairman of the Supreme Soviet, adviser to President Nazarbayev as one of his most important ideologues in the 1990s, secretary of state from 1996 to 2002, and long-term senator. In his memoirs, Gerold Belger remembered the first days of independence as "exciting" moments of change but he soon left the ideological apparatus to focus on writing and translations in the mid- and late 1990s.

73. President Nazarbeayev's speech, in Transcript of the meeting of the national committee for state policy under the president of the Republic of Kazakhstan, who was present (at the meeting), about the concept of developing state policies, September 29, 1993 [*Stenogramma zasedaniia natsional'nogo soveta po gosudarstvennoi politike pri Prezidente RK s uchastiem Prezidenta RK Nursultana Abishevicha Nazarbaeva po voprosu razrabotki kontseptsii gosudarstvennoi politiki ot 29 sentiabria 1993 goda*, F5H, Op.1, D. 1754, p. 47, National Presidential Archive of the Republic of Kazakhstan.

74. See "Ia vas uslyshal," podcast, April 25, 2019, on the issue of imprisoned activists who called for open and fair elections in June 2019, accessed April 26, 2019, https://www.youtube.com/watch?v=hMY_SLpuDFE&feature=youtu.be&fbclid=IwAR1ixXdOBPXkuZb3hsquSg7wDZm-hwK5Gcg6hyutUk7mOi4uoqsE8Glikpec&app=desktop.

75. Van Dijk, "Ideology and Discourse Analysis," 116. Teun Van Dijk notes that regardless of the differences in ideologies and values and beliefs they propagate, ideologies are defined as "socially shared." He notes, for example, that "sometimes ideologies become shared so widely that they seem to have become part of the generally accepted attitudes of an entire community, as obvious beliefs or opinion, or common sense" ("Ideology and Discourse Analysis," 117).

76. Linz, *Totalitarian and Authoritarian Regimes*, 54.

77. "Bar Brawl Death Touches Off Caustic Ethnic Tension Debate in Kazakhstan," *Diplomat*, January 2019, https://thediplomat.com/2019/01/bar-brawl-death-touches-off-caustic-ethnic-tension-debate-in-kazakhstan/. "Kazakhstan: Local Ethnic Conflict Exposes National Fault Lines," https://eurasianet.org/kazakhstan-local-ethnic-conflict-exposes-national-fault-lines.

78. The APK deputies responded to the events only after a week, https://rus.azattyq.org/a/kazakhstan-karaganda-killing-during-the-brawl-in-a-restaurant-and-reactions/29697493.html.

79. Following the first anti-Soviet manifestations in Almaty in December 1986, the ideological officials of the Communist Party established a "sociological-monitoring" group to probe social

perceptions and protest moods (*protestnye nastroeniia*) as well as ethnic tolerance levels in major cities of Soviet Kazakhstan in 1988. Archival documents on the Communist Party of the KazSSR (F.708, Almaty, 1995) trace the establishment of the Center for Political-Sociological Processes under Dmitry Tolstukhin's leadership. The goal of the center was to conduct opinion polls and send these reports directly to Gennady Kolbin, the leader of the Communist Party of the KazSSR from 1986 to 1989.

80. Until 1993–1994, President Nazarbayev defended the use of "ideology" as a concept, but not within the frame of "Soviet ideology," which, according to him, was "erroneous" and "manipulative" (see *Ideinaia konsolidatsiia*). However, the regime gradually moved away from using "ideology" as a concept and instead posited the murky definition of a set of ideas, programs, and visions. I write separately on this concept of "ideological shifts" in "Compartmentalized Ideology."

81. Brubaker, "Nationhood and the National Question," 48.

82. Mills, *Power Elite*, 3.

83. In Kazakhstan the Communist Party was not banned as in Latvia but it did become formally transformed into a new entity. The formal and informal mechanisms of political mobility via the career structures of mobility (*gorkoms* and *obkoms* of the party, etc.) were completely lost in the formal structure of the dominant party. The Communist Party was reinstated under the leadership of the communist Serikbolsyn Abdildin, but the party lost the dominant structures that were available during the previous regime. New parties emerged but, most important, the formal leadership of the new independent regime, under the already formally noncommunist Nazarbayev, provided a new framework for political mobility and competition.

84. Lane, *Capitalist Transformation*, 101.

85. See Laruelle, "Which Future for National-Patriots?" 155; Cummings, *Kazakhstan*; Dave, *Kazakhstan*.

86. Chicherina, *Grazhdanskie dvizheniia*, 22.

87. Lane, *Capitalist Transformation*, 102.

88. In contrast, Latvia had already declared the restoration of its prewar independence on May 4, 1990.

89. The term "Baltic syndrome" was used in official Soviet media, especially in discussions published in the official newspaper *Kazakhstankaya Pravda*, to describe the development of radical far-right nationalism in Estonia and Latvia that excluded the majority of ethnic Russians. In these early 1990s discussions of Baltic nation-building, the discourse on Russian-speakers in Latvia did not exist in Kazakhstan, where minorities were simply defined by their presumed ethnic identity, as Russians.

90. Data in the tables based on Cummings, *Kazakhstan*; and Zhussupov, *Dinamika* survey in *Politicheskaia analitika*.

91. A. Nysanbaev has argued that these amendments were democratizing in Kazakhstan (see *Philosophiia vzaimoponimaniia*, 138–201), "The structural evolution of state power" in Kazakhstan. On Latvia, see Chicherina *Grazhdanskie dvizheniia*.

92. Timur Suleimenov is the head of the Designers' Union of Kazakhstan. He initiated and was in charge of restorations of the Khoja Akhmet Yassavi Mausoleum in the ancient city of Turkestan, in charge of the design of national currency, the tenge, and other national identification projects. He is a well-known expert in the field and a powerful member of the intellectual elite. He was part of the Zhas Tulpar movement of cultural elites who were educated in Moscow and St. Petersburg. A group of young indigenous Kazakh intellectuals, including Murat Auezov, Olzhas Suleimenov, Timur Suleimenov, and Aida Kunanbay, were members of this movement and were concerned with the authentic national character of their local culture and country. This intellectual network devel-

oped abroad, in Russia where they were educated. Other networks of those back at home included different networks within the Writers' Union.

93. Interview with the author, April 2011, Almaty.

94. Chicherina, *Grazhdanskie dvizheniia*.

95. The December 1986 events were the first open manifestation against Moscow's decision to replace local leadership from above. On December 17, 1986, a mass protest took place. The police cracked down on it and the protestors were accused of being "nationalists." The famous Kazakh-speaking writer Mukhtar Shakhanov took an active role in seeking to investigate the reasons for the events as well as the outcomes. See also Ponomarev and Dzhukeeva, *Documents*.

96. Kuttiqadam, "Early Political Landscape," 43.

97. Isaacs, *Party System Formation*, 48.

98. The political struggle started in 1993; Abdildin was prime minister (*Predsedatel' Verkhovnogo Soveta*) from 1991 to December 1993. At the time he had already disagreed with President Nazarbayev on many economic and political policies, ideological matters. The political analysts described this as a "battle of generations"—of the old communism and new *reformator* (reformer) Nazarbayev. In my interview with Serikbolsyn Abdildin, he accused Nazarbayev and the whole regime of being undemocratic and of dominating the parliament and rearranging the parliamentary elections. By 1994 Abdildin was officially opposing President Nazarbayev. Zhasaral Kuanyshalin, currently a member of the Alga! opposition (allegedly on the Mukhtar Ablyazov team) was one of the December 1986 activists and an active member of the 1993 parliament. His political career as a parliamentarian ended with the dissolution of what he called "the most democratic parliament in the history of Kazakhstan" in 1993. Gaziz Aldamzharov had a promising career as a speaker of the parliament but he lost in a follow-up vote (which is widely considered fraud). Abish Kekilbayev, a famous Kazakh writer who in the 1990s became a prominent political figure in the Nazarbayev regime, is now a member of the Senate. The "old" Communist Party (Abdildin, Kuanyshalin, and Aldamzharov) has split up; Kuanyshalin is still in the opposition, but Adamzharov, now a nationalist, is a party leader (since 2010).

CHAPTER 2. THE ARCHAEOLOGY OF NATIONALIZING REGIMES

Epigraph: Ronald Grigor Suny, "Contructing Primoridalism," 868.

1. Castells, *Communication Power*, 10.

2. See McGlinchey *Chaos, Violence, Dynasty*.

3. The power elites have the most power in decision making and in determining the limit and the frameworks of national ideology or ideologies. The power elite are thus "composed of men [and women] whose positions enable them to transcend the ordinary environments of ordinary men and women; they are in positions to make decisions having major consequences" (Mills, *Power Elite*, 3). Anonymous interview with a former member of the power elite, series of interviews, August 2012–September 2013, Almaty.

4. Dave, *Kazakhstan*, 5.

5. Chinn and Kaiser, *Russians as the New Minority*; Danzer, "Battlefields of Ethnic Symbols"; Diener, "Assessing Potential Russian Irredentism; Diener, "Kazakhstan's Kin State Diaspora"; Diener, "National Territory" ; Koch, "Why Not a World City?"

6. Adamson, *Hegemony and Revolution*; Forgacs, *Gramsci Reader*; Hoare, *Antonio Gramsci Selections*; and March, "State Ideology."

7. March, "State Ideology," 211.

8. Anonymous interview with a former member of the power elite under Nazarbayev's transition, August 22, 2012, Kazakhstan. (These power elites have the most power in decision making and in determining the limit and the frameworks of national ideology or ideologies.)

9. In his 1990 publications of essays and thoughts, the famous Soviet Latvian writer and chairman of the Latvian Writers' Union, Jānis Peters mentions a slogan of that time, "Migrants—Latvia's Chernobyl," which according to him was a "sign of a very low culture which balances on the edge of the cynical racism" (Peters, *Ordena i infarkty,*17).

10. OSCE Mission to Latvia repository of confidential reports on the 1993–1994 Saeima (Parliament) discussions about the Citizenship Law and quota-based system of naturalization specifically outline this argument of the far-right parties such as LNNK and TB (at the time still separate movements), who opposed even the mere possibility of naturalization for those without advanced proficiency in Latvian. Their initial proposal was to allow no more than 0.1 percent of the noncitizen population so as not to endanger the Latvian core of the new polity. On democracy and exclusion in divided societies, see Aasland, "Citizenship Status" and Horowitz, "Challenge of Ethnic Conflict"; on access to electoral rights in Latvia, see Kruma "Access to Electoral Rights."

11. Data on noncitizens drawn from OSCE and Latvian Citizenship and Naturalization Board reports, direct numbers quoted from OSCE document, Reference No.: 376/97/L.

12. Naturalization Board (NB) data for 1996.

13. Rose, *Baltic Barometer III.*

14. From author's interview with a pro-Russian activist, August 2013, Riga.

15. Rose, *Baltic Barometer III;* Rose, *Baltic Barometer V.*

16. Anna Stroy, *Diena,* August 6, 1997.

17. Reports of the Naturalization Board of the Republic of Latvia and the OSCE Mission to Latvia.

18. These domains were top priority for OSCE High Commissioner on National Minorities Max van der Stoel's recommendations and long-term negotiations with Latvian elites.

19. TB/LNNK expressed the most rigid position regarding the Latvian language-acquisition policy by non-Latvian ethnic minorities during the naturalization process and in educational reform. The OSCE mission statements reveal that the TB/LNNK fraction in the parliament constantly opposed the idea of allowing Russian-speaking high school students to waive the language test during the naturalization process and present school exams in the Latvian state language instead.

20. The majority of those applications were, however, made outside the window system: for the first three years 81 percent of applications were through extraordinary naturalization (by a spouse or child of a citizen), 11 percent were through window 1 (between the ages of sixteen and twenty), 5.5 percent through window 2 (between the ages of twenty-one and twenty-five21–25), and 2.5 percent through window 3 (between the ages of twenty-six and thirty).

21. See Kolstø, *Nation-Building;* and Solska "Citizenship."

22. Author's interview with the parliamentary leader from Vienotiba (Unity) party, May 2013, Riga.

23. Ross, *Baltic Barometer III* results.

24. Author's interview with Brigita Zepa, February 2013, Riga.

25. Kohn, *Idea of Nationalism;* Miley, "Against the Thesis."

26. Miley "Against the Thesis," 23.

27. See Brubaker, "Nationalizing States Revisited."

28. From author's interview with a pro-Russian activist, August 2013, Riga.

29. From author's interviews February–May 2013, Riga, and OSCE Secretariat archival data consulted in October–December 2013.

30. See Rozenvalds, *How Democratic Is Latvia.*

31. Baltic post-Soviet postcolonialism dismissed the vast industrialization of the country during the Soviet period, which brought economic development in Latvia and contributed to its privatization in the 1990s. See Nissinen, *Latvia's Transition.*

32. From archival data on discussions of the Ideological Committee under the President's Administration, Republic of Kazakhstan, Presidential Archive, Fund 5N, Almaty, Kazakhstan.

33. From archival data on discussions in the Ideological Committee under the President's Administration, Fund 5N.

34. Constitution of the Republic of Kazakhstan, 1993 (abolished with the adoption of the new Constitution on August 30, 1995).

35. Article 4, paragraph 3 of the 1993 Constitution stated: "All citizens of the Republic who were forced to leave the territory of the Republic as well as Kazakhs living in other states are recognized for the right of citizenship of the Republic of Kazakhstan along with the citizenship of other states if it is not contrary to the laws of the State of which they are part."

36. Cummings, *Kazakhstan: Power and the Elite*; and Kuttiqadam, "Kazakh Drama."

37. Constitution of the Republic of Kazakhstan, August 30, 1995.

38. Author's anonymous interview with a leader of the Kazakh national-patriot movement, January 2013, Almaty.

39. Sarym, "Povestka kazakhskih natsionalistov dolzhna obnovit'sia" [Kazakh nationalists' agenda requires renewal of ideas], *Sayasat*, January 23, 2015, http://sayasat.org/articles/1121-ajdjos-sarym-povestka-kazahskih-nacionalistov-djolzhna-obnovitsja.

40. See Kudaibergenova, "Use and Abuse."

41. Malesevic, *Identity as ideology*, 27.

42. Brubaker, "Nationhood and the National Question" and "Nationalizing States Revisited."

43. Author's interview with Pyotr Svoik, opposition politician, August 2012, Almaty. His article "Russian Is the State Language in Kazakhstan" in summer 2012 created much controversy in Kazakhstan's society.

44. Fierman, "Language and Identity," 179.

45. Abdigaliev, "Iazikovaia politika v Kazakhstane" [Language policy in Kazakhstan], *Kazakhskaia missiia*. In an interview with the author (September 2014, Almaty), Abdigaliev voiced this opinion again, recounting that "for more than twenty years of independence the regime only achieved language divisions where many Russian-speaking people do not speak and are not able to understand and communicate in Kazakh language." Abdigaliev believed this situation presented a threat to the future stable development of Kazakhstan as a unified society.

46. Abdigaliev, *Kazakhskaia missiia*, 238.

47. Fierman, "Language and Identity," 178-79.

48. See, for example, Nysanbaev, *Evraziiskaia doktrina*.

49. Steen, "Ethnic Relations," 79.

50. I use this concept of contemporary Kazakhstan's ideology to identify a technique that employs a controlled ambiguity of the discursive field of identities issued and used by the regime. In this manner two opposing identities of supposedly Kazakhstani (civic and depoliticized ethnic identity under the state-belonging identity) and Kazakh (predominantly ethnic calling for legitimation via primordialism) are used interchangeably based on audiences and contexts in which these messages and discourses are addressed by the regime and President Nazarbayev.

51. Junisbai and Junisbai, "Democratic Choice of Kazakhstan."

52. In December 2011 on the eve of the Independence Day celebration (the twentieth anniversary) a six-month labor conflict of oil workers resulted in bloodshed after unknown demonstrators attacked the main square. This became one of the darkest, most violent incidents in post-1991 Kazakhstan.

53. See Bissenova, "Post-Socialist Dreamworlds"; Koch, "Monumental and the Miniature"; and Laszczkowski, "Building the Future."

54. See Kudaibergenova, "Compartmentalized Ideology and Nation-Building."

55. Author's interview with a Kazakh national-patriots, anonymous, January 2013, Almaty.

56. Sarym, "Povestka kazakhskih natsionalistov."

57. See the "anti-heptyl" movement website, http://antigeptil.com. It is a rather spontaneous movement with no clear present leadership. It is identified with provocative manifestations against Russia's position and inaccurate calculations of rocket launches from the Baikonur cosmodrome that have resulted in spills of the toxic substance heptyl. For further discussion of the Baikonur disputes, see Ganga, "Baikonur, Bagys and the Legacy of Soviet-Era Territorial Leases."

58. Author's interview with the leading parliamentary fraction of the Ak Zhol party, August 2012, Almaty. The interview source who wished to remain anonymous stated that "the regime started making systematic mistakes in terms of not stopping political gossip about lending land to China or preparing a "half-baked" Doctrine of National Unity (2009) demonstrate that it is no longer capable of producing new ideas or sustaining its quasi-ideology."

59. Author's interview with a Kazakh national-patriot, anonymous, January 2013, Almaty.

60. Author's interview with the leading parliamentary fraction of the Ak Zhol party, August 2012.

61. See Kudaibergenova, "Use and Abuse."

CHAPTER 3. APPROPRIATING AND CONTESTING THE NATION

1. Rudenshiold, "Ethnic Dimensions," 609.

2. See also Adams, *Spectacular State*, for a similar argument in Uzbekistan.

3. The 2016 terrorist attacks in the major Kazakh cities of Aqtobe and Almaty demonstrate this growing threat adding to the previous attacks in Taraz and even the country's capital Astana in 2014. Whether continuous attacks are possible or not, the danger discourse creates significant support for believing in this danger. For further discussion on the discourse of danger, see Totaro, "To Protect or to Nightmarize?"

4. The cities of Aqtobe and Aktau are located close to the town of Zhanaozen where, in December 2011, an ongoing labor dispute resulted in clashes with the policy (for unknown reasons) and led to at least seventeen deaths and numerous imprisonments of labor union activists.

5. S. Duvanov, "Kuda delis' blednolitsye?" (http://www.respublika-kaz.info/news/politics/47028/, last accessed on July 25, 2016. The link no longer works, as the site, and whole oppositional paper, has been blocked); Central Asia Monitor, "Pochemu nekazakhi ne podderzhali aktsii protesta i voobshche anolitichny?" [Why did non-Kazakhs not support the protest and why are they apolitical?], June 10, 2016, accessed July 25, 2016, http://camonitor.kz/23731-pochemu-neka zahi-ne-podderzhali-akcii-protesta-i-voobsche-apolitichny.html; Polovinko, Radio Free Europe Report on Land Reform in Kazakhstan, 2016, accessed July 25, 2016, http://rus.azattyq.org/a/kazakhstan-prodazha-zemli-protest-v-atyrau/27695526.html; Kazakh diaspora living in Russia also wrote an open letter to President Nazarbayev asking him not to sell or lend Kazakh land, Radio Free Europe, accessed July 25, 2016, http://rus.azattyq.org/a/kazakhi-v-rossii-o-zemelnom -voprose/27736678.html.

6. See Burkhanov and Chen, "Kazakh Perspective"; Laruelle and Peyrouse, *Chinese Question*; and Syroezhkin, "Social Perceptions."

7. Anonymous interview with the author, August 2012, Almaty.

8. Salyq Zimanov, "Ne nado rasshatyvat' godusarstvennye ustoi" [No need to shake the state foundation], *Kazakhstanskaya Pravda*, January 21, 1995, 3. The author is the chairman of the Committee for Constitutional Law-making and Human Rights of the Verkhovnogo Soveta of the Republic of Kazakhstan.

9. Cummings, "Legitimation and Identification"; and Ó Beacháin and Kevlihan, "Threading a Needle."

10. Adams, *Spectacular State*.

11. See, for example, Cummings, "Legitimation and Identification."

12. Marat, "Nation Branding in Central Asia"; and Solska, "Citizenship."

13. Shortly after independence, Latvian officials introduced language tests for the employees of all official offices (including the airports). Those who did not pass the language test were dismissed from their jobs. This was followed by regular language checks by language officials, and fines were issued for inability to communicate in Latvian with customers (see, e.g., Kolstø, *Nation-Building*). Testimonies of noncitizens during my fieldwork in Latvia confirmed that language checks are still a norm of everyday life, and constitute the main reason that non-Latvian speakers and those who fail to master the language seek jobs outside the city center in Riga (where the parliament and most ministries are situated) and work in special Russian-speaking urban enclaves such as like Kengaraks or Maskavas iela in Riga. The situation is slightly better in the predominantly Russian-speaking regions and cities such as Daugavpils.

14. From the first official elections to the fifth parliament (with a renewed structure as of 1937) in 1993 to more recent victories of the Harmony Party in the mid-2000s, there were about twelve representatives of Russian elites (out of one hundred in total) in the Latvian Parliament (Saeima) (Bela et al., "Latvija").

15. Author's interview with Yuriy Petropavlovsky, a PCTVL leader, noncitizen, August 2013, Riga.

16. Author's anonymous interview with a former member of the Latvian Supreme Council (1990–1993) and a member of the pro-Russian movement to save minority schools, August 2013, Riga.

17. Author's anonymous interview, August 2013, Riga.

18. Author's interview with an anonymous Russian-speaking political activist, August 2013, Riga.

19. Anonymous interview with the leader of the pro-minority rights party, August 2013.

20. Kudaibergenova, "Compartmentalized Ideology"; and Kudaibergenova, "Compartmentalized Ideology and Nation-Building."

21. See Kudaibergenova, "Use and Abuse."

22. For more details, see Masanov, Zhulduzbek, and Erofeeva, *Nauchnoe znanie*.

23. See Adams, *Spectacular State*; Cummings, *Symbolism and Power*; Kudaibergenova, "'Imagining Community'"; Marat "Nation Branding in Central Asia"; Marat, "State-Propagated Narratives"; and Matveeva "Legitimising Central Asian Authoritarianism."

24. For example, the Soviet Encyclopedia entries on Latvians, Kazakhs, Estonians, Ukrainians, and other Soviet republics describe them as "historically predetermined" communities and territories bound by the ancestral and historical connection.

25. Ó Beacháin and Kevlihan, "Threading the Needle."

26. By Kazakh-type monuments I mean the depiction of ethnic Kazakh legendary warriors and rulers, which became ubiquitous reminders of the Kazakhified public sphere in major urban centers of Kazakhstan. I discuss this issue separately in the context of nationalism and gender representation in "Between the State and the Artist," but similar arguments can be found in Ibrayeva, *Iskusstvo Kazakhstana* and Fauve "Tale of Two Statues."

27. See, for example, Adams, *Spectacular State*; March, "Use and Abuse of History"; and March, "State Ideology."

28. For example, Karimov, "Ne postroiv novyi dom—ne razrushai starogo," February 12, 1993, in Karimov, "Uzbekistan na poroge XXI veka."

29. Interview with political analyst, April 2011, Almaty.

30. From Programma Sotsial-Demokraticheskoi partii Soglasie [Program of the Social-

Democratic Party Harmony], http://www.saskana.info/o-soglasii/programmy/polnaja-program
ma/ [no longer available].

31. Centrala Velesanu Komisija (Latvian Central Electoral Commission) election results.

32. According to SKDS opinion polls, results for 2015, http://baltictimes.delfi.lv/opinion_poll
_shows_usakovs_has_high_approval_ratings_in_riga__despite_latvian_pm_labelling_him
____pinocchio___/ and at http://bnn-news.com/73-riga-residents-approve-usakovs-15383.

33. SKDS opinion poll results, http://www.leta.lv/eng/home/important/80ECF258–2F56–4A
8B-BD03–104658EF64D8/?text.

34. Author's interview with political analyst, April 2013, Riga.

35. Programma Sotsial-Demokraticheskoi partii Soglasie, 16, in "Integration and the development of inclusive society."

36. This percentage included only citizens of the Republic of Latvia age eighteen or older who
were able to vote in the referendum.

37. Author's interview with a leader of the National Alliance, April 2014, Riga. Dombrovskis
was one of the long-surviving prime ministers in Latvian political history post-1991. However, the
political opinions shared by my interviewees suggest that Dombrovskis remained in power because
of the persistence of the Unity party's rule. In November 2013 he resigned after a tragic event in
Zolitude, a district in Riga where a supermarket building collapsed, killing fifty-four people.

38. Programma Sotsial-Demokraticheskoi partii Soglasie, 16, in "Integration and the development of inclusive society."

39. Centrala Velesanu Komisija (Latvian Central Electoral Commission).

40. Interview with the political analyst Juris Rosenvalds, April 2013, Riga.

41. Steen, "Elite and Mass Confidence," 128.

42. Steen, "Elite and Mass Confidence," 144.

43. Steen "Elite and Mass Confidence," 144.

44. Linz and Stepan, Problems of Democratic Transition.

CHAPTER 4. "LOST IN TRANSLATION"

1. Series of interviews with Anna, a middle-aged ethnic Russian from the Kengaraks district in
Latvia, February 2013, March 2013, August 2013, and February 2014, Riga.

2. Anonymous interview with Alyona (name changed), March 2013, Riga.

3. Interview with a Kazakh resident who had a Russian passport obtained in the late 1990s,
August 2018, Almaty region.

4. Here I quote Tatjana Zhdanok, a European member of parliament (MP) from Latvia and
a legendary Russian-speakers' human rights activist in Demurin, Sovremennaia evropeiskaia et-
nokratiia, 8. Zhdanok is a very famous and controversial figure in Latvian politics. She was an active
member of the Latvian Communist Party and in 1998 was stripped of her MP position in the Riga
municipality due to her support of the Communist Party after the collapse of the Soviet Union and
her participation in the opposition Interfront organization on the eve of Latvian independence.
Interfront was held in high disregard in Latvian history as an enemy of the state that impeded independence. Following Article 25 of the Latvian Citizenship Law, which prohibits anyone opposed
to Latvian independence or actively involved in the Communist Party of Latvia from applying for
citizenship and thus from political rights, Zhdanok was officially stripped of her duties. Previously
she had already gained Latvian citizenship in court. In 2002 her name was removed from the parliamentary election list following the similar findings of the Inner Audit Commission of the Latvian
Communist Party committee (in Latvia, it is also described as a black list). She appealed to the
European Court of Human Rights and won her case against Latvia five days after her first election

to the European Parliament as the only pro-Russian MP from Latvia in 2004. Before that she was actively involved as a leader of Equal Human Rights for All People in Latvia (Za Prava Cheloveka v Latvii—abbreviated ZaPCHEL or PCTLV). See Alena Vysotskaya's analysis in "'Alliance for Human Rights in a United Latvia'"; and Cheskin, "Synthesis and Conflict."

5. In reality the migration to the Baltic states was restricted and available only based on a specific legal application or professional mobility (*professional'noe raspredelenie*) for highly skilled workers and professionals, such as engineers, military personnel, industrial managers, and so on. But this upward professional mobility was predominantly Russian or Slavic. For example, the demographic composition of Latvia's minorities consists of European minorities (Russians, Belarusians, Ukrainians, Germans, Poles, Lithuanians, and Jews) with almost no Caucasian or Central Asian minority groups, such as Georgians, Kazakhs, Uzbeks. During my archival search on the Europeanization of values in Latvian legislation I came across a confidential 1994 Council of Europe report on recommendations regarding the Latvian parliament's heated debates on the matter of quota system. Unfortunately, confidentiality prohibits direct citations from the report. Paraphrasing the document, however, indicates a very "understanding" position toward Latvia's restricted citizenship policy in regard to migrants it never wanted to have on its soil but had no power to decide at the time of the Soviet occupation.

6. Marat, "Nation Branding in Central Asia."

7. Constitution of the Republic of Kazakhstan, January 28, 1993. Invalidated with acceptance of the new constitution in 1995.

8. The war on monuments is a distinct and fascinating field of discussion in all post-Soviet states, including Latvia and Kazakhstan. In Riga the Pushkin Monument behind the Russian theater caused mass public "allergy" and discontent among local Latvian residents. In June 2014 the dwarf version of the classic Kazakh figure Abay next to the much bigger figure of Evgeniy Mihaelis in the Eastern town of Ust-Kamenogorsk sparked a wave of scandals on Kazakh-speaking blogs and social media (see http://tengrinews.kz/picture_art/pamyatnik-abayu-i-mihaelisu-v-ust-kamenogorske-vozmutil-ka-zahstantsev-257539/). Finally, a lawsuit was prompted by a poster advertising a gay club at the intersection of two streets, Kurmangazy (named for a famous Kazakh musician) and Alexander Pushkin (the famous Russian poet). The two were portrayed kissing on the lips, which came to the attention of Human Rights Watch (see http://www.hrw.org/news/2014/10/01/kazakhstan-lawsuits-over-same-sex-kiss-poster). For an analytical discussion of the war on monuments, see Danzer 2009 review of minority response; on war monuments in Estonia, see Burch and Smith, "Empty Spaces"; on the Kyrgyz elite approach to Lenin's statue, see Cummings "Leaving Lenin"; on Tashkent, see Bell, "Redefining National Identity"; and on monument art in Kazakhstan, see Ibrayeva, *Iskusstvo Kazakhstana*.

9. Cummings, "Legitimation and Identification," 184.

10. In my sociological and demographic analysis, I rely on official data defining ethnocultural groups by their ethnicity, for example, as Germans or ethnic Russians. In the official discourse, the out-migration of ethnic Russians and Germans was also documented as the first destination, for example, the Russian Federation or Germany, which were considered their ethnic homelands (also known as *ethnicheskaia rodina*). The ethnic denominator remained a significant influence in the categorizing groupings and identities of citizens in post-Soviet states like Kazakhstan.

11. KISI 2010 report, "The Social-Political Stratification of Kazakhstani Society," 9.

12. CIA Factbook estimates of language background in Kazakhstan (2001 data). The level of Kazakh language proficiency and application in the public sphere is predicted to grow even further. Data from the Ministry of Education of Kazakhstan (2010) show that in 2004 more than 55 percent of all schoolchildren studied in Kazakh language and 39 percent in Russian; in the 2008–9 academic year, Russian-speaking education dropped to 35 percent and the Kazakh-speaking sector grew to 60

percent. In the 2004–5 academic year ethnic Kazakhs constituted 69 percent of all schoolchildren, and ethnic Russians—almost 20 percent; in 2008–9 Kazakhs were the vast majority, 73 percent, and Russians represented 19 percent of all schoolchildren.

13. Data based on Estonian Statistics Agency and www.estonia.eu (Citizenship section) and the Police and Border Guard Board, Estonia.

14. The numbers were provided by the CSCE [OSCE] Mission to Latvia in January 1994.

15. In the period from 1995 to 2010, 16,207 of candidates for naturalization who took the Latvian language test failed to pass it. The failing rate for the history test is even lower than that—approximately 4 percent or 5,459 out of 114,104.

16. See Grigas, *Beyond Crimea*; Knott, "Quasi-Citizenship"; Laruelle, "Why No Kazakh Novorossiya?"; and Sasse, *Crimea Question*.

17. The problem of human rights abuse of the Russian-speaking population in Latvia is a key feature of the PCTVL web presence (see http://www.pctvl.lv) and of the ZaRYA micro-blog at http://www.imhoclub.lv/ru/material/doktor_berdnikov_i_latishskaja_politzoologija. One of ZaRYA's leaders, Illarion Girs, shared his opinion with me in an online discussion by pointing to my previous connection with one of the movement's actors who in his latest interview said: "The project of political nation in Latvia is dismantled. This is my feeling [about it]. This idea was supported by many Latvian liberals and many Russian-speaking opinion leaders. But I think that the only possibility [for Latvian society to exist] is a model of ethnopluralism. Every [ethno]community should develop on its own. Maybe this is not the best way but if the united society is not working then what else should we hope for?"

18. CSCE Helsinki Document 1992, "The Challenges of Change" High Commissioner on National Minorities, Mandate, point 3, p. 9.

19. "Early Warning and Early Action: Preventing Inter-Ethnic Conflict," speech by Max van der Stoel, OSCE High Commissioner on National Minorities at the Royal Institute of International Affairs, London, July 9, 1999. Source: HCNM.GAL/5/99.

20. Helsinki Document 1992, part II, CSCE High Commissioner on National Minorities, "Early Warning," points 11a, 11b, p. 9.

21. CSCE Mission to Latvia, Activity Report No. 2, January 1994.

22. This categorization of "Soviet-era migrants," the majority of whom were non-Latvian and thus qualified as both the ethnic minority and a minority group (under the hegemony of the dominant pro-Latvian group) was justified by the legal continuity of the Latvian pre-Soviet state, which, according to confidential data and recommendations of the Council of Europe (CoE), for example, was widely supported in many European observer organizations. The unspoken policy of noninvolvement in domestic dealings with migrants framed as observers' desire not to intervene in domestic policymaking and decisions was highlighted in the CoE recommendations on the 1994 Citizenship Law, for example. The counter-rhetoric of the majority of Latvian parties who were present in the parliament beginning in 1993 up to the 2000s when Latvia joined the EU also highlighted and even exacerbated anti-involvement and "sovereign" decision-making in Latvia as a state and as a nation. These debates were highlighted in *Diena*'s op-eds and interviews and confirmed in my content analysis of the newspaper, especially in 1997–99.

23. Russian delegation to the CSCE Forum, Press Conference by Deputy Minister of Foreign Affairs of the Russian Federation, V. I. Churkin, January 27, 1994, about the Russian Federation's relations with the Baltic states, available in the OSCE archives.

24. CSCE Delegation of Latvia, Statement made at the Twenty-Eight Meeting of the Permanent (CSCE) Committee and distributed at the request of the CSCE Delegation of Latvia, Vienna, July 14, 1994, p. 3.

25. Author's interview with a PCTVL leader, anonymous, August 2013, Riga.

26. Although this particular respondent did not object to having his name used in the publication, in light of intensifying debates about the Latgale People's Republic, for example (see Paul Goble's "Pro-Moscow Groups Launch Websites for 'Peoples Republics' in Latvia and Lithuania"), I have maintained the anonymity of the majority of my Russian-speaking activist respondents for their security.

27. Just before the extraordinary fourth reading of the Citizenship Law (July 22, 1994) the coalition of the ruling party Latvia's Way and Farmer's Union dissolved. President Ulmanis who was in contact with OSCE and Council of Europe high officials urged the parliament to accept the law, which was done on July 22, 1994. After that the president asked the leader of the far-right LNNK, Andrejs Krastins, to form the government. The party soon formed a list for the proposed government, which included two American-Latvian businessmen—Aristids Lambergs and Pauls Dzintars Kalins. The LNNK proposed the government in coalition with the Farmer's Union and TB far-right party (after 1994 TB united with LNNK and formed a national bloc currently known as TB-LNNK-Visu Latvija representing far-right Latvian politics and a long-lived party). The LNNK coalition government failed to gain confidence and a new government proposed by Latvia's Way was voted in only on August 15, 1994, after more than two months with no government. The new government won forty-nine votes in favor, thirty-three against, and seven abstentions. Information from the OSCE Mission to Latvia Reports No. 6 (July 19, 1994), No. 7 (August 1, 1994), No. 8 (August 18, 1994), Spot Report (August 22, 1994), and Spot Report (September 16, 1994).

28. Initial naturalization rates, which were based on quotas prioritizing the younger population of noncitizens, did not reach even 10 percent of anticipated rates.

29. Pettai, "Explaining Ethnic Politics," 129.

30. Latvia and Russia were able to sign the border agreement only in 2007, after a series of internal and foreign policy disputes, including Russia's disapproval of the Latvian parliament's passing of the resolution on its Soviet occupation and a local dispute in the transborder region of Abrene, which was supposed to be returned to Russia in exchange for a different part of territory.

31. I specifically draw more attention to the work of the OSCE in this chapter because the Council of Europe and other European organizations did not focus on the monitoring throughout the whole period before Latvia's accession to the EU. The organizational as well as the structural separation in this sense make the pressure from different networks clearer in the European context.

32. But the role of the HCNM in the post-Yugoslav or Nagorno-Karabakh conflicts was of course quite different from that in Latvia, Ukraine (until 2000), Hungary, Slovakia, Romania, Kyrgyzstan, and Kazakhstan or Estonia because it related to conflict resolution in the latter case and to conflict prevention in the former cases. There were several matters in the northeastern part of Estonia (with Russian-speaking secession activism) and in Crimea (formerly an autonomous republic in Ukraine), but these did not rise to the level of conflict resolution in other parts of Europe at the time.

33. Report by the head of the OSCE Mission to Latvia, Ambassador Peter Semneby to the Permanent Council of the OSCE, December 14, 2000.

34. OSCE Mission to Latvia, Report No. 61, December 3, 1999.

35. PC.DEC/28, OSCE Permanent Council Twelfth Plenary Meeting, PC Journal No. 12, point 5, Decision No. 28, p. 1.

36. Eglitis, Imagining the Nation.

37. Tokayev, Svet i ten', 10.

38. See http://www.osce.org/odihr/elections/78750.

39. ODIHR Interim Report No. 2, on early parliamentary elections, see http://www.osce.org/odihr/elections/Kazakhstan/86898?download=true.

40. Statement by the Permanent Representative of the Republic of Kazakhstan to the OSCE, Ambassador Doulat Kyanyshev at the 595th Permanent Council Meeting, March 2, 2006, PC.DEL /170/06, http://www.osce.org/pc/18377?download=true.

41. The ODIHR Interim Report on the 2019 presidential elections cites this requirement as "according to the 2005 CEC resolution, the language test consists of writing an essay, reading with appropriate diction, and public speaking for 15 minutes. There are no precise assessment criteria for the language test," June 9, 2019, presidential elections, ODIHR Interim Report, https://www.osce .org/odihr/elections/kazakhstan/420857?download=true.

42. See Kudaibergenova, "Body Globalized," for a discussion of the growing influence of Instagram and social media on activism in Kazakhstan.

43. See Almaz Kumenov's report on the rise of activism before the June 2019 presidential elections in Kazakhstan: https://eurasianet.org/kazakhstan-piles-pressure-on-activists-ahead-of-election.

44. The series with banners and posters in Kazakhstan started on April 23, with Asya Tulesova and Beibarys Tolymbekov's banner at the Almaty marathon. After they were arrested the artistic and activist community began broad support for them and protests against their arrests. On April 29, the Almaty-based contemporary artist Roman Zakharov posted a banner on the central Almaty street, quoting Kazakhstan's constitution: "The only source of state power is people"; he too was arrested but then released amid protests. On May 6, 2019, Aslan Sagutdinov was arrested in the Kazakh city of Uralsk for carrying an empty poster protesting what he saw as unfair and staged presidential elections. Zhanbota Alzhanova was arrested on May 9, 2019, for posting a photo of an "imaginary" poster in Astana on her Facebook page at the beginning of May.

45. From the Oyan, Qazaqstan manifesto, https://www.the-village.kz/village/city/news-city /5961-grazhdanskie-aktivisty-prezentovali-deklaratsiyu-oyan-kazahstan (in Russian).

46. On June 21, 2019, during the "30 Years of Leadership" conference with the participation of the former president Nazarbayev, the head of the Almaty Zhas-Otan subgroup of the ruling Nur Otan party suggested erecting another monument to the first president, https://holanews.kz/view/ news/39129. Nursultan A. Nazarbayev said he was against such initiatives unless people wanted to do it.

47. Tokayev, *Svet i ten'*.

48. The fact that Kazakhstan has experienced harmonious interethnic relations for a long time, almost throughout the twentieth century, was acknowledged by the HCNM, for example, in his correspondence with Kazakh officials in the 1990s.

49. Civic ideas of "Kazakhstani" patriotism are still closely tied to the ethnic specifications of various groups, such as Tatars, Russians, Koreans, and so on, where the ritualization of ethnic differences is promoted by the state (through the Assembly of Peoples of Kazakhstan and their cultural subgroups in every oblast), which creates a very strange model of semi-civic nation-building. This is largely a construct of the Soviet (civic) man, which overcomes cultural and ethnic distinctions but still celebrates them in the form of spectacular politics of the Peoples' Friendship (Adams, *Spectacular State*).

50. Recommendations to the Government of Kazakhstan; letter of the CSCE High Commissioner on National Minorities, CSCE Communication No. 26, April 29, 1994. HCNM letter to the Foreign Minister of the Republic of Kazakhstan His Excellency Mr. Kanat Saudabayev. Ref: No. 2357/94/L.

51. Except for the dispute over the use of any nonstate language in the private sphere, which was continuously debated by the HCNM and Latvian officials (e.g., President Vike-Freiberga in 1999–2001), the domain of Latvian language superiority over any other language in the country was almost never questioned by the European organizations. The legitimacy of the Latvian trauma of

occupation and its rightful return to Fortress Europe defined the frameworks of the pressure that could exerted in that field.

52. Fierman, "Identity, Symbolism, and the Politics of Language"; and Fierman, "Russian in Post-Soviet Central Asia." See also Peyrouse, "Nationhood."

53. The issue of total indigenization of public offices (from the Saeima to strategic bases like airports) that happened right after independence in Latvia was never raised in any of the recommendations or reports. The representation of minority groups in official offices was never a prerequisite either to Latvian democratization or its membership in any European organizations.

54. A good example of this ethnolingual mapping is Gerold Belger, a noted Kazakh writer and translator and an ethnic German from the first wave of Stalinist deportations. He grew up in a Kazakh village in Northern Kazakhstan and is fluent in his native German and his native Kazakh (as he regards it) and he speaks Russian fluently but with a very distinguishable Kazakh accent. He has translated many Kazakh-language classic Soviet literature, such as Nurpeisov's *Kan men Ter* (Blood and Sweat) and has become known as an influential Kazakh philosopher and opinion leader on Kazakh nationalism. Gera-aga, as Kazakhs tenderly call him (Belger is very popular and highly regarded among most Kazakh nationalists) publishes a lot in the Kazakh-speaking opposition press. Yet in many contexts when the name of Gera-aga came up during my interviews, all my respondents (even Russians) referred to him as an ethnic German who "brilliantly speaks Kazakh" (*velikolepno vladeet kazakhskim iazikom*). The persistence of ethnic identification regardless of the language spoken is also seen in analyses of the census and other sociological data used in this study.

55. Laitin, *Identity in Formation*, x.

56. As Bhavna Dave observed (*Kazakhstan: Ethnicity and Power*), Kazakh language proficiency (99.4 percent of knowledge stated in the 1999 census among ethnic Kazakhs) does not always represent the real picture. Ethnic Kazakhs appropriate Kazakh language as *native* sometimes without at least an intermediate level of proficiency. Ethnolingual entitlement to a specific language like Kazakh to ethnic Kazakhs is one of the strongholds of the Soviet codification of ethnicity practices.

57. Cummings, "Legitimation and Identification"; Ó Beacháin and Kevlihan, "Threading a Needle"; and Schatz, "Framing Strategies."

58. Badalov, " Oralmans"; Cerny, "Going Where the Grass Is Greener"; Diener, "Kazakhstan's Kin State Diaspora"; Dubuisson Genina, "Claiming an Ancestral Homeland"; and Kuscu, "Kazakhstan's Oralman Project."

CHAPTER 5. HOMOGENIZING THE NATION

1. In their study on the post-Nazarbayev regime change, a group of local political analysts (Satpayev et al., *Sumerechnaia zona*) established that the roots of this anxiety are in "the complex situation" that has no formal political mechanisms for regime change or delegation of power, in which "the ruling elite is divided into competing groups" and thus "cannot be expected to provide a viable scenario of power continuity" (8–9). According to the experts and their opinion polls, this has led to a situation in which "not only experts and opposition but also members of the ruling elites" and ordinary citizens "are startled by this question" (9). The sociological findings of this study show that intra-elite competition and debates are the leading possible risks for the country (91.7 percent of respondents believed this in 2011–13). See chapter 3 on risks in Satpayev et al., *Sumerechnaia zona*, 128. When President Nazarbayev resigned, many in Kazakhstan expressed a sense of anxiety about who would replace the first president. It was expressed in responses, posts, and comments on social media but also in news outlets.

2. OECD Country Notes: Recent Changes in Migration Movements and Policies, http://www .oecd.org/els/mig/LATVIA.pdf.

3. Latvian Centrala Velesanu Komisija (Central Electoral Commission of Latvia), the Twelfth Saeima election results.

4. It is widely accepted in the field that Kazakhstan's regime and identity are "based on positive aspirations" instead of negative discussions and legacies of "whether the Soviet past was good or bad, but rather endorse[ed] it in its entirety as a shared historical experience which made the country what it is" (Matveeva, "LegitimisingCentral Asian Authoritarianism," 1105). The regime specifically focuses on future-oriented projects such as Kazakhstan-2030 and Kazakhstan-2050 (modernizing projects) rather than on the tragic recounting of the Soviet past. However, as other commentators, including myself have pointed out, this opinion is not entirely popular among Kazakh nationalists, who do not openly oppose modernizing projects but challenge the regime to nationalize the ideology even further.

5. Castells, *Communication Power*; quote from Zepa and Kļave, "National Identity," 18.

6. Zepa and Kļave, "National Identity."

7. From an interview with a Russian activist, anonymous, August 2013, Riga.

8. Valery Kravtsov in an interview quoted in the report "The Last Prisoners of the Cold War: The Stateless People of Latvia in Their Own Words," 2006, 13–14; emphasis added.

9. Interview with Russian political activist, August 2013, Daugavpils.

10. Rose, *Baltic Barometer III*, and *V*, surveys from 1997, 2000.

11. Zepa and Kļave, "National Identity," 27.

12. Zepa and Kļave, "National Identity," 36.

13. Zepa and Kļave, "National Identity," 24.

14. Zepa and Kļave, "National Identity," 83–89.

15. Author's interview with a Russian-speaking Latvian political activist, anonymous, August 2013, Riga.

16. *Doktrina natsional'nogo soglasiia Kazakhstana*, 1. Project of the Assembly of Peoples of Kazakhstan, downloaded from the Kazinform official news agency on November 5, 2009. (Doctrine of National Unity of Kazakhstan Project, November 2009—initial project not the second amended project in January 2010).

17. Dave, "Shrinking Reach of the State"; Fierman, "Language and Identity in Kazakhstan"; and Fierman "Identity, Symbolism, and the Politics of Language."

18. *Doktrina natsional'nogo soglasiia Kazakhstana*, 4.

19. *Doktrina natsional'nogo soglasiia Kazakhstana*, 4.

20. *Doktrina natsional'nogo soglasiia Kazakhstana*, 7; and more on languages, 6–7.

21. *Doktrina natsional'nogo soglasiia Kazakhstana*, 2.

22. "Osobennosti identitchnosti i konsolidatsii naseleniia Kazakhstana (mart 2009)" [Features of identity and consolidation of the population of Kazakhstan, March 2009]. This study also included four bilingual focus groups among a randomly chosen sample.

23. "Osobennosti identitchnosti," 16.

24. Kudaibergenova, "Use and Abuse."

25. The presidential announcement of the Doctrine of National Unity in December 2009 had activated the political participation of Kazakh national-patriots. The Kazakh writer Mukhtar Shakhanov became the main standard-bearer of this dispersed movement of Kazakh nationalists. They threatened to organize a public hunger strike on the main Republican Square in the center of Almaty in protest against the Kazakhstani nation, which was supposed to become the main state-forming political community. The threat remained active until new amendments were promised, and Kazakh nationalists replaced Kazakhstani concept of Kazakh nation. See "Doktrina natsional'nogo razdora" [Doctrine of national dispute], http://www.kursiv.kz/freshkursiv/details/tendencii-weekly/doktrina-nacionalnogo-razdora/.

26. For the discussion, see the report *Kazakhstan sporit o natsional'noi politike* [Kazakhstan debates about the national policy], February 2, 2010, http://www.dw.de/dw/article/0,,5204291,00 .html, accessed September 25, 2012.

27. For more information on Vladimir Kozlov's prosecution, see http://www.vladimirkozlov .org/about/biography.aspx, accessed November 13, 2014.

28. Interview with Burikhan Nurmukhambetov, August 2012, Almaty.

29. I discuss this in precise detail in Kudaibergenova, "Mankurts, Kazakh "Russians" and "Shala" Kazakhs," where I precisely argue that the ethnolingual distinction no longer plays a crucial role in dividing the two groups or identifying their agenda. In many respects regarding national development, corruption scandals, ecological protection movements, and identity-related problems (where we belong and where are we going) are identical in the addresses of various Kazakh-nationalist-led and cosmopolitan movements. Some of my key respondents on both sides of this "artificial" divide also do not consider themselves to be solely divided based on these categorizations of nationality or language acquisition. Furthermore, in the paper, which is based on my extended fieldwork in Kazakhstan and novels (I use the example of *Mankurtstan*, a recent novel about the generation of Kazakhstan's citizens who lost their identification with the country and nation), I conclude that belonging to a specific group in most recent generations is related to other factors such as education, lifestyle, and class rather than language acquisition skills.

30. *Strategiia* sociological survey "Osobennosti identitchnosti," based on a representative sample of 1,537 respondents in all fourteen regions and two principal cities.

CONCLUSION

1. Interview with the author, September 2012, Almaty.

2. Isaacs, *Party System Formation*, 159.

3. Muižnieks, "Daugavpils Hydro Station"; Plakans, *Latvians*.

4. See Edward Schatz's discussion of "soft authoritarianism," in "Soft Authoritarian Tool Kit"; and Cummings, *Kazakhstan*.

5. I demonstrate the seeming shift in the opposition agenda in Kudaibergenova, "Use and Abuse."

BIBLIOGRAPHY

Aasland, Aadne. "Citizenship Status and Social Exclusion in Estonia and Latvia." *Journal of Baltic Studies* 33, no. 1 (2002): 57–77.

Abdigaliev, Berik. *Kazakhskaia missiia: sbornik statei* [The Kazakh mission: a collection of articles]. Almaty: Dayk Press, 2007.

Abdigaliev, Berik. *Politizatsiia ethnichnosti: protsessy, mekhanizmi, posledstviia* [The politicization of ethnicity: processes, mechanisms, and outcomes]. Almaty: Ush Qiyan, 2003.

Abuseitova, Meruyet, Nurbulat Masanov, and Anatoly Khazanov. *Istoriia Kazakhstana i Tsentral'noi Azii* [History of Kazakhstan and Central Asia]. Almaty: Dayk-Press, 2001.

Abylkhozhin, Zhuldyzbek. *Istoriia Kazakhstana: narodi y kulturi* [A history of Kazakhstan: people and culture]. Almaty: Dayk-Press, 2000.

Adams, Laura L. "Globalization, Universalism, and Cultural Form." *Comparative Studies in Society and History* 50, no. 3 (2008): 614–40.

Adams, Laura L. "Modernity, Postcolonialism, and Theatrical Form in Uzbekistan." *Slavic Review* 64, no. 2 (2005): 333–54.

Adams, Laura L. *The Spectacular State: Culture and National Identity in Uzbekistan.* Durham, NC: Duke University Press, 2010.

Adams, Laura, and Assel Rustemova. "Mass Spectacle and Styles of Governmentality in Kazakhstan and Uzbekistan." *Europe-Asia Studies* 61, no. 7 (2009): 1249–76.

Adamson, Walter L. *Hegemony and Revolution: A Study of Antonio Gramsci's Political and Cultural Theory.* Berkeley: University of California Press, 1983.

Akiner, Shirin. *The Formation of Kazakh Identity: From Tribe to Nation-State.* London: Royal Institute of International Affairs, 1995.

Alexander, Jeffrey C. *Trauma: A Social Theory.* Hoboken, NJ: John Wiley, 2013.

Amanzholova, Dina. *Na izlome: Alash v etnopoliticheskoi istorii Kazakhstana* [On the edge: Alash in the ethnopolitical history of Kazakhstan]. Almaty: Taymas, 2009.

Anacker, Shonin. "Geographies of Power in Nazarbayev's Astana." *Eurasian Geography and Economics* 45, no. 7 (2004): 515–33.

Anderson, Benedict. *Imagined Communities: Reflections on the Origin and Spread of Nationalism.* London: Verso Books, 1993.

Angrick, Andrej, and Peter Klein. *The "Final Solution" in Riga: Exploitation and Annihilation, 1941–1944.* War and Genocide, Book 14. New York: Berghahn Books, 2009.

Annus, Epp. "The Ghost of Essentialism and the Trap of Binarism: Six Theses on the Soviet Empire." *Nationalities Papers* 43, no. 4 (2015): 595–614.

Annus, Epp. "Layers of Colonial Rule in the Baltics: Nation-Building, the Soviet Rule and the Affectivity of a Nation." In *(Post) Colonialism across Europe: Transculturl History and National Memory,* edited by Dirk Göttsche and Axel Dunker, 353–78. Bielefeld: Aisthesis Verlag, 2014.

Annus, Epp. "The Problem of Soviet Colonialism in the Baltics." *Journal of Baltic Studies* 43, no. 1 (2012): 21–45.

Anonymous. "Latvia Unlikely to Ban Soviet Symbols Before Victory Day." RIA Novosti report, April 19, 2013. Accessed October 28, 2014, http://en.ria.ru/world/20130419/180720727/Latvia-Unlikely-to-Ban-Soviet-Symbols-Before-Victory-Day.html.

Anonymous. "Voices in Latvia Mobilizing for a Memory Contest on the 9th of May . . . ." Sites of Memory Blog, 2012. Accessed October 28, 2014, http://sitesofmemory.twoday.net/stories/5639312/.

Arel, Dominique. "Interpreting 'Nationality' and 'Language' in the 2001 Ukrainian Census." *Post-Soviet Affairs* 18, no. 3 (2002): 213–49.

Azadi, Almat. "V etoi voine klanov samoe glavnoe—vizhyt, ili, po krainei mere ne ne byt' ubitymi" [In this clan war, the most important thing is to survive, or at least not to get killed]. *DAT*, October 2010,

Badalov, Ulugbek. "The Oralmans: Migration of Ethnic Kazakhs from China to Europe." *Washington Review of Turkish and Eurasian Affairs*, November 2012. http://www.thewashingtonreview.org/articles/the-oralmans-migration-of-ethnic-kazakhs-from-china-to-europe.html.

Badie, Bernard, Dirk Berg-Schlosser, and Leonardo Morlino, eds. *International Encyclopedia of Political Science*. Thousand Oaks, CA: Sage, 2011.

Balibar, Etienne. "The Nation Form: History and Ideology." *Review (Fernand Braudel Center)* 13, no. 3 (Summer 1990): 329–61.

Bauman, Zygmunt. "Love in Adversity: On the State the Intellectuals, and the State of the Intellectuals." *Thesis Eleven* 31, no. 1 (1992): 81–104.

Beissinger, Mark, and Young, Crawford, eds. *Beyond State Crisis: Postcolonial Africa and Post-Soviet Eurasia in Comparative Perspective*. Washington, DC: Woodrow Wilson Center Press, 2002.

Bela, Baiba, Līga Rasnača, Mareks Niklass, Olga Rajevska, Feliciāna Rajevska, Didzis Stāvausis, Ilmārs Mežs et al. 2013 "Latvija. Pārskats par tautas attīstību 2012/2013: Ilgtspējīga nācija". Riga.

Bell, James. "Redefining National Identity in Uzbekistan: Symbolic Tensions in Tashkent's Official Public Landscape." *Ecumene* 6, no. 2 (1999): 183–213.

Bendix, Reinhard. "Concepts and Generalizations in Comparative Sociological Studies." *American Sociological Review* 28, no. 4 (August 1963): 532–39.

Best, Heinrich. "Marx or Mosca? An Inquiry into the Foundations of Ideocratic Regimes." *Historical Social Research/Historische Sozialforschung* 37, no. 1 (2012): 73–89.

Billig, Michael. *Banal Nationalism*. London: Sage, 1995.

Bissenova, Alima. "The Master Plan of Astana: Between the 'Art of Government' and the 'Art of Being Global.'" In *Ethnographies of the State in Central Asia: Performing Politics*, edited by Madeleine Reeves, Johan Rasanayagam, and Judith Beyer, 127–48. Bloomington: Indiana University Press, 2014.

Bissenova, Alima. "Post-Socialist Dreamworlds: Housing Boom and Urban Development in Kazakhstan." PhD diss., Cornell University, 2012.

Bogushevitch, Tatyana, and Aleksejs Dimitrovs. "Elections in Latvia: Status Quo for Minorities Remains." *JEMIE* 9, no. (2010): 72–89.

Brown, David. "Are There Good and Bad Nationalisms?" *Nations and Nationalism* 5, no. 2 (1999): 281–302.

Brubaker, Rogers. *Citizenship and Nationhood in France and Germany*. Cambridge, MA: Harvard University Press, 1992.

Brubaker, Rogers. *Ethnicity without Groups*. Cambridge, MA: Harvard University Press, 2004.

Brubaker, Rogers. "National Minorities, Nationalizing States, and External National Homelands in the New Europe." *Daedalus* 124, no. 2 (1995): 107–32.

Brubaker, Rogers. *Nationalism Reframed: Nationhood and the National Question in the New Europe.* Cambridge: Cambridge University Press, 1996.

Brubaker, Rogers. "Nationalizing States Revisited: Projects and Processes of Nationalization in Post-Soviet States." *Ethnic and Racial Studies* 34, no. 11 (2011): 1785–814.

Brubaker, Rogers. "Nationhood and the National Question in the Soviet Union and Post-Soviet Eurasia: An Institutionalist Account." *Theory and Society* 23, no. 1 (1994): 47–78.

Buchli, Victor. "Astana: Materiality and the City." In *Urban Life in Post-Soviet Asia*, edited by Catharine Alexander, Victor Buchli, and Caroline Humphrey, 52–81. New York: UCL Press, 2007.

Bunce, Valerie. "Subversive Institutions: The End of the Soviet State in Comparative Perspective." *Post-Soviet Affairs* 14, no. 4 (1998): 323–54.

Burch, Stuart, and David J. Smith. "Empty Spaces and the Value of Symbols: Estonia's 'War of Monuments' from Another Angle." *Europe-Asia Studies* 59, no. 6 (2007): 913–36.

Burkhanov, Aziz, and Yu-Wen Chen. "Kazakh Perspective on China, the Chinese, and Chinese Migration." *Ethnic and Racial Studies* 39, no. 12 (2016): 2129–48.

Calhoun, Craig. *Nations Matter: Culture, History and the Cosmopolitan Dream.* London: Routledge, 2007.

Cameron, Sarah. *The Hungry Steppe: Famine, Violence, and the Making of Soviet Kazakhstan.* Ithaca, NY: Cornell University Press, 2018.

Carlson, Richard. "The Failure of Liberal Democratisation in Kazakhstan: The Role of International Investment and Civil Society in Impending Political Reform." In *Social and Cultural Change in Central Asia: The Soviet Legacy*, edited by Sevket Akyildiz and Richard Carlson, 139–56. London: Routledge, 2013.

Castells, Manuel. *Communication Power.* Oxford: Oxford University Press, 2009.

Cerny, Astrid. "Going Where the Grass Is Greener: China Kazaks and the Oralman Immigration Policy in Kazakhstan." *Pastoralism* 1, no. 2 (2010): 218–47.

Chatterjee, Partha. *Nationalist Thought and the Colonial World: A Derivative Discourse.* London: Zed Books, 1986.

Cheskin, Ammon. "Exploring Russian-Speaking Identity from Below: The Case of Latvia." *Journal of Baltic Studies* 44, no. 3 (2013): 287–312.

Cheskin, Ammon. "History, Conflicting Collective Memories, and National Identities: How Latvia's Russian-Speakers Are Learning to Remember." *Nationalities Papers* 40, no. 4 (2012): 561–84.

Cheskin, Ammon. "Synthesis and Conflict: Russian-Speakers' Discursive Response to Latvia's Nationalising State." *Europe-Asia Studies* 64, no. 2 (2012): 325–47.

Chicherina, Nina, ed. *Grazhdanskie dvizheniia v Latvii 1989: nauchno-issledovatel'skii proekt "Sovremennye natsional'nye dvizheniia v SSR"* [Civil movements in Latvia 1989: research project "Modern National Movements in the USSR"]. Moscow: TsIMO, 1990.

Chinn, J., and R. Kaiser. *Russians as the New Minority: Ethnicity and Nationalism in the Soviet Successor States.* Boulder, CO: Westview Press, 1996.

Clowes, Edith. *Russia on the Edge: Imagined Geographies and Post-Soviet Identity.* Ithaca, NY: Cornell University Press, 2011.

Collins, Katherine. *Clan Politics and Regime Transition in Central Asia.* Cambridge: Cambridge University Press, 2006.

Commercio, Michele. *Russian Minority Politics in Post-Soviet Latvia and Kyrgyzstan: The Transformative Power of Informal Networks.* Philadelphia: University of Pennsylvania Press, 2010.

Conquest, Robert. *Harvest of Sorrow: Soviet Collectivization and the Terror-Famine.* London: Hutchinson, 1986.

Constitution of the Republic of Kazakhstan. 1993.

Constitution of the Republic of Kazakhstan. 1995.

Cummings, Sally N. "Eurasian Bridge or Murky Waters between East and West? Ideas, Identity and Output in Kazakhstan's Foreign Policy." *Journal of Communist Studies and Transition Politics* 19, no. 3 (2003): 139–55.

Cummings, Sally N. *Kazakhstan: Centre-Periphery Relations.* London: Royal Institute of International Affairs, 2000.

Cummings, Sally N. *Kazakhstan: Power and the Elite.* London: I. B. Tauris, 2005.

Cummings, Sally N. "Leaving Lenin: Elites, Official Ideology and Monuments in the Kyrgyz Republic." *Nationalities Papers* 41, no. 4 (2013): 606–21.

Cummings, Sally N. "Legitimation and Identification in Kazakhstan." *Nationalism and Ethnic Politics* 12, no. 2 (2006): 177–204.

Cummings, Sally N., ed. *Symbolism and Power in Central Asia: Politics of the Spectacular.* London: Routledge, 2010.

Dadabaev, Timur. "Post-Soviet Realities of Society in Uzbekistan." *Central Asian Survey* 23, no. 2 (2004): 141–66.

Danzer, Alexander. "Battlefields of Ethnic Symbols: Public Space and Post-Soviet Identity Formation from a Minority Perspective." *Europe-Asia Studies Journal* 61, no. 9 (2009): 1557–77.

Dave, Bhavna. *Kazakhstan: Ethnicity and Power.* London: Routledge, 2007.

Dave, Bhavna. "The Shrinking Reach of the State: Language Policy and Implementation in Kazakhstan and Kyrgyzstan." In Jones Luong, *Transformation of Central Asia*, 120–57.

Dawson, Jane I. "Latvia's Russian Minority: Balancing the Imperatives of Regional Development and Environmental Justice." *Political Geography* 20, no. 7 (2001): 787–815.

Demurin, Mikhail. *Sovremennaia evropeiskaia etnokratiia: narushenie prav natsional'nykh men'shinstv v Estonii i Latvii* [Modern European ethnocracy: national minority rights abuse in Estonia and Latvia]. Moscow: Istoricheskaia pamiat, 2009.

Diener, Alexander. "Assessing Potential Russian Irredentism and Separatism in Kazakhstan's Northern Oblasts." *Eurasian Geography and Economics* 56, no. 5 (2015): 469–92.

Diener, Alexander. "Kazakhstan's Kin State Diaspora: Settlement Planning and the Oralman Dilemma." *Europe-Asia Studies Journal* 57, no. 2 (2005): 327–48.

Diener, Alexander. "National Territory and the Reconstruction of History in Kazakhstan." *Eurasian Geography and Economics* 43, no. 8 (2002): 632–50.

Doktrina natsional'nogo soglasiia Kazakhstana [The Doctrine of National Unity]. Project of the Assembly of Peoples of Kazakhstan, 2009.

Drifelds, Juris. *Latvia in Transition.* Cambridge: Cambridge University Press, 1996.

Dubuisson, Eva-Marie, and Anna Genina. "Claiming an Ancestral Homeland: Kazakh Pilgrimage and Migration in Inner Asia." *Central Asian Survey* 30, no. 3–4 (2011): 469–85.

Edgar, Adrienne Lynn. "Marriage, Modernity, and the 'Friendship of Nations': Interethnic Intimacy in Post-War Central Asia in Comparative Perspective." *Central Asian Survey* 26, no. 4 (2007): 581–99.

Edgar, Adrienne Lynn. *The Tribal Nation: The Making of Soviet Turkmenistan.* Princeton, NJ: Princeton University Press, 2006.

Eglitis, Daina S., and Laura Ardava. "The Politics of Memory: Remembering the Baltic Way 20 Years after 1989." *Europe-Asia Studies* 64, no. 6 (2012): 1033–59.

Eglitis, Daina Stukuls. *Imagining the Nation: History, Modernity, and Revolution in Latvia.* University Park: Pennsylvania State University Press, 2002.

Eley, Geoff, and Ronald Grigor Suny. *Becoming National: A Reader.* New York: Oxford University Press, 1996.

Engels, Friedrich. *The Origin of the Family, Private Property and the State*. London: Penguin UK, 2010.

Etkind, Alexander. *Internal Colonization: Russia's Imperial Experience*. Hoboken, NJ: John Wiley, 2013.

Evans, Peter, Dietrich Rueschemeyer, and Theda Skocpol, eds. *Bringing the State Back In*. Cambridge: Cambridge University Press, 1985.

Fauve, Adrien. "A Tale of Two Statues in Astana: The Fuzzy Process of Nationalistic City Making." *Nationalities Papers* 43, no. 3 (2015): 383–98.

Fierman, William. "Identity, Symbolism, and the Politics of Language in Central Asia." *Europe-Asia Studies* 61, no. 7 (2009): 1207–28.

Fierman, William. "Language and Identity in Kazakhstan: Formulations in Policy Documents 1987–1997." *Communist and Post-Communist Studies* 31, no. 2 (1998): 171–86.

Fierman, William. "Russian in Post-Soviet Central Asia: A Comparison with the States of the Baltic and South Caucasus." *Europe-Asia Studies* 64, no. 6 (2012): 1077–100.

Forgacs, David, ed. *A Gramsci Reader: Selected Writings 1916–1935*. London: Lawrence and Wishart, 1988.

Foucault, Michele. *The Archaeology of Knowledge*. London: Tavistock, 1972.

Galbreath, David J., and Mary Elizabeth Galvin. "The Titularization of Latvian Secondary Schools: The Historical Legacy of Soviet Policy Implementation." *Journal of Baltic Studies* 36, no. 4 (2005): 449–66.

Ganga, Paula. "Baikonur, Bagys and the Legacy of Soviet-Era Territorial Leases in Contemporary Central Asia." *Cambridge Central Asia Reviews*, no. 1 (2015): 1–18.

Geizis, Gederts. "Latvia's Victory Day Shows Security Tensions." *Al Jazeera*, May 14, 2014. Accessed October 28, 2014, http://www.aljazeera.com/indepth/features/2014/05/latvia-victory-day-shows-security-tensions-20145148193896938p.html.

Gellner, Ernest. *Nations and Nationalism*. Ithaca, NY: Cornell University Press, 1983.

Gellner, Ernest. "The Nomadism Debate." In *State and Society in Soviet Thought*, 92–114. Oxford: Basil Blackwell, 1988.

Gellner, Ernest. *State and Society in Soviet Thought*. Oxford: Basil Blackwell, 1988.

Graziosi, Andrea. *Stalinism, Collectivization and the Great Famine*. Cambridge, MA: Ukrainian Studies Fund, 2009.

Grigas, Agnes. *Beyond Crimea: The New Russian Empire*. New Haven, CT: Yale University Press, 2016.

Grzymala-Busse, Anna, and Pauline Jones Luong. "Reconceptualizing the State: Lessons from Post-Communism." *Political Theory* 30, no. 4 (2002): 529–54.

Hale, Henry E. "Cause without a Rebel: Kazakhstan's Unionist Nationalism in the USSR and CIS." *Nationalities Papers* 37, no. 1 (2009): 1–32.

Higley, John, and Gyorgy Lengyel, eds. *Elites after State Socialism: Theories and Analysis*. Lanham, MD: Rowman and Littlefield, 2000.

Higley, John, and Pakulski, Jan. "Elite Theory versus Marxism: The Twentieth Century's Verdict." In Higley and Lengyel, *Elites after State Socialism*, 320–32.

Hirsch, Francine. *Empire of Nations: Ethnographic Knowledge and the Making of the Soviet Union*. Ithaca, NY: Cornell University Press, 2005.

Hoare, Quintin, ed. *Antonio Gramsci Selections from Political Writings (1921–1926)*. Translated and edited by Quintin Hoare. London: Lawrence and Wishart, 1978.

Hobsbawm, Eric. *Nations and Nationalism since 1780: Programme, Myth, Reality*. Cambridge: Cambridge University Press, 1990.

Hogan-Brun, Gabrielle. "At the Interface of Language Ideology and Practice: The Public Discourse surrounding the 2004 Education Reform in Latvia." *Language Policy* 5, no. 3 (2006): 315–35.

Horowitz, Donald L. "The Challenge of Ethnic Conflict: Democracy in Divided Societies." *Journal of Democracy* 4, no. 4 (1993): 18–38.

Hroch, Miroslav. *Social Preconditions of National Revival in Europe: A Comparative Analysis of the Social Composition of Patriotic Groups among the Smaller European Nations.* Cambridge: Cambridge University Press, 1985.

Ibañez-Tirado, Diana. "'How Can I Be Post-Soviet If I Was Never Soviet?' Rethinking Categories of Time and Social Change: A Perspective from Kulob, Southern Tajikistan." *Central Asian Survey* 34, no. 2 (2015): 190–203.

Ibrayeva, Valeria. *Iskusstvo Kazakhstana: Postsovetskii period* [Art in Kazakhstan: post-Soviet period]. Almaty: Tonkaya Gran, 2014.

Igmen, Ali. *Speaking Soviet with An Accent: Culture and Power in Kyrgyzstan.* Pittsburgh: University of Pittsburgh Press, 2012.

Ikstens, Jānis. "Latvia: Disclosure Yet Abuse, Volatility Yet Stability." In *Public Finance and Post-Communist Party Development*, ed. Steven D. Roper and Jānis Ikstens, 61–78. Hampshire: Ashgate, 2008.

Isaacs, Rico. "Bringing the 'Formal' Back In: Nur Otan, Informal Networks, and the Countering of Elite Instability in Kazakhstan." *Europe-Asia Studies* 65, no. 6 (2013): 1055–79.

Isaacs, Rico. "'Papa': Nursultan Nazarbayev and the Discourse of Charismatic Leadership and Nation-Building in Post-Soviet Kazakhstan." *Studies in Ethnicity and Nationalism* 10, no. 3 (2010): 435–52.

Isaacs, Rico. *Party System Formation in Kazakhstan: Between Formal and Informal Politics,* London: Routledge, 2011.

Ivans, Dainis. "Before We Were Recognized." In *Sarezgitais gajums: The Complicated Road: A Dedication to the Restoration of Independence of the Republic of Latvia*, conceived and compiled by Meldra Usenko, n.p. Riga: Tautas Frontes muzeijs, 2002.

Ivans, Dainis. *Voin ponevole* [Reluctant warrior]. Riga: Vieda, 1996.

Jones Luong, Pauline. *Institutional Change and Political Continuity in Post-Soviet Central Asia: Power, Perceptions and Pacts.* Cambridge: Cambridge University Press, 2002.

Jones Luong, Pauline, ed. *The Transformation of Central Asia: States and Societies from Soviet Rule to Independence.* Ithaca, NY: Cornell University Press, 2004.

Junisbai, Barbara. "Market Reform Regimes, Elite Defections, and Political Opposition in the Post-Soviet States: Evidence from Belarus, Kazakhstan, and Kyrgyzstan." PhD diss., Indiana University, 2009.

Junisbai, Barbara, and Azamat Junisbai. "The Democratic Choice of Kazakhstan: A Case Study in Economic Liberalization, Intraelite Cleavage, and Political Opposition." *Demokratizatsiya* 13, no. 3 (2005): 373–92.

Kamp, Marianne. *The New Woman in Uzbekistan: Islam, Modernity, and Unveiling under Communism.* Seattle: University of Washington Press, 2006.

Kandil, Hazem. *The Power Triangle: Military, Security, and Politics of Regime Change.* Oxford: Oxford University Press, 2016.

Kandiyoti, Deniz. "Between the Hammer and the Anvil: Post-Conflict Reconstruction, Islam and Women's Rights." *Third World Quarterly* 28, no. 3 (2007): 503–17.

Kandiyoti, Deniz. "How Far Do Analyses of Postsocialism Travel? The Case of Central Asia." In *Postsocialism: Ideals, Ideologies and Practices in Eurasia*, ed. Christopher Hann, 238–57. London: Routledge, 2002.

Karabel, Jerome. "Towards a Theory of Intellectuals and Politics." *Theory and Society* 25, no. 2 (1996): 205–33.

Karimov, Islam. "Uzbekistan na poroge XXI veka" [Uzbekistan on the threshold of the twenty-first century]. *Ugroza bezopasnosti, uslovia i garantii progresa* [Security threats, conditions and guarantees of progress]. Tashkent: Uzbekiston 1997.

Karimov, Islam. *Uzbekistan: natsional'naia nezavisimost', ekonomika, politika, ideologiia* [Uzbekistan: national independence, economics, politics, ideology]. Vol. 1. Tashkent: Uzbekiston, 1996.

Karklins, Rasma. "Ethnopluralism: Panacea for East Central Europe?" *Nationalities Papers* 28, no. 2 (2000): 219–41.

Karklins, Rasma. *Ethnopolitics and Transition to Democracy. The Collapse of the USSR and Latvia.* Baltimore: Johns Hopkins University Press, 1994.

Karklins, Rasma, and Brigita Zepa. "Political Participation in Latvia 1987–2001." *Journal of Baltic Studies* 32, no. 4 (2001): 334–46.

Kasekamp, Andres. *A History of the Baltic States.* Basingstoke: Palgrave Macmillan, 2010.

Kasekamp, Andres. "Radical Right-Wing Movements in the North-East Baltic." *Journal of Contemporary History* 34, no. 4 (1999): 587–600.

Kazakhstan Institute for Strategic Studies (KISI). *Sotsial'no-politicheskaia stratifikatsiia kazakhstanskogo obshchestva: po rezultatam sotsiologicheskogo issledovaniia KISI i nauchno-issledovatel'skogo proekta IFiP* [The social-political stratification of Kazakhstani society: based on a sociological study project conducted by the Kazakhstan Institute for Strategic Studies and IFiP]. Almaty: KISI, 2011.

Kelertas, Violeta, ed. *Baltic Postcolonialism: On the Boundary of Two Worlds, Identity, Freedom, and Moral Imagination in the Baltics.* Amsterdam: Rodopi, 2006.

Kelley, Judith. *Ethnic Politics in Europe: The Power of Norms and Incentives.* Princeton, NJ: Princeton University Press, 2004.

Kendirbaeva, Gulnar. "'We Are Children of Alash . . .': The Kazakh Intelligentsia at the Beginning of the 20th Century in Search of National Identity and Prospects of the Cultural Survival of the Kazakh people." *Central Asian Survey* 18, no. 1 (1999): 5–36.

Kendirbay, Gulnar. "The National Liberation Movement of the Kazakh Intelligentsia at the Beginning of the 20th Century." *Central Asian Survey* 16, no. 4 (1997): 487–515.

Kindler, Robert. *Stalin's Nomads: Power and Famine in Kazakhstan.* Pittsburgh: University of Pittsburgh Press, 2018.

Khalid, Adeeb. "Backwardness and the quest for civilization: early Soviet Central Asia in comparative perspective." *Slavic Review* 65, no. 2 (2006): 231–51.

Khalid, Adeeb. "Introduction: Locating the (Post-) Colonial in Soviet History." *Central Asian Survey* 26, no. 4 (2007): 465–73.

King, Charles, and Neil Melvin, eds. *Nations Abroad: Diaspora Politics and International Relations in the Former Soviet Union.* Boulder, CO: Westview Press, 1998.

King, Gundar J., Edvins Vanags, Inga Vilka, and David E. McNabb. "Local Government Reforms in Latvia, 1990–2003: Transition to a Democratic Society." *Public Administration* 82, no. 4 (2004): 931–50.

Kivelson, Valerie A., and Ronald Grigor Suny. *Russia's Empires.* Oxford: Oxford University Press, 2017.

Klyashtornyi, Sergey. *Istoriia Tsentral'noi Azii i pamiatniki runicheskogo pis'ma* [History of Central Asia and runic script monuments]. St. Petersburg: Aziatika, 2003.

Knott, Eleanor. "Quasi-Citizenship as a Category of Practice: Analyzing Engagement with Russia's Compatriot Policy in Crimea." *Citizenship Studies* 21, no. 1 (2017): 116–35.

Koch, Natalie. "Bordering on the Modern: Power, Practice and Exclusion in Astana." *Transactions of the Institute of British Geographers* 39, no. 3 (2014): 432–43.

Koch, Natalie. "The Monumental and the Miniature: Imagining 'Modernity' in Astana." *Social and Cultural Geography* 11, no. 8 (2010): 769–87.

Koch, Natalie. "Why Not a World City? Astana, Ankara, and Geopolitical Scripts in Urban Networks." *Urban Geography* 34, no. 1 (2013): 109–30.

Kohn, Hans. *The Idea of Nationalism: A Study in Its Origins and Background.* New York: Macmillan, 1944.

Kolstø, P., ed. *Nation-Building and Ethnic Integration in Post-Soviet Societies: An Investigation of Latvia and Kazakhstan.* Boulder, CO: Westview Press, 1999.

Kravtsov, V. "The Last Prisoners of the Cold War: The Stateless People of Latvia in Their Own Words." Riga, 2006.

Kruma, Kristine. "Access to Electoral Rights: Latvia." EUDO Citizenship Observatory, Robert Schuman Centre for Advanced Studies, 2013.

Kruma, Kristine. "EU Citizenship: Unresolved Issues." RGSL Working Papers, no. 22, 2004.

Kudaibergenova, Diana T. "Between the State and the Artist: Representations of Femininity and Masculinity in the Formation of Ideas of the Nation in Central Asia." *Nationalities Papers* 44, no. 2 (2016): 225–46.

Kudaibergenova, Diana T. "The Body Globalized and Re-Traditionalized: A Digital Ethnography of Instagram in Kazakhstan and Russia." *Central Asian Survey* 38, no. 2 (2019): 363–80.

Kudaibergenova, Diana T. "Compartmentalized Ideology and Nation-Building in Non-democratic States." *Communist and Post-Communist Studies* 52, no. 3 (2019): 247–57.

Kudaibergenova, Diana T. "Compartmentalized Ideology: Presidential Addresses and Legitimation in Kazakhstan." In *Theorizing Central Asian Politics,* edited by Rico Isaacs and Alessandro Frigerio, 145–66. Cham: Palgrave Macmillan, 2019.

Kudaibergenova, Diana T. "The Ideology of Development and Legitimation: Beyond 'Kazakhstan 2030.'" *Central Asian Survey* 34, no. 4 (2015): 440–55.

Kudaibergenova, Diana T. "'Imagining Community' in Soviet Kazakhstan: An historical Analysis of Narrative on Nationalism in Kazakh-Soviet Literature." *Nationalities Papers* 41, no. 5 (2013): 839–54.

Kudaibergenova, Diana T. "Mankurts, Kazakh 'Russians' and 'Shala' Kazakhs: Language, National Identity and Ethnicity Revisited." In Laruelle, *Nazarbayev Generation,* 89–111.

Kudaibergenova, Diana T. "Modernizing the Past in the Present: Early Soviet Kazakh Literature, Education and Soviet Orientalism." *Cambridge Central Asia Reviews* 2, no. 1 (October 2016): 20–30.

Kudaibergenova, Diana T. "'My Silk Road to You': Re-imagining Routes, Roads, and Geography in Contemporary Art of "Central Asia." *Journal of Eurasian Studies* 8, no. 1 (2017): 31–43.

Kudaibergenova, Diana T. *Rewriting the Nation in Modern Kazakh Literature: Elites and Narratives.* Lanham, MD: Lexington Books, 2017.

Kudaibergenova, Diana T. "The Use and Abuse of Postcolonial Discourses in Post-Independent Kazakhstan." *Europe-Asia Studies* 68, no. 5 (2016): 917–35.

Kudaibergenova, Diana T., and Boram Shin. "Authors and Authoritarianism in Central Asia: Failed Agency and Nationalising Authoritarianism in Uzbekistan and Kazakhstan." *Asian Studies Review* 42, no. 2 (2018): 304–22.

Kuscu, Isik. "Kazakhstan's Oralman Project: A Remedy for Ambiguous Identity?" PhD diss., Indiana University, 2008.

Kuttiqadam, Seidakhmet. "Early Political Landscape." In *Kazakhskaia drama na tsene i zakulisami: istoriia sovremennogo Kazakhstana* [Kazakh drama on the stage and backstage: history of contemporary Kazakhstan]. Almaty: Dayk Press, 2010.

Laitin, David. *Identity in Formation: The Russian-Speaking Populations in the New Abroad.* Ithaca, NY: Cornell University Press, 1998.

Lane, David. *The Capitalist Transformation of State Socialism: The Making and Breaking of State Socialist Society, and What Followed.* London: Routledge, 2014.

Lane, David. *Elites and Classes in the Transformation of State Socialism.* London: Transaction, 2011.

Laruelle, Marlène. *In the Name of the Nation: Nationalism and Politics in Contemporary Russia.* New York: Palgrave Macmillan, 2009.

Laruelle, Marlène, ed. *Kazakhstan in the Making: Legitimacy, Symbols, and Social Changes.* Lanham, MD: Lexington Books, 2019.

Laruelle, Marlène, ed. *Nazarbayev Generation: Studies on Youth in Kazakhstan.* Lanham, MD: Lexington Books, 2019.

Laruelle, Marlène, "Which Future for National-Patriots? The Landscape of Kazakh Nationalism." In Laruelle, *Kazakhstan in the Making,* 155–80.

Laruelle, Marlène. "Why No Kazakh Novorossiya? Kazakhstan's Russian Minority in a Post-Crimea World." *Problems of Post-Communism* 65, no. 1 (2018): 65–78.

Laruelle, Marlène, and Sébastien Peyrouse. *The Chinese Question in Central Asia: Domestic Order, Social Change, and the Chinese Factor.* Vol. 29. New York: Columbia University Press, 2012.

Laruelle, Marlène, and Sébastien Peyrouse. *Les russes du Kazakhstan.* Paris: Maisonneuve & Larose, 2004.

Laszczkowski, Mateusz. "Building the Future: Construction, Temporality, and Politics in Astana." *Focaal* 2011, no. 60 (2011): 77–92.

Laszczkowski, Mateusz. "State Building(s): Built Forms, Materiality, and the State in Astana." In *Ethnographies of the State in Central Asia: Performing Politics,* 149–72. Bloomington: Indiana University Press, 2014.

Linderman, Vladimir. "Linderman: Ushakov Won but Rejected His Principles." Delfi news agency, June 3, 2013. Accessed October 29, 2014. http://rus.delfi.lv/news/daily/latvia/linderman-ushakov-pobedil-no-otkazalsya-ot-principov.d?id=43371651.

Linz, Juan J. "State Building and Nation Building." *European Review* 1, no. 4 (1993): 355–69.

Linz, Juan. *Totalitarian and Authoritarian Regimes.* Boulder, CO: Lynne Rienner, 2000.

Linz, Juan, and Alfred Stepan. *Problems of Democratic Transition and Consolidation: Southern Europe, South America, and Post-Communist Europe.* Baltimore: Johns Hopkins University Press, 1996.

Lynch, Julia F. "Aligning Sampling Strategies with Analytic Goals." In Mosley, *Interview Research,* 31–44.

Maksloo, Maria. *The Politics of Becoming European: A Study of Polish and Baltic Security Imaginaries.* London: Routledge, 2010.

Malesevic, Sinisa. *Identity as Ideology: Understanding Ethnicity and Nationalism.* Houndmills: Palgrave Macmillan, 2006.

Mamashuly, Asylkhan. "Vosstaniiu kazakhov v 1916 godu predshestvoval raskol shtannoi intelligentsii" [The Kazakh revolt of 1916 was preceded by a split in the intellectual intelligentsia]. Radio Free Europe, Kazakh version, June 24, 2011, in the section "Newest History/Grey Areas."

Marat, Erica. "Kyrgyzstan's Fragmented Police and Armed Forces." *Journal of Power Institutions in Post-Soviet Societies,* no. 11 (2010). https://journals.openedition.org/pipss/3803.

Marat, Erica. "Nation Branding in Central Asia: A New Campaign to Present Ideas about the State and the Nation." *Europe-Asia Studies* 61, no. 7 (2009): 1123–36.

Marat, Erica. "State-Propagated Narratives about a National Defender in Central Asian States." *Journal of Power Institutions in Post-Soviet Societies,* no. 6/7 (2007). https://journals.openedition.org/pipss/545.

March, Andrew F. "State Ideology and the Legitimation of Authoritarianism: The Case of Post-Soviet Uzbekistan." *Journal of Political Ideologies* 8, no. 2 (2003): 209–32.

March, Andrew F. "The Use and Abuse of History: 'National Ideology' as Transcendental Object in Islam Karimov's 'Ideology of National Independence.'" *Central Asian Survey* 21, no. 4 (2002): 371–84.

Marples, David. *Heroes and Villains: Creating National History in Contemporary Ukraine*. Budapest: Central European University Press, 2007.

Masanov, Nurbulat. *Kochevaia tsivilizatsiia Kazakhov: osnovy zhiznedeiatel'nosti nomadnogo obshchestva* [Kazak nomadic civilization: basis of the social life of nomadic society]. Moscow: Gorizont, 1995.

Masanov, Nurbulat, Zhulduzbek Abylkozhin, and Irina Erofeeva. *Nauchnoe znanie i mifotvorchestvo v sovremennoi istoriografii Kazakhstana* [Scientific knowledge and mythmaking in the contemporary historiography of Kazakhstan]. Almaty: Dayk Press, 2007.

Matveeva, Anna. "Legitimising Central Asian Authoritarianism: Political Manipulation and Symbolic Power." *Europe-Asia Studies* 61, no. 7 (2009): 1095–1121.

McGlinchey, Eric. *Chaos, Violence, Dynasty: Politics and Islam in Central Asia*. Pittsburgh: University of Pittsburgh Press, 2011.

McGlinchey, Eric. "Paying for Patronage: Regime Change in Post-Soviet Central Asia." PhD diss., Princeton University, 2003.

Melvin, Neil. *Russians beyond Russia: The Politics of National Identity*. London: Royal Institute of International Affairs, 1995.

Miley, Thomas Jeffrey. "Against the Thesis of the 'Civic Nation': The Case of Catalonia in Contemporary Spain." *Nationalism and Ethnic Politics* 13, no. 1 (2007): 1–37.

Miley, Thomas Jeffrey. "The Politics of Language and Nation: The Case of Catalans in Contemporary Spain." PhD diss., Yale University, 2004.

Mills, Wright. *The Power Elite*. Oxford: Oxford University Press, 1956.

Mole, Richard. *The Baltic States from the Soviet Union to the European Union: Identity, Discourse and Power in the Post-Communist Transition of Estonia, Latvia and Lithuania*. London: Routledge, 2012.

Morris, Helen M. "President, Party and Nationality Policy in Latvia, 1991–1999." *Europe-Asia Studies* 56, no. 4 (2004): 543–69.

Mosley, Layna, ed. *Interview Research in Political Science*. Ithaca, NY: Cornell University Press, 2013.

Mosley, Layna. "Just Talk to People? Interviews in Contemporary Political Science." In Mosley, *Interview Research*, 1–28.

Motyl, Alexander J. "Inventing Invention: The Limits of National Identity Formation." In Suny and Kennedy, *Intellectuals*, 57–75.

Muižnieks, Nīls R. "The Daugavpils Hydro Station and 'Glasnost' in Latvia." *Journal of Baltic Studies* 18, no. 1 (1987): 63–70.

Muiznieks, Nils, Juris Rozenvalds, and Ieva Birka. "Ethnicity and Social Cohesion in the Post-Soviet Baltic States." *Patterns of Prejudice* 47, no. 3 (2013): 288–308.

National Statistical Agency of Kazakhstan. "Results of the 2009 National Population Census of the Republic of Kazakhstan: Analytical Report." based on the 2009 All-National Census of the Republic of Kazakhstan, 2009.

Nazarbayev, Nursultan. *Ideinaia konsolidatsiia obshchestva kak uslovie progressa Kazakhstana* [The ideational consolidation of society as a condition of progress in Kazakhstan]. Almaty: Foundation for Political Research, Kazakhstan XXI Century, 1993.

Nazarbayev, Nursultan. *The Kazakhstan Way*. London: Stacey International, 2008.

Nissinen, Marja. *Latvia's Transition to a Market Economy: Political Determinants of Economic Reform Policy*. London: Macmillan, 1999.

Northrop, Douglas. *Veiled Empire: Gender and Power in Stalinist Central Asia*. Ithaca, NY: Cornell University Press, 2004.

Nysanbaev, A. *Evraziiskaia doktrina Nursultana Nazarbayeva* [The Eurasian doctrine of Nursultan Nazarbayev]. Almaty: Institute of Philosophy, 2010.

Nysanbaev, A. *Philosophiia vzaimoponimaniia* [The philosophy of mutual understanding]. Almaty: Kazakh Encyclopedia, 2001.

Ó Beacháin, Donnacha, and Rob Kevlihan. "Threading a Needle: Kazakhstan between Civic and Ethno-nationalist State-Building." *Nations and Nationalism* 19, no. 2 (2013): 337–56.

Organization for Economic Cooperation and Development (OECD). Country Notes: Recent Changes in Migration Movements and Policies. http://www.oecd.org/els/mig/LATVIA.pdf.

Ostrowski, Wojciech. *Politics and Oil in Kazakhstan*. London: Routledge, 2010.

Peters, Jānis. *Ordena i infarkty: rechi, esse, razmyshleniia. I. A. Peters* [Orders and heart attacks: speeches, essays, reflections. J. A. Peters, compiled by M. Melberg. Riga: Avots, 1990.

Petrunin, Sergey. "Sredneaziatskii inorodnyi front" [Central Asian alien front]. Russkaia Planeta. http://rusplt.ru/ww1/history/sredneaziatskiy-inorodnyiy-front-13531.html.

Pettai, Vello. "Explaining Ethnic Politics in the Baltic States: Reviewing the Triadic Nexus Model." *Journal of Baltic Studies* 37, no. 1 (2006): 124–36.

Peyrouse, Sébastien. "Nationhood and the Minority Question in Central Asia: The Russians in Kazakhstan." *Europe-Asia Studies* 59, no. 3 (2007): 481–501.

Pianciola, Niccol. "Décoloniser l'Asie centrale? Bolcheviks et colons au Semirech'e (1920–1922)." *Cahiers du monde russe. Russie-Empire russe-Union soviétique et États indépendants* 49, no. 1 (2008): 101–44.

Pianciola, Niccolò. "Famine in the Steppe: The Collectivization of Agriculture and the Kazak Herdsmen 1928–1934." *Cahiers du monde russe. Russie-Empire russe-Union soviétique et États indépendants* 45, no. 1–2 (2004): 137–92.

Plakans, Andrejs. *A Concise History of the Baltic States*. Cambridge: Cambridge University Press, 2011.

Plakans, Andrejs. *The Latvians: A Short History*. Stanford, CA: Hoover Press, 1995.

Plakans, Andrejs. "Regional Identity in Latvia: The Case of Latgale." In *Forgotten Pages in Baltic History: Diversity and Inclusion*, edited by Martyn Housden and David J. Smith, 49–70. Amsterdam: Rodopi, 2011.

Ponomarev, V., and S. Dzhukeeva. *Documents and Materials about the December 1986 Events in Kazakhstan*. Almaty: Panorama, 1993.

Procevska, Olga, Vita Zelče, and Klinta Ločmele. "Celebrations, Commemorative Dates and Related Rituals: Soviet Experience, Its Transformation and Contemporary Victory Day Celebrations in Russia and Latvia." In *The Geopolitics of History in Latvian-Russian Relations*, edited by N. Muižnieks, 109–38. Riga: Academic Press of the University of Latvia, 2011.

Przeworski, Adam, and Henry Teune. *Logic of Comparative Social Inquiry*. Malabar, FL: Krieger, 1982.

Rasanayagam, Johan, Judith Beyer, and Madeleine Reeves. "Introduction: Performances, Possibilities, and Practices of the Political in Central Asia." In Reeves Rasanayagam, and Beyer *Ethnographies of the State*, 1–26.

Reeves, Madeleine. *Border Work: Spatial Lives of the State in Rural Central Asia*. Ithaca, NY: Cornell University Press, 2014.

Reeves, Madeleine, Johan Rasanayagam, and Judith Beyer, eds. *Ethnographies of the State in Central Asia: Performing Politics*. Bloomington: Indiana University Press, 2014.

Rivers, William P. "Attitudes towards Incipient Mankurtism among Kazakhstani College Students." *Language Policy* 1, no. 2 (2002): 159–74.

Robinson, William I. "Gramsci and Globalisation: From Nation-State to Transnational Hegemony." *Critical Review of International Social and Political Philosophy* 8, no. 4 (2005): 559–74.

Ro'i, Yakov "The Soviet and Russian Context of the Development of Nationalism in Soviet Central Asia." *Cahiers du monde russe et soviétique* 32, no. 1 (1991): 123–41.

Rose, Richard. *New Baltic Barometer III: A Survey Study.* No. 284. University of Strathclyde, Centre for the Study of Public Policy, 1997.

Rose, Richard. *New Baltic Barometer V: A Pre-Enlargement Survey.* No. 368. University of Strathclyde, Centre for the Study of Public Policy, 2002.

Rozenvalds, Juris, ed. *How Democratic Is Latvia: Monitoring of Democracy.* Riga: Zinātne, 2007.

Rudenshiold, Eric. "Ethnic Dimensions in Contemporary Latvian Politics: Focusing Forces for Change." *Soviet Studies* 44, no. 4 (1992): 609–39.

Sarsembayev, Azamat. "Imagined Communities: Kazak Nationalism and Kazakification in the 1990s." *Central Asian Survey* 18, no. 3 (1999): 319–46.

Sarym, Aidos. "Kazakhskosti budet vse bolshe" [There will be more Kazakh-ness]. Interview, *Esquire Kazakhstan*, April 2014. http://esquire.kz/content/1185-aydos_saryim_kazahskosti _budet_vse_bol'she.

Sarym, Aidos. "My lish' trebuet, chtoby ispolnialis' zakony strany" [We only demand that the country's laws be enforced]. *Central Asian Monitor*, http://old.camonitor.com/archives/8403.

Sasse, Gwendolyn. *The Crimea Question: Identity, Transition, and Conflict.* Cambridge, MA: Harvard University Press, 2007.

Satpayev, Dosym. "An Analysis of the Internal Structure of Kazakhstan's Political Elite and an Assessment of Political Risk Levels." In *Empire, Islam and Politics in Central Eurasia*, edited by Tomohiko Uyama, 283–300. Sapporo: Slavic Research Centre, Hokkaido University, 2007.

Satpayev, Dosym, and Tolganai Umbetaliyeva. "The Protests in Zhanaozen and the Kazakh Oil Sector: Conflicting Interests in a Rentier State." *Journal of Eurasian Studies* 6, no. 2 (2015): 122–29.

Satpayev, Dosym, Tolganai Umbetaliyeva, Andrey Chebortarev, Rasul Zhumaly, Aidos Sarym, Aiman Zhusupova, Zamir Karazhanov, and Rustem Kadyrzhanov. *Sumerechnaia zona ili "lovushki" perekhodnogo perioda* [The twilight zone or "traps" of the transition in Kazakhstan]. Almaty: Rakurs, 2013.

Schatz, Edward. "Access by Accident: Legitimacy Claims and Democracy Promotion in Authoritarian Central Asia." *International Political Science Review* 27, no. 3 (2006): 263–84.

Schatz, Edward. "Framing Strategies and Non-conflict in Multi-ethnic Kazakhstan." *Nationalism and Ethnic Politics* 6, no. 2 (2000): 71–94.

Schatz, Edward. *Modern Clan Politics: The Power of "Blood" in Kazakhstan and Beyond.* Seattle: University of Washington Press, 2004.

Schatz, Edward. "Notes on the 'Dog That Didn't Bark': Eco-internationalism in Late Soviet Kazakstan." *Ethnic and Racial Studies* 22, no. 1 (1999): 136–61.

Schatz, Edward. "Reconceptualizing Clans: Kinship Networks and Statehood in Kazakhstan." *Nationalities Papers* 33, no. 2 (2005): 231–54.

Schatz, Edward. "The Soft Authoritarian Tool Kit: Agenda-Setting Power in Kazakhstan and Kyrgyzstan." *Comparative Politics* 41, no. 2 (2009): 203–22.

Schatz, Edward. "What Capital Cities Say about State and Nation Building." *Nationalism and Ethnic Politics* 9, no. 4 (2004): 111–40.

Scott, James. *Seeing Like a State: How Certain Schemes to Improve the Human Condition Have Failed.* New Haven, CT: Yale University Press, 1998.

Silova, Iveta. "Bilingual Education Theater: Behind the Scenes of Latvian Minority Education Reform." *Intercultural Education* 13, no. 4 (2002): 463–76.

Silova, Iveta. *From Sites of Occupation to Symbols of Multiculturalism: Reconceptualizing Minority Education in Post-Soviet Latvia.* Scottsdale, AZ: Information Age, 2006.

Silova, Iveta. "The Manipulated Consensus: Globalisation, Local Agency, and Cultural Legacies in Post-Soviet Education Reform." *European Educational Research Journal* 1, no. 2 (2002): 308–30.

Skultans, Vieda. "Remembering to Forget: Commemoration of Atrocities in the Baltic States." *Central Europe* 12, no. 1 (2014): 32–46.

Smith, Anthony. *The Ethnic Origins of Nation.* Oxford: Wiley-Blackwell, 1988.

Smith, Anthony. *Myth and Memories of the Nation.* New York: Oxford University Press, 1999.

Smith, Anthony. *National Identity.* London: Penguin Books, 1991.

Solska, Magdalena. "Citizenship, Collective Identity and the International Impact on Integration Policy in Estonia, Latvia and Lithuania." *Europe-Asia Studies* 63, no. 6 (2011): 1089–108.

Soucek, Branko, and Svat Soucek. *A History of Inner Asia.* Cambridge: Cambridge University Press, 2000.

Steen, Anton. *Between Past and Future: Elites, Democracy and the State in Post-Communist Countries: A Comparison of Estonia, Latvia and Lithuania.* Aldershot: Ashgate, 1997.

Steen, Anton. "Consolidation and Competence: Research on the Politics of Recruiting Political Elites in the Baltic States." *Journal of Baltic Studies* 27, no. 2 (1996): 143–56.

Steen, Anton. "Elite and Mass Confidence in New Democracies: Towards Congruence? The Baltic states 1992–2007." *Historical Social Research/Historische Sozialforschung* 37, no. 1 (2012): 127–47.

Steen, Anton. "Ethnic Relations, Elites and Democracy in the Baltic States." *Journal of Communist Studies and Transition Politics* 16, no. 4 (2000): 68–87.

Stepan, Alfred. *The State and Society: Peru in Comparative Perspective.* Princeton, NJ: Princeton University Press, 1978.

Sztompka, Piotr. "Cultural Trauma: The Other Face of Social Change." *European Journal of Social Theory* 3, no. 4 (2000): 449–66.

Sztompka, Piotr. "On the Decaying Moral Space: Is There a Way Out?" *European Review* 10, no. 1 (2002): 63–72.

Suny, Ronald Grigor. "Constructing Primordialism: Old Histories for New Nations." *Journal of Modern History* 73, no. 4 (2001): 862–96.

Suny, Ronald Grigor. "Incomplete Revolution: National Movements and the Collapse of the Soviet Empire." *New Left Review* 189 (1991): 111–25.

Suny, Ronald Grigor, and Michael D. Kennedy, eds. *Intellectuals and the Articulation of the Nation.* Ann Arbor: University of Michigan Press, 1999.

Suny, Ronald Grigor, and Terry Martin, eds. *A State of Nations: Empire and Nation-making in the Age of Lenin and Stalin.* New York: Oxford University Press, 2001.

Surucu, Cengiz. "Modernity, Nationalism, Resistance: Identity Politics in Post-Soviet Kazakhstan." *Central Asian Survey* 21, no. 4 (2002): 385–402.

Syroezhkin, Konstantin. "Social Perceptions of China and the Chinese: A View from Kazakhstan." In *China and Eurasia Forum Quarterly* 7, no. 1 (2009): 29–46.

Tilly, Charles. *Democracy.* New York: Cambridge University Press, 2012.

Tilly, Charles. *Stories, Identities, and Political Change.* Lanham, MD: Rowman and Littlefield, 2002.

Tlostanova, Madina. *What Does It Mean to be Post-Soviet? Decolonial Art from the Ruins of the Soviet Empire.* Durham, NC: Duke University Press, 2018.

Tokayev, Kasymzhomart. *Svet i ten': ocherki kazakhstanskogo politika* [Light and shadow: essays of Kazakhstani politicians]. Moscow: Vostok-Zapad, 2008.

Tolybekov, Sabit. *Obshchestvenno-ekonomicheskii stroi kazakhov v XVII–XIX vekakh* [Socioeconomic structure of Kazakhs in the seventeenth–nineteenth centuries]. Alma-Ata: Kazakhskoe Gosudarstvennoe Izdatel'stvo, 1957.

Totaro, Maurizio. "To Protect or to Nightmarize? Counter-Extremism, Affects, and the State in Kazakhstan." *Problems of Post-Communism.* Forthcoming.

Tsilevich, Boris. "Development of the Language Legislation in the Baltic States." *International Journal on Multicultural Societies* 3, no. 2 (2001): 137–54.

Tsygankov, Andrei P. "Modern at Last? Variety of Weak States in the post-Soviet World." *Communist and Post-Communist Studies* 40, no. 4 (2007): 423–39.

Tutumlu, Assel. "Governmentalization of the Kazakhstani State: Between Governmentality and Neopatrimonial Capitalism." In *Theorizing Central Asian Politics*, edited by Rico Isaacs and Alessandro Frigerio, 43–64. Cham: Palgrave Macmillan, 2019.

Tutumlu, Assel. "The Rule by Law: Negotiating Stability in Kazakhstan." In Laruelle, *Kazakhstan in the Making*, 3–28.

Uyama, Tomohiko. "The Geography of Civilizations: A Spatial Analysis of the Kazakh Intelligentsia's Activities, from the Mid-Nineteenth to the Early Twentieth Century." In *Regions: A Prism to View the Slavic-Eurasian World*, edited by Kimitaka Matsuzato, 70–99. Sapporo: Slavonic Research Centre, 2000.

Van Dijk, Teun A. "Ideology and Discourse Analysis." *Journal of Political Ideologies* 11 (2006): 115–40.

Verdery, Katherine. "Civil Society or Nation? 'Europe' in the Symbolism of Romania's Postsocialist Politics." In Suny and Kennedy, *Intellectuals*, 301–44.

Verdery, Katherine. *What Was Socialism and What Came Next?* New Haven, CT: Yale University Press, 1996.

Vilka, Inga, Maris Pukis, and Edvins Vanags. "Indicators of Local Democracy in Latvia." Course Literature for Baltic and Nordic Local Governments, Tartu University, Department of Baltic Studies, 2006.

Vysotskaya, Alena. "The 'Alliance for Human Rights in a United Latvia' in the European Parliament: Europeanisation of a Soviet Legacy?" 2005. https://www.academia.edu/19081822/_2005_The_Alliance_For_Human_Rights_in_a_United_Latvia_in_the_European_Parliament_Europeanisation_of_a_Soviet_Legacy.

Weber, Max. *Economy and Society: An Outline of Interpretive Sociology.* Edited by Guenther Roth and Claus Wittich. New York: Bedminster Press, 1968.

Wedeen, Lisa. *Ambiguities of Domination: Politics, Rhetoric, and Symbols in Contemporary Syria.* Chicago: University of Chicago Press, 1999.

Wedeen, Lisa. *Peripheral Visions: Publics, Power, and Performance in Yemen.* Chicago: University of Chicago Press, 2008.

Weinthal, Erika, and Pauline Jones Luong. "Energy Wealth and Tax Reform in Russia and Kazakhstan." *Resources Policy* 27, no. 4 (2001): 215–23.

Werner, Cynthia, Holly Barcus, and Namara Brede. "Discovering a Sense of Well-Being through the Revival of Islam: Profiles of Kazakh Imams in Western Mongolia." *Central Asian Survey* 32, no. 4 (2013): 527–41.

Wolfel, Richard L. "North to Astana: Nationalistic Motives for the Movement of the Kazakh (stani) Capital." *Nationalities Papers* 30, no. 3 (2002): 485–506.

Yessenova, Saulesh. "'Routes and Roots' of Kazakh Identity: Urban Migration in Postsocialist Kazakhstan." *Russian Review* 64, no. 4 (2005): 661–79.

Zake, Ieva. "Inventing Culture and Nation: Intellectuals and Early Latvian Nationalism." *National Identities* 9, no. 4 (2007): 307–29.

Zardykhan, Zharmukhamed. "Russians in Kazakhstan and Demographic Change: Imperial Legacy and the Kazakh Way of Nation Building." *Asian Ethnicity* 5, no. 1 (2004): 61–79.

Zaslavsky, Victor. "Nationalism and Democratic Transition in Postcommunist Societies." *Daedalus* 121, no. 2 (1992): 97–121.

Zepa, Brigita. *Integration Practices and Perspectives.* Riga: Baltic Institute of Social Sciences, 2006.

Zepa, Brigita, and E. Kļave, eds. "National Identity, Mobility and Capability: Latvia." Human Development Report, 2010/2011.

Zhussupov, Sabit. *Politicheskaia analitika issledovaniia* [Political research analytics]. Almaty, 2011.

INDEX